"St. David is a thoughtful observer and generous teacher who is always asking how we might say 'yes' to the Spirit. This book is an answer: beautifully imagined, beautifully written, at once deeply theological and deeply scientific, this faithful attempt to reconcile our brains and our souls will offer beauty to anyone who reads it."

—GREG GARRETT
Author of A Long Long Way: Hollywood's Unfinished Journey from Racism to Reconciliation

"St. David takes us on pilgrimage through the brain of a Christian, pointing out where neurons are firing and where transformation is happening as the good news does its work. Her curiosity, creativity, facility with neuroscience, and deep affection for the elements of the Christian faith are all on display as she helps us see why trust, forgiveness, and integration in Christ are also patterns of an emotionally healthy and happy life."

—ANTHONY D. BAKER
Professor of Systematic Theology, Seminary of the Southwest

"The consummate storyteller, with the elegant aesthetics of ancient tapestry, the dramatic romance of a symphonic maestro, the contemplative energies of desert amas, and the mathematical insights of a quantum physicist, Gena St. David integrates neuroscience, Scripture, art, poetry, and theology to grapple with how we perceive God, signal trust, and embrace the capacity to forgive. Dr. St. David's lyrical, intimate, rhythmic style of quiet listening and inspired writing makes reading the systematic theological categories of creation, humanity, sin, Christ, salvation, Spirit, and the body of Christ (church) meaningful and accessible. This volume, which engages autobiographical, contemplative spirituality is a must-read for academicians and laypersons alike interested in the connections between lived spirituality, contemplation, trauma, and stress management toward embodied forgiveness, where one loves with an open heart."

—CHERYL A. KIRK-DUGGAN
Author of Baptized Rage, Transformed Grief: I Got Through, So Can You

"In a time of rampant distrust and widespread trauma, this is a book we desperately need. Gena St. David combines scientific savvy with spiritual insight to help us imagine what healing, trust, and transformation can look like. She carries us along as she makes her own story a bridge between the narratives of Scripture and the insights of science. She is a gifted writer, a first-rate storyteller, and a careful researcher. I'll never see my brain the same way again! If all truth is God's truth, then St. David is helping the rest of us pull diverse pieces of that truth together in unexpected ways. Readers who enter from the world of psychology will be invited to contemplate the mystery that exceeds observation. Readers who enter from the world of spirituality will be invited to engage the science that can explain us to ourselves and make us more compassionate toward others. Reading this book is an invitation to joy."

—SCOTT BADER-SAYE
Academic Dean, Professor of Christian Ethics and Moral Theology,
Seminary of the Southwest

"In this beautiful, healing book Gena St. David shows the spiritual and material are so interwoven it becomes impossible to draw a line. The human brain displays a structural capacity to reconfigure itself and its dynamic relations to the world in response to sacred Scripture. St. David retells the biblical story in key topics and episodes, laying out multiple examples of scriptural revelation both modeling and producing human well-being through changed connections in the brain. As she aptly quotes, 'What fires together wires together!' This book is an acutely timely, revolutionizing account of biblical narrative from the perspective of neurobiology and its profound potential to integrate and practice new modes of human life, away from reflex violence, punishment, and trauma. . . . A vital addition to emerging theological accounts of transformative humanity."

—ANTHONY BARTLETT
Theologian and author of *Theology Beyond Metaphysics*

"I am offering a Hemingway-inspired six-word story of this beautiful book: Neuroscience and God, trusting restoration: a tapestry. St. David has woven together two worlds which are, too often and unnecessarily, divided. Her work explores the neuroscience of emotion, healing, trust, and reconnection with nuance and clarity, while interweaving biblical and spiritual depth with poetic thread. Whether you are called to this work through the spirit, the science, or both, it promises to open your curiosity, stir your ability to listen deeply, and awaken your capacity for reconnection."

—JULIANE TAYLOR SHORE
Founder of IPNB Psychotherapy

THE BRAIN AND THE SPIRIT

THE BRAIN AND THE SPIRIT

Unlocking the Transformative Potential
of the Story of Christ

Gena St. David

CASCADE *Books* · Eugene, Oregon

THE BRAIN AND THE SPIRIT
Unlocking the Transformative Potential of the Story of Christ

Cascade Books
An Imprint of Wipf and Stock Publishers
199 W. 8th Ave., Suite 3
Eugene, OR 97401

www.wipfandstock.com

PAPERBACK ISBN: 978-1-7252-7508-9
HARDCOVER ISBN: 978-1-7252-7509-6
EBOOK ISBN: 978-1-7252-7510-2

Cataloguing-in-Publication data:

Names: St. David, Gena, author.

Title: The brain and the spirit : unlocking the transformative potential of the story of Christ / Gena St. David.

Description: Eugene, OR : Cascade Books, 2021 | Includes bibliographical references and index.

Identifiers: ISBN 978-1-7252-7508-9 (paperback) | ISBN 978-1-7252-7509-6 (hardcover) | ISBN 978-1-7252-7510-2 (ebook)

Subjects: LCSH: Jesus Christ—Psychology. | Neuropsychology—Religious aspects. | Brain—Religious aspects. | Theology. | Salvation—Christianity.

Classification: BL624 .S72 2021 (paperback) | BL624 .S72 (ebook)

10/27/21

Dedicated to the scapegoats.

If you believe that Jesus, the crucified victim, is God, you stop believing in the gods . . . and you get closer and closer to seeing things as they really, humanly, are.

—JAMES ALISON

Contents

Copyright Notices | ix
List of Illustrations | x
Acknowledgments | xi
Introduction | xiii

1 **Dirt Roads and Highways** | 3
   Mapping the Brain | 5
   The Stress Continuum | 10
   The Neuroscience of Stress | 11
   In the Beginning | 11
   Time, Why? | 16
   Reflecting God | 17
   The Story of Creation | 21

2 **A Trustworthy Compass** | 26
   Regulating the Brain | 27
   The Brain on Trust | 29
   The Trust Compass | 31
   The Neuroscience of Trust | 34
   The Garden | 34
   Knowledge of Evil | 37
   The Story of Humanity | 41

3 **A Cup of Stress; A Cup of Safety** | 47
   Teaching the Brain | 48
   The Learning Continuum | 48
   The Brain on Punishment | 49
   The Neuroscience of Learning | 53
   Misperceiving God | 53
   God and the Law | 64
   The Triangle of Punishment | 67
   The Story of Sin | 71

4 **A Borrowed Body** | 77
   Mirroring the Brain | 78
   The Brain on Desire | 80
   The Neuroscience of Desire | 82
   The Scapegoat Mechanism | 82
   Jesus Christ | 90
   Forgiveness | 91
   The Story of Jesus | 96

5 **A Healing Story** | 102
   Healing the Brain | 104
   The Brain on a Story | 105
   The Neuroscience of Healing | 106
   Saved from What? | 107
   A Transformative Story | 114
   The Story of Salvation | 118

6 **Integration** | 123
   Integrating the Brain | 125
   The Brain on Spirituality | 129
   The Neuroscience of Integration | 131
   The Spirit as Movement | 132
   Giving Consent | 135
   Breath Prayer | 136
   The Lord's Prayer | 138
   The Story of the Spirit | 141

7 **Reconnection** | 146
   Growing the Brain | 148
   The Brain on Relationship | 150
   The Neuroscience of Relationship | 151
   The Body of Christ | 152
   Baptism | 156
   Eucharist | 157
   Sanctuary | 159
   The Story of the Body of Christ | 161

Postscript: The Shape of the Story | 165
Bibliography | 173
Index | 183

Copyright Notices

List of Illustrations

Christ Pantocrator | xii

Cosmology | 1

Mapping the Brain | 6

The Stress Continuum | 10

Theological Anthropology | 24

The Trust Compass | 31

Hamartiology | 45

The Learning Continuum | 49

The Triangle of Punishment | 69

Christology | 74

The Scapegoat Mechanism | 87

Jesus, the Rescuer | 93

Jesus, the Victim | 94

Jesus, the Forgiver | 95

Soteriology | 100

Transforming the Triangle | 115

Pneumatology | 122

Right and Left Brain Hemispheres | 125

Ecclesiology | 145

Growth-Fostering Relationships | 149

"Fight to the Death" Plot Diagram | 166

"Epiphany" Plot Diagram | 169

Acknowledgments

THANKS TO THE MANY individuals who supported this project with your time, feedback, and inspiration, especially Jordan and Grace Minnix for your encouragement, patience, humor, creativity, and authenticity. Thanks to parents, siblings, and in-laws who have encouraged me.

Much gratitude to the following colleagues and conversation partners who informed or offered feedback on drafts or excerpts of this manuscript: Scott Bader-Saye, Anthony Baker, Anthony Bartlett, Steve Bishop, Cynthia Briggs Kittredge, Claire Colombo, Kimberly Culbertson, Greg Garrett, Danielle Tumminio Hansen, Nathan Jennings, Daniel Joslyn-Siemiatkoski, Melanie Jones, Cheryl Kirk-Duggan, Laura Kirk, Rachel Lee, Weylin Lee, Jason Minnix, Cheryl Navarrete, Jane Patterson, Andrew Reed, Janice Reed, Kathleen Russell, Juliane Taylor Shore, Steven Tomlinson, and Karen Tsang.

And thank you to supportive colleagues and friends at Seminary of the Southwest and the Vox Veniae community. Thank you to Ashley Colley and Tracy Elizabeth Guthrie who worked as research assistants, and to Liz Dowling-Sendor who edited early drafts. And thank you to the William Shubael Conant Fund for a sabbatical grant that supported the research on this project.

Thank you to Charlie Collier and the editorial team at Wipf and Stock for investing in this project. And a heart-filled thanks to Father James Alison whose theology, mentorship, and friendship have enriched my life, and whose trust, forgiveness, and joy inspired me to become curious how I might come to encounter God as he does.

Christ Pantocrator

Introduction

LAST WINTER, I SAT in a room full of pastors and community leaders, many of whom I was meeting for the first time. I had been invited because of my background in psychological and spiritual wellness; many of the others in the room were clergy with a theology background. Each of us had driven or flown in from around the country and the communities we represented were culturally and geographically diverse. Outside it was snowing, and inside we nestled close and waited for our time to begin. Our goal in coming together was to spend a few days praying and reflecting on some seismic shifts we sensed were occurring in many of our churches; we were there to reflect on patterns we were noticing and endeavor to discern together what the Spirit might be doing in our time and how we could say "yes" to it. I felt curious how our time would unfold, attentive to the reasons for which we had gathered, and slightly awkward, huddled so close together with a roomful of adults whom I did not know well.

To break the ice, our host suggested we go around the room and each of us tell a "six-word story" about why we had come. I had never heard of this practice; later that night back in my room I would Google it and read that the idea may have been inspired by this one of Ernest Hemingway's: "For sale, baby shoes, never worn." It's a story that moves me each time; I cannot even type those words now without tearing up—well-played, Hemingway.

The stories I heard that day from folks who would soon become friends were quite touching as well. Gradually, the awkwardness I initially felt was replaced by an easy intimacy. I do not remember my story, but I do recall one man's vividly. He had been pastoring for many years, and expressed a mourning over how the larger faith community he loved—one that had been characterized by kindness and generosity—was suddenly asking for up-or-down votes to decide who was "in" or "out." In the wake of this shift in ethos, some community members were being pushed out, and others who advocated for them were being disciplined, stripped of credentials, and sometimes terminated from employment.

"Far from home; I never left." This was the grieving pastor's story.

He began to paint a picture of the faith community he had loved, one in which his family had been invested for generations. The community had traditionally practiced what I sometimes call "slow listening"—practices like silent prayer and spiritual discernment, rooted in contemplative Christian traditions. For centuries, slow listening has guided Christian communities to discern complex turning points together. It is a practice that invites us to patiently listen to the Spirit, to one another, and to Scripture. It is also a humbling practice; I say that because it invites us to acknowledge that we need each other in order to discern truth and calibrate our compasses together. It is a practice that helps groups carefully avoid the trap of organizing around the agenda of a charismatic leader in the center, to the detriment of the welfare of those on the margins.

Experience has taught me that slow listening is essential for discernment, but difficult to sustain. For one thing, it is just that—it's slow; rational discourse and up-or-down votes are definitely quicker. Slow listening requires time before, during, and after a discussion to allow for individuals to care well for ourselves and our instruments for discernment, which can be our whole bodies.[1] Slow listening helps groups make better-informed decisions because it allows us the opportunity to access information from the right and left hemispheres of the brain, individually and collectively, and from as many social locations as there are people engaged in the practice. As a result, slow listening can bring forth creative solutions to complex dilemmas at which we would never have arrived otherwise; and these solutions tend to emerge when we are at our most calm, relaxed, trusting, and trustworthy. That state of being can be challenging to enter into during times of extreme anxiety and stress.

That day while the snow fell outside, we listened to my new friend wonder out loud whether the shift in his church's practices might have been fueled by anxiety. Global measures of health tell us that the United States and other industrialized countries are displaying many indicators of mental and emotional distress these days.[2] Racial trauma exacts a high toll.[3] Neighborhoods are plagued by racial disparities in income, housing, education, health, and safety;[4] and for the privileged, excess income and luxury do not

1. For reflection, Ign. *Spirit.* 2.328–36.8.
2. Institute for Health Metrics and Evaluation, "Share of Population."
3. Williams et al., "Assessing Racial Trauma," 245–48.
4. "Williams and Jackson, "Social Sources of Racial Disparities," 325.

appear to be factors that increase happiness and mental wellness.[5] Our surplus many times adds to our troubles, rather than alleviating them.

In addition, as I sit here, we are enduring a global pandemic. And the climate crisis is an ever-present backdrop. We have much about which to feel anxious. And that stress and anxiety is poured on top of individual and collective traumas that statistics tells us that a significant number of us have endured in our respective lifetimes.[6] We are a beautiful people, and we are a hurting people.

It has been said that much of spiritual wisdom is about what we do with our pain;[7] a few years ago I encountered a theologian who expanded my understanding of what that means. But before we get to that story, I will provide a little context, as Krista Tippett has taught us to do, by offering a bit of the spiritual background of my own childhood.[8] Our parents attended a Catholic church in Austin when I was born; our mother had converted so that she and our father could be married in the church. My early memories of Catholicism are warm and comforting—dinner table and bedside prayers, visits from the local priest, and catechism classes. My brother Gabriel attended with me; we were close in age and raised together until I was around three years old. He was my foster brother and our parents thought they might adopt him. I feel affection whenever I think of him now. Gabriel was funny and kind and in photos we are often holding hands.

Our parents were caring and attentive to us both, and I thought we would always be a family. I remember someone telling me once that Gabriel's medical records indicated he had sustained a head injury as an infant. Gabriel's eyes were crossed at first and our parents arranged for surgery to correct his vision, but as time progressed it became evident he also had learning delays to overcome. My sense is that it was difficult for Gabriel to remember things he was taught, like how to ride a tricycle or how to chew with his mouth closed. I overheard someone say once, "It's like the boy goes to sleep and forgets everything he learned the day before!"

As the severity of Gabriel's needs grew, the painful time came for him to be adopted by a more experienced caregiver. When the day arrived for us to take him to his new home, he and I crawled into the back seat of our family's blue station wagon. I do not remember if we talked much on the drive there. Upon our arrival, Gabriel and I stayed outside and played with

5. Jebb et al., "Happiness, Income Satiation," 34; Kuhn et al., "Own and Social Effects," 22.

6. Sacks and Murphy, "Prevalence of Adverse Childhood Experiences," 1.

7. Rhor, *Things Hidden*, 101.

8. Tippett, *Becoming Wise*, 23.

the chickens in the yard. Our parents chatted for a while with Gabriel's new mother, and then brought us inside. The woman had a large piano in her living room and I wondered if she would allow us to play it. Before I could ask, we were saying our goodbyes and then we drove home, leaving Gabriel behind

In the years that followed, I longed for Gabriel in a way I could not articulate. Our mother soon gave birth to two more babies and there was much laughter in our home. The house was bright and full of activity and I relished the happy times when we were all together; there was also an undercurrent of sadness, however, that I could not precisely name. A child tries to cope with a grief through play, and around this time our parents remember that I made up an imaginary friend, a little boy. When houseguests came over, I told them that our father had brought the boy home from the office in the pocket of his suit. Sometimes when a painful story is too complex, a child's brain fills in the gaps with explanations that are less rooted in reality than we might imagine. In this case, I grew up with the vague sense that Gabriel had been given away because he could not chew with his mouth closed nor ride a tricycle. My sense of belonging never felt as secure after that.

When my other siblings and I were in elementary school, our parents divorced and our father moved away, and we moved with our mother to a different city. Our mother worked as a school teacher during the week, and took us on Sundays to the Methodist church down the street. I thought the grown-ups in this faith community were kind and welcoming to an unmarried mother and her three children. Over time, the care and belonging we experienced in this community came to feel surprisingly trustworthy.

When I was thirteen, I signed up for confirmation classes, and enjoyed learning the history of some of the Christian traditions. I soon after developed a nightly routine of reading the Scriptures by candlelight, contemplating the creeds, and writing mini-sermons in a spiral notebook. Sometimes I would carry these pages to a pond near our house and practice "preaching" when no one was around but the ducks and the geese. My sense of God's nearness in those times felt grounding and comforting.

A few more years passed, and one night some high school friends knocked on my door and invited me to their Southern Baptist youth group. I squeezed into the backseat of their car and went with them and was intrigued; I had never heard preaching like that before! It was passionate and precise and compelling, and I soon involved myself in that community. My practice of reading the Scriptures deepened even further, and I developed a hunger for theology. I wanted to learn everything I could.

Those spiritual practices sustained me when I moved back to Austin and started college; I spent warm nights at a café by the river annotating books by C. S. Lewis, Augustine of Hippo, Spurgeon, Calvin, Bonhoeffer, Thomas Aquinas, and R. C. Sproul along with my Bible, the pages of which had became softened with daily use and dotted with coffee. I studied New Testament Greek and church history. My interest in Scripture and theology continued to deepen.

During my graduate training in the Pacific Northwest, I met a contemplative Quaker community. The kind individuals in that community introduced me to the Christian contemplative tradition of slow listening and spiritual discernment. One night, a contemplative prayer group in Portland invited us to join them for dinner. Father Thomas Keating was the guest. He sat dressed in monks' robes and talked about centering prayer as a practice of awareness; he led us in a prayer where he encouraged us to quietly observe our thoughts like leaves floating by on a stream. I was less comprehending of what he was saying that night as much as I was intrigued by his warm smile and non-anxious presence.

Now having practiced contemplative prayer for several years, I understand the difficulty of articulating an experience that takes place mostly on the inside of us. The psalmist once wrote "I have calmed and quieted my soul, like a weaned child with its mother; my soul is like the weaned child that is with me."[9] That may be a helpful description of what contemplative prayer can be like. It is a practice of quieting ourselves, and "being" with God, and experiencing our souls to be at peace.

I continued learning from the Quaker contemplatives during those years, but my graduate training was focused on psychology, systems theory, and interpersonal neurobiology. During graduate school, a couple of professors recognized my interest in theology as well and introduced me to Miroslav Volf, Ignatius of Loyola, and Julian of Norwich. Down the road, I would also discover James Cone, Katie Cannon, Óscar Romero, Gustavo Gutiérrez, and Rowan Williams. Theology remained an interest, even as I continued to develop as a therapist, researcher, and counselor educator in the era when neuroscience was just beginning to revolutionize the field of psychology.

I first entered graduate school in the late 1990s, when functional magnetic resonance imaging (fMRI) technology and other forms of technology were ushering in a new understanding of how the brain functions. Prior to this, we had theories about how complex learning occurs and how memories are stored, recalled, and changed. But therapy in those days was

9. Ps 131:2 (NRSV)

still often like tossing spaghetti against the wall—when it stuck, we did not know precisely why. (And when it didn't, we would often blame the wall.) Neuroscience gave us a new pair of glasses to see with greater clarity aspects of human functioning that had been blurry up till then. And we still have much to learn. But the insights gained over the past few decades, distilled by scholars like Dan Siegel, Stephen Porges, Allan Schore, Jean Baker Miller, and Amy Banks have transformed almost every branch of our field. Neuroscience is correcting and updating our theories, so that our interventions can be more consistently beneficial. Science writer Erik Vance put it this way: "Brain scientists are like astronomers of old. They unsettled humanity's sense of itself by redrawing our picture of the cosmos out there."[10]

We are coming to understand better the mechanisms by which our neural circuitry is established, impacted by relationships, and transformed. The process of altering our neural circuitry so that it links up differently is what we typically refer to as "healing," "growth," or "maturity." This is a core focus of those of us trained to be healers, educators, or spiritual care givers. We are in want of theories that are grounded in the data about how healing, growth, and maturity occur—and under what conditions—so that we can hold ourselves accountable to ensuring that our work is contributing to those conditions. Equipped with data about how our brain forms new linkages between neural networks, and how those networks impact how we feel and behave, we can now revisit and update previously held notions about what is good and helpful for human beings so that our "helpfulness" can be more consistently helpful.

For many years, I have wanted to carve out time to practice slowly listening to theology through the earpiece of brain science, to see if the practice might generate anything worthwhile. I have wondered how the insights from neuroscience might help us to hear with greater clarity aspects of theology that may have been faint or muffled before. Theology shapes and informs our notions about God, ourselves, and others, and is a factor that influences our physical, mental, emotional, psychological, relational, and spiritual wellness. My understanding of the human brain has only deepened my appreciation for theological reflection; and likewise, my sense that God is active in processes like healing, growth, and maturity has further enhanced my curiosity about the relationship between theology and neuroscience.

In the spring of 2013, I began teaching at an Episcopal seminary and I was suddenly surrounded by conversation partners with similar interests. My faculty position was as a counselor educator, and I was teaching classes in research, traumatic stress, family systems, and interpersonal neurobiology. I

---

10. Erik Vance. interviewed by Tippett, "Drugs Inside Your Head," 1:21–30.

enjoyed lively discussions with colleagues who taught theology and biblical studies and these conversations enriched my thinking about how these two fields might relate to one another. My list of curiosities expanded. But I was teaching and running a clinical practice, raising a family, and volunteering in our faith community; I was not sure if I would ever be able to carve out time for the slow theological listening I wanted to pursue, or where exactly I would begin if I did.

Then I met Father James Alison.

One warm night in March of 2017, a mutual friend named George introduced us at a dinner party. Our host, named Dorsey, owned a small, urban farm in East Austin. Before the meal, she walked our group through rows of flowers, vegetables, and herbs to introduce us to a miniature donkey and a spirited goose. When George called us to dinner, I was happy to be seated next to Father Alison. I was familiar with his writings; I had just finished a paper in which he contrasted worshipful gatherings that transform our violent inclinations with group rituals that fuel and reinforce them.[11] Over dinner, I asked about a word he had used, *interdividuality*,[12] and our conversation unfolded from there. I had experienced Alison in his writings as funny, kind, and clear-minded, and I found him equally so in person. I also thought he was unexpectedly gracious and humble, for the scholar I knew him to be.

Over the months that followed, we continued chatting and I gradually learned more of Alison's story. He grew up in a conservative, Evangelical Anglican family in Britain. He studied theology in Brazil at the Jesuit School of Philosophy and Theology and was ordained a Catholic priest of the Dominican order in 1988. A few years later, James wrote to Rome expressing a dilemma of conscience: he had discovered that the church's teaching about gay people being "objectively disordered" was untrue and that meant his vows had been taken under a false conscience. But did that mean he was then not a priest? Priesthood came by ordination and was relatively independent of the state of mind of the one being ordained. Meticulously honest and desiring of integrity in all things, Alison wrote to Rome asking for advice. And he waited decades for an answer.

In the years since that letter to Rome, one might imagine that "what to do with James Alison" became a topic of some debate in Curial circles. Those in power erected walls to shut him out, and others fought to tear down those walls, and the back and forth ended up inflicting much suffering. My sense

11. Alison, "Worship in a Violent World," 133–46.

12. Girard and Oughourlian are credited with having coined the term; Oughourlian, *Mimetic Brain*, xiii.

is that Alison would have preferred a quieter life; he seems most at peace when he is communicating God's love across a dinner table, or celebrating the Eucharist with a neighborhood church, or tending to the sick and suffering whom Jesus loved. He would have likely preferred to fulfill his calling outside of the spotlight of notoriety that he has paradoxically received while being given a nonperson status by many of his peers.

And yet transformative love is often sparked at the margins. As I came to know Alison better, I felt intrigued by one thing above all: his forgiveness toward those who had injured him. Parker Palmer once said our hearts can break in one of two ways: either we shatter into shards of shrapnel that may injure others, or we break open at our core and love pours out.[13] And forgiveness appears to be the enduring *heartsong* of Alison's life; which is to say, when he is broken, extraordinary love pours out. Time and again, I found Alison's forgiving response toward those who had injured him both inspiring to witness, and intriguing from a neuropsychological perspective.

My background in trauma studies has fueled a long-time interest in the subject of forgiveness. I used to think forgiveness meant that someone was willing to be reconciled if their enemy wished to make amends. But I gradually came to see that forgiveness has to be something more robust—something that stands alone, independent of the actions of another. Observing Alison's process of working through his pain, sourcing something from his trust in God, and—through an alchemy I did not yet understand—producing love and joy on the other side, independent of anything else changing, expanded my thinking on this. I was not yet sure exactly how forgiveness functioned for Alison, but it left an impression on me.

I also used to think forgiveness involved something of a heart-softening, a dropping of one's armor. But over time I came to think that forgiveness has to be something wiser—something more like Alison's practice of opening his heart-door to the trustworthy, while parrying the jabs of the untrustworthy. And he somehow accomplished this with lightness, skill, and humor. I noticed Alison did not attempt to fully secure the door of his heart, while at the same time he was thoughtful about when and to whom he handed over the keys. I was intrigued.

A significant development in my thinking about forgiveness took place one day in a conversation with Alison. He made the off-hand comment that by living as we are called, we will have enemies; otherwise Jesus would not have mentioned it. He went on, almost as an aside, to say that when an enemy means us harm, it does no good to pretend we are friends; Jesus did not teach us to befriend our enemies but to *love* them. For me in

13. Palmer, *On the Brink of Everything*, 161.

that moment, it was like hearing something for the first time—and in the presence of someone I had been witnessing do precisely that. So now I had a new umbrella question: what does loving our enemies mean and, neuro-biologically speaking, how does one pull that off?

As a clinician who studies the neuroscience of trauma, I try to under-stand and respect the capacities and limitations of our human brain. When an enemy inflicts harm on us, we can expect a particular part of our brain to take over in effort to protect us. When this happens, I knew there existed a finite range of responses that our brain would permit us to manufacture. And in the love of Jesus, echoed in the forgiveness that poured out of James Alison, I recognized a neurobiological response that defied that expectation. And neither my background in neuroscience, nor my grasp of theology at the time, could sufficiently explain how that was possible.

In the fall of 2018, I was offered a sabbatical to take up any research project that interested me and I knew immediately what I wanted to pursue. I thought the chances were slim, however, that the scheduling and logistics would work out. Still, I had to try. I called up James and asked, "Would you take me on as a theology student?"

By then my affection for James had grown strong. And I had read more of his writings and developed a couple of working theories about the inner functioning of his neurobiology. I thought, for instance, that the qualities I marveled at—his love, forgiveness, compassion, and humor—appeared to be fueled by two practices I had witnessed him exercising with impressive consistency. The first was his practice of contemplating the Hebrew and Greek Scriptures, and the second was a practice of communicating with God, whom James maintained was made known to us in the person and story of Jesus. I understood this second piece to be the crux of James' theol-ogy, and this is what I wanted to understand better. It was not clear to me precisely how the threads of his theology wove together to produce in his brain the love and forgiveness I had witnessed first-hand. I was eager to flip the tapestry of his theology over and observe it from underneath.

Despite my hope that James would grant my request, I felt worried about two things: the logistics with me being in Austin and James in Spain, and the basic level at which the lessons would need to begin—given that I had no formal training in theology and my background was in a completely different discipline. I knew James would be gracious, but I worried he might grow weary of having to start at such a granular level with me as a student. James seemed to share neither of these concerns, however, and appeared intrigued by the request. He did have one question for me though, which I was not anticipating: what did I mean by "theology?"

This gave me pause. I told James I wanted to understand better how he had come to think about God's love the way he did. For instance, how did his understanding of the Christian story, as he encountered it in the Scriptures, inform how he thought about God and life and relationships? I wanted to understand how the pieces came together for him, how he arrived at the trust that he embodied, and what he encountered in the Christian story that permitted such trust. I said all this to James, and then there was a pause on his side.

Finally, he broke the silence with his infectious voice that frequently spills into laugher. "Ah well," he began, "you know, a theologian is someone who wakes up one day to find themselves on the inside of a communication that they know did not originate with them. So the first task of a theologian is to listen. And after some time of listening, one might practice living out that communication. And only after that, one might dare to speak about it."

I was not aware, but the lesson had begun.

In the years to come, James became a generous and patient teacher who never seemed to tire of my curiosities and questions, however tedious. He was also surgical when it came to providing critique on my attempts to articulate my understanding of a text. His attention to detail and commitment to integrity taught me to listen slowly and allow the Scriptures to "read us" as much as the other way around. And when I reached a point of articulating something that I was observing, James taught me to be meticulous about showing my work. In social science research, we are taught two techniques that came in handy here. First, we use procedures for surfacing and bracketing off our preconceived notions, in order to minimize our influence on the subject we are observing. Second, we use procedures for documenting each source, decision, and procedure of discovery; this is so that researchers can come behind us and replicate our methods to either confirm or disconfirm our results. In this manuscript, I have tried to leave a clear trail of breadcrumbs for each turn I took, in the hopes that others may pick up the trail and see if it leads them to the same destination or someplace else.

Certainly there is more to be "fleshed out"; at the same time, my endeavor to practice listening slowly to the Scriptures through the earpiece of neuroscience has brought me into a different sort of encounter with the Christian story, and one that has made forgiveness appear to be an option in places where it seemed impossible before. It has also sparked in me a sense of trust, curiosity, and hope about the future. I have come to think that theology that is grounded in something true will be helpful for all, at the expense of none. I also think it will be discerned collectively, and I look forward to continuing to learn from and collaborate with others along the way. Here are some of the questions that have guided my process of listening thus far:

What enabled Jesus to respond nonviolently when threatened?
How did Jesus perceive himself, God, and others?
What practices might allow us to perceive reality more as Jesus did?
If we became more like Jesus, how might that benefit our health,
society, and planet?

As I describe what I encountered when I listened to the various parts of the Christian story, through the earpiece of neuroscience, I will contribute some thoughts on these questions, and add a few more questions. Along the way, I will use the words "theology" and "the Christian story" interchangeably because that is how I have encountered theology—as a story unfolding over time. And I want us to notice that calling something "a story" is different than calling it "fiction"; we often encounter truth in the form of a narrative. And while there can be many approaches to theology, the Christian story is the one with which I am most familiar; therefore I will be drawing from the Hebrew and Greek Scriptures that are the bedrock of the Christian tradition. And by exploring this story sequentially, beginning in Genesis, it will produce for us something of a systematic theology—which is to say, at the end we will find ourselves with a cohesive story, with the Christ narrative in the middle, informing our understanding of all that came before.

Each chapter then will open with a discussion of how the brain works; here is a list of seven insights informed by neuroscience that I will invite us to explore:

1. The map of our brain consists of dirt roads and highways.

2. Trust is like a thermostat for the nervous system.

3. A cup of stress + a cup of safety = a recipe for learning.

4. You borrow my body, and I borrow yours.

5. A story's ending changes our understanding of what came before it.

6. We heal through integration.

7. The brain grows through reconnection.

After examining the brain science, I will then invite us to hold that piece of research in mind while we turn our attention to the Scriptures and take up a particular theological question or set of questions in each chapter. So here then is an idea of what to expect:

In chapter 1, "Dirt Roads and Highways," we will consider how science is helping us map the brain and then hold this in mind while listening to Genesis and considering questions of cosmology and the creation story.

In chapter 2, "A Trustworthy Compass," we will explore the neuroscience of trust and hold this in mind as we listen to the story of the garden of Eden and engage questions about theological anthropology and the story of humanity.

In chapter 3, "A Cup of Stress; a Cup of Safety," we will look at the neuroscience of punishment and learning, and hold this in mind while listening to the Exodus story of Moses receiving the law, and taking up questions of hamartiology—the study of sin.

In chapter 4, "A Borrowed Body," we will examine the neuroscience of our mirror systems, and hold this in mind while listening to the story of Jesus' life, and considering matters related to scapegoating and Christology, the story of Christ.

In chapter 5, "A Healing Story," we will consider the impact of a story on the human brain and hold this in mind while listening to Jesus' teachings about salvation and engaging questions of soteriology and the story of salvation.

In chapter 6, "Integration," we will look at how the brain establishes linkages—top to bottom and right to left—and we will hold this in mind while listening to the stories of the Spirit and reflecting on questions of pneumatology.

In chapter 7, "Reconnection," we will explore the neuroscience of growth-fostering relationships that cycle through connection, disconnection, and reconnection, and hold this in mind while listening to stories of the body of Christ and considering matters related to ecclesiology.

In our time together, I would like to offer us a whole-bodied experience. I find the exploration of scholarship intriguing to the rational parts of our brain, the parts of us that enjoy the work of being a detective, following a trail of clues. I also find that the stress and anxiety of our daily lives and collective traumas renders the emotional parts of our brain in need of care, inspiration, and transcendent encounters with beauty. I am of the mind that helpful theology will nourish all parts of us—the rational and emotive, the intellectual and embodied. And so between chapters, I will offer up images from artists, and words of poetry, prayers, and blessings that may invite us into an embodied experience with the theology upon which we are reflecting.

So perhaps we might find it helpful to begin this way:

Take a moment
to place awareness

on your breath;
many consider this a way
to become aware
of the Spirit within.
When ready, say (or think) to God
"I'm listening . . ."
Begin to notice
thoughts, emotions, sensations,
and allow them to float by
as if on a stream.
When distracted
return to
your breath,
and the Spirit
and say to God once again
"I'm listening . . ."

A friend of mine once said something that stayed with me: "Beautiful theology doesn't speak, it sings." We were sitting outside a coffee shop and I thought at the time he meant we needed a poetic phrase for a piece of writing we were working on, but I think differently about his comment now. I think he may have meant that when theology is true and helpful, it will move us bodily, as beautiful music does. It will resonate with both the logical and the emotional parts of us. It will help us to discern the harmonic patterns and chords of reality, which surprisingly consist of the very same notes as cacophony and discord, suggesting perhaps that nothing new or different is needed and the pieces just need rearranging.

Over time, I have come to think that beautiful theology will move us bodily toward something reminiscent of the *heartsong* of James Alison's forgiveness. It will nourish us and nudge us toward integration, healing, and trust. Simply put, when theology is true for our souls, we can expect it will be true for our bodies as well. And perhaps that is part of the reason for the need to live our theology before we begin to speak about it, and why we must listen to it before we can live it. This practice may span our whole lives, but we can begin now by listening to the Christian story as communicated through the sacred Scriptures, using the earpiece of brain science, and then discerning together if the practice has proved worthwhile.

THE FOURTH DAY OF CREATION

WE EACH ONE, ARE ALL THE SOILS.

AND EACH ONE, ALL THE WORLDS

WEED-CHOKED AND STONY, DEEP AND FERTILE.

Cosmology

Hover

The ocean reflects the sky
by which we charted our way
to our own displacement.

Off-kilter from the stars,
we awakened inside our own skin
to discover:

It is a thin divide
between the universe without
and the one within.

1

Dirt Roads and Highways

I was running with a mind to see God
and so it was that I ascended the mount.

—St. Gregory of Nazianzus (ca. 330–90)[1]

One Saturday morning when I was sixteen, I woke early and borrowed the keys to our mother's station wagon. A guy on whom I had a crush had invited me to come see him that day; he was staying at a farmhouse about forty-five miles outside the city limits. My mother and siblings were still asleep, so I laced up my tennis shoes and left a note on the kitchen counter. Then I tiptoed into the garage, with butterflies in my belly.

It was still dark outside and the street lamps were lit as I steered through my neighborhood. Once I reached the highway, I increased my speed. Lightning flashed overhead, followed by a thunderclap, and then the sky broke open and it began to rain. I slowed down, but kept driving. I had no cell phone or navigation system, but my crush had drawn a map on a square of red paper. I clutched the map in one hand as I gripped the steering wheel, peering through the storm to find my way.

After some time, I pulled off the interstate at an exit that looked right, and I turned onto a two-lane farm road lined with cotton fields. I drove for what seemed a long distance, squinting through the rain. Finally, I spotted a turn-off that appeared to match my map; it was a long gravel path between

1. Gregory of Nazianzus, *Orat.* 28.3.

3

two fields. About half a mile down, the thunderstorm intensified; the gravel path disappeared beneath puddles and my tires lost traction with the road. I braked hard and the car swerved. My wheels started spinning, splattering mud across the windshield. I stepped on the accelerator again; no movement. "Oh no," I thought, throwing the gearshift into reverse, then drive, then reverse . . . I wasn't going anywhere.

I sat for a while, stuck in the mud with the engine running, and ran plays in my head. I could search the ground for a piece of wood to put under the wheel. Or I could try to scoop up enough gravel to sprinkle around the tires. Rain was falling in sheets. On the horizon, I thought I spotted the farmhouse that was my destination. It crossed my mind that maybe if I just turned off the engine and stayed put, someone would come find me. But I decided that was improbable; more likely, my crush would decide I had changed my mind or that my mother had refused to let me come. Seeing no other alternative, I stepped into the downpour.

Within seconds, I was soaked; my shoes sank into the mud. The house I had spotted stood a half-mile across a cotton field. Other than that, it was farmland in all directions. An old fast food commercial floated up in my mind then; it featured a person walking through a ghost town saying, "Where is everyone?"

I trekked through rows of cotton until I reached a chest-high fence of barbed wire that I had not noticed before. The house lay about a quarter mile further beyond the fence. I looked both directions and saw no way around, so I gingerly pinched the middle wire and lifted it to step through. When I placed my foot down on the other side, it slid in the mud; the downward motion propelled me backward and one of the barbs snagged a ring I wore on one finger.

The ring was silver with a heart charm. My crush had given it to me as a Valentine's Day gift and it was too big. When the barb snagged the ring, it yanked it off and left a deep slice down the inside of my finger. I caught a glimpse of the shiny ring as it landed in a muddy puddle. I froze then; part of me wanted to kneel down and hunt for the ring. Another part was aware I was now bleeding and needed to find help. I cleared the fence and resumed my mission to reach the farmhouse. To slow the bleeding of my finger, I wrapped the bottom part of my shirt around it. As I walked, I comforted myself with the thought that I might return later to this spot to search for the ring. (That would never happen.)

Finally, I reached the front porch of the farmhouse. My t-shirt was soaked through and blood-stained; my shoes were caked with mud. I felt lightheaded from the injury and embarrassed because my makeup was running. But I was eager to see my crush and explain why I had been delayed.

And visions of hot cocoa or maybe apple cider may have been on my mind as well. I climbed the steps to the front door, but to my disappointment it was all boarded up. The windows were broken; the farmhouse was abandoned.

I saw no other option then but to navigate the field and the barbed wire once more, and attempt to reach the two-lane country road where I hoped to cross paths with someone who could help me. To find my bearings, I fished through my pocket for the map, but it wasn't there. Had I dropped it? I didn't know. But in the commotion, that little red square of paper had vanished. I resisted the temptation to go searching then for my ring, and instead, I headed in the direction of the two-lane farm road. Once I reached it, I walked another mile or so before I heard the sound of a pickup truck rolling to a stop behind me. A kind-looking couple offered me a ride. When I described the house where my crush was staying, the couple said they might know the owners. They made a U-turn, and sailed past the gravel road where my car sat, and then took another turn after that. I realized then that I would have never found the house on my own; my original turn had been a mistake and ever since I had been traveling in the wrong direction.

Mapping the Brain

In the era right before I entered graduate school, the field of psychology was navigating without a map much of the time when it came to the human brain. We could measure electric activity on the surface, and the amounts of chemicals in the brain. But our brains are three-dimensional, and to accurately map what was occurring, we needed a way to look *inside*. The development of brain-imaging technology has allowed us to do just that, and now we are able to map the pathways along which brain activity travels. Bessel van der Kolk has described the magnitude of this development this way: "Measuring brain chemicals like serotonin or norepinephrine enabled scientists to look at what fueled neural activity, which was a bit like trying to understand a car's engine by studying gasoline. Neuroimaging made it possible to see inside the engine."[2]

We now have the capacity to look—not *at* the brain, but *into* it. As technology improves, we are learning increasingly more about how our brain functions, how memories are stored and rewired, how emotions are regulated, and how our brain changes as a result of relational interactions between us. Here is how Dan Siegel has articulated the relationship between neural activity and interpersonal relationships: "The brain is the embodied neural *mechanism* shaping the flow of energy and information;

2. van der Kolk, *Body Keeps the Score*, 39–40.

relationships are the *sharing* of that flow."[3] For our purposes, it might be helpful for us to picture the flow of energy and information inside our brain as traveling along a system of pathways resembling roads and highways:

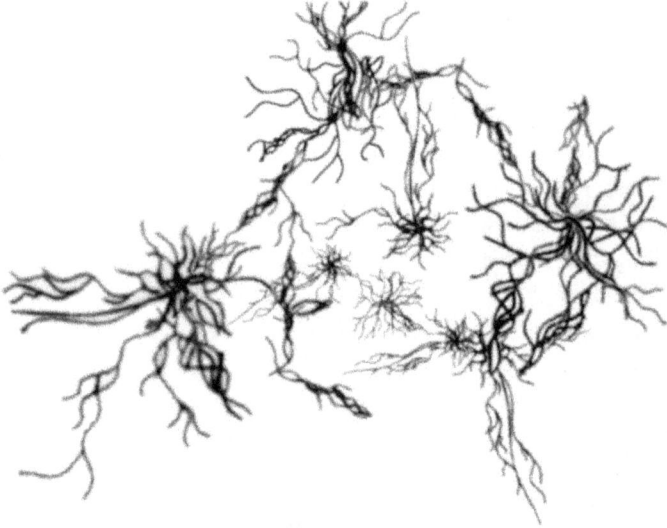

Mapping the Brain

Some of our neural pathways may function like super-highways where energy and information travels at great speeds across relatively far distances. The networks in our brain that see more traffic tend to become extra slick. Other pathways may be like rocky gravel roads where activity slows down, or sometimes meets with a dead end, forcing it to loop back. In a major city, traffic flows in all directions using highway flyovers, ground-level streets, and underground subway tunnels. As we move farther away from the city, we may encounter dirt roads and gravel paths that do not link up with the urban high system, or perhaps only in isolated spots. All of this may be a helpful way for us to think about the neural networks in the brain as well.

The pathways in our brain link up to form neural networks, and new linkages between networks are taking place all the time. When we encounter cues in our environment—sights, sounds, smells, tastes, or information through touch—our brain fires in a pattern along networks that were established the previous times we encountered similar cues. Our body may then produce similar emotions and sensations to those that we felt the last time our brain fired in a similar pattern. Our brain then gathers up these bits of information as well, and constructs an explanation for what

3. Siegel, *Developing Mind*, 7.

is occurring inside us: "I feel sad because this situation is tragic," or "I feel nervous because this person is dangerous," etc. While all this is occurring, new environmental cues to which our brain is attending may now get linked up with this pre-existing network, or as Siegel puts it, "What fires together, wires together."[4]

We used to think our brain perceived cues in our environment, then constructed an explanation, and then we felt the emotions related to that explanation, and took action in response. We now understand the process to be more recursive. Instead, it appears that our brain perceives something in our environment, activates networks established the last time we encountered those cues, and fires in a pattern that produces similar emotions and sensations to those we felt in the past. We often then take action in response to how we're feeling *internally*, to regulate our stress and increase our sense of safety. Only then does our brain construct an explanation of what has already occurred, which means *we* become a key environmental cue to which we are responding.[5]

It is difficult to overstate the ramifications of the difference between the more linear way we used to think about this sequence, and the more recursive way in which we now understand the brain to function. Recognizing that the brain responds to environmental cues and fires in patterns that produce felt emotions and sensations in our body prior to us arriving at an explanation or story about what has occurred has helped us to better understand human behavior. If we wish to correct harmful behavior and teach more helpful behavior, then we must take into consideration environmental cues and the brain's perception of them.

Fortunately, brain imaging has given us the tools by which we can begin to take notice of which networks are firing when, and in what pattern, and that can help us develop a mental "map" of someone's brain. But that's perhaps not even the most helpful part. Understanding better how the brain functions has helped us learn to "map" our own brain for ourselves, without using technology. By the simple practice of paying attention to our own thoughts, emotions, sensations, memories, and embodied reactions to environmental cues, we can begin to "map" our own brain networks and develop some awareness of which networks are linked up and how.[6] As human beings, we share some networks in common, while others are entirely unique to our own life and story. For example, my early beach memories are mostly pleasant, and so now when I encounter sandy shores and the sound

4. Siegel, *Developing Mind*, 49.

5. Feldman Barrett, *How Emotions Are Made*, 59.

6. Thompson, *Anatomy of the Soul*, 184.

of waves, my body automatically produces peaceful emotions and relaxed sensations. These networks in the brain once fired together, so they are now wired together. If these networks were linked up differently, my body would produce different emotions. My early memories of fried chicken, for instance, are unpleasant, and so now when I encounter fried chicken, my body produces the emotion of repulsion. If you love fried chicken, you might find this difficult to understand. How could our two brains function so differently? Well, if my brain networks were linked up exactly like yours, I would love all same things you love. But the networks in our brain are clustered in unique patterns according to our environment, and largely determined by the emotions, sensations, and relational interactions we associated early in childhood with various environmental cues.

We are not held captive to our memory networks, however; they can be helped to link up differently and this neural flexibility may continue our whole life long.[7] It can be difficult to establish new linkages between slick networks and rocky unpaved ones, but it can be accomplished through practice and repetition, if the proper conditions for learning are present. And when that happens, the emotions and sensations we feel when those networks are activated will change.[8] As our networks form new linkages, a wider range of behavioral responses that "feel right" and appropriate to the situation will open up to us. And the first step in that direction may be to pay attention to what we're thinking, feeling, and remembering in a given moment, so we can develop some idea of how our brain's networks are linked up now.

This practice can be beneficial for a few reasons. First, as we develop a map for our own unique brain, we can begin to practice creating the conditions that may help our networks link up in more helpful ways. This awareness can allow us to work with our brain's anatomy instead of against it, which is useful because our brain is the only instrument we have for exerting any influence over our brain to begin with. Second, as we develop appreciation for how delicate this process is, we can begin to practice small experiments, recognizing that a tiny link in the right direction can expand over time into a whole new network that we may think of as "transformation." Third, as we spend time mapping our own brain, we may find compassion for ourselves and others, recognizing that we cannot force our brain to do something that it presently lacks the network linkages to do.

Some linkages in my own brain were revealed a few weeks ago, and the insight emerged as I was contemplating my reaction to encountering a

7. Siegel, *Developing Mind*, 4–5.

8. Ecker et al., *Unlocking the Emotional Brain*, 4.

roach. My children often find my over-the-top reactions to roaches entertaining. But I'd like my brain to have a wider range of responses to choose from. As I was reflecting on this, an unrelated memory occurred to me of a time when I was eight years old, and our father had been taking care of the three of us children for the afternoon. He took us to the grocery store for some items. The store was hot and crowded; the lines were long. As we waited for our father to check out, my brother and sister and I became restless and noisy. We started teasing each other, trying to make the other laugh or cry. We were beginning to annoy the other customers, and our dad told us to knock it off. It would have been a stressful afternoon for any parent, and I imagine our father was feeling challenged and overwhelmed.

We left the grocery story, and our father drove us to our great-grandmother's house. When we got there, he took me to a spare room and disciplined me physically and severely. Earlier generations of parents were often advised to use discipline techniques that are now discouraged.[9] Some of these may have been benign under conditions of low or moderate stress. But this particular afternoon, I am guessing that we were both under especially high stress, because this physical assault felt uncommonly frightening and unresolved.

When I speak with our parents now about times like these, I try to communicate the compassion I feel for the stress they were under. And if a childhood memory produces distress now, I try to spend time helping these networks link up with other networks associated with present-day awareness and kindness. So when this particular memory surfaced of the frightening incident in the spare room of my great-grandmother's house, I took some time to reflect on it and two things occurred to me. The first was that I had gone to bed later that night in the same room where the earlier terror had occurred. The second was that my great-grandmother's house had a roach problem.

That night after the incident, I had trouble falling asleep and lay there thinking, while also being aware that roaches were crawling the walls and occasionally flying by. This was an element of the memory that I had never noticed before, and it gave me a clue as to how these networks had linked up in my brain, and what I might do to help them link up differently. To help our brain networks rewire requires that the proper networks be activated. If one of those networks is associated with a distressing memory, then we can expect to feel a bit of that distress upon activation. The key then is to activate that distressing network while also activating other networks—perhaps ones associated with adult awareness, compassion, or humor—at the

9. Straus, "Prevalence, Societal Causes, and Trends," 7.

very same time. If our stress then is just right, we can expect these networks may link up.

Whenever we say, "I feel better," or "I see some humor in it now," it is because our networks have managed to link up in a new way. It is the new linkages that produce a felt change in our emotions and sensations. Therefore, when we speak of "healing," "growth," or "maturity," we can understand ourselves to be referring to changes taking place at the level of our neural anatomy; effectively, different thinking requires different linking.

So here are three things we might find helpful to remember about mapping the brain: 1) the networks we use more frequently become slicker and more efficient; 2) when networks become activated at the same time, they may link up; and 3) by directing attention and awareness to the networks we wish to link up, we can help them do so.

The Stress Continuum

When it comes to linking up networks in our brain, we find a bit of stress is helpful. This is because stress activates our brain networks, causing them to "fire," which is essential to the linking-up process. So what is stress? I like a definition I came across recently: stress is "the nonspecific response of the body to any demand made upon it."[10] And we can think of stress as the energy that catalyzes our neural networks to stretch and form new linkages. But in order for our brain to form new linkages in a helpful way, our stress needs be in the "Goldilocks" range—not too low, nor too high. Stress exists on a continuum between pleasant and unpleasant,[11] and we need the "just right" amount to optimally grow our brain; too little or too much stress narrows the options for when, how, and which neural networks will link up. In other words, optimal learning, healing, and growth for human beings occurs when our stress is "just right."[12]

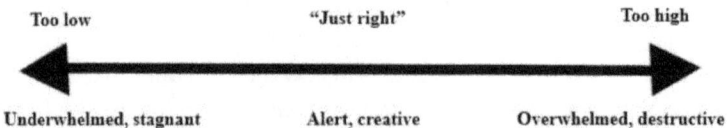

Too low	"Just right"	Too high
Underwhelmed, stagnant	Alert, creative	Overwhelmed, destructive

The Stress Continuum

10. Selye, *Stress without Distress*, 27.

11. For reflection, Selve, *Stress without Distress*, 33.

12. Immordino-Yang and Damasio, "We Feel, Therefore We Learn," 3; Selve, *Stress without Distress*, 70–82.

With too little stress, we may feel bored and underwhelmed; in that case growth stagnates and we might find few helpful linkages getting established. But with too much stress, we're at risk of being overwhelmed and tossed into a state of physiological agony. Linkages may occur when our stress is too high but if the stress is activating only certain networks, say the ones concerned about our physical survival alone, then we can expect these will be the networks that link up. If other networks, such as those related to relationality, kindness, creativity, and access to joy, are not also activated under extreme stress, then we would not expect new linkages with these networks to get established or reinforced.

So here is a summary of this first earpiece:

The Neuroscience of Stress

Stress exists on a continuum.
With too little stress, we may feel bored and underwhelmed; growth stagnates.
With too much stress, we're at risk of being overwhelmed by our agony.
With just right stress, new helpful linkages occur,
and we learn and grow in maturity.

Holding this awareness of stress and its impact on our brain in mind, I began listening to the Christian story at the very beginning in Genesis—the story of our creation; and I was curious what I might encounter.

In the Beginning

In the beginning God created the heavens and the earth . . .
and the Spirit of God was moving over the surface of the waters.[13]

This is the opening line of the sacred text that invites us into an encounter with God the Creator at the beginning of the story of creation. When I first listened to these words, I found myself trying to imagine the difference between created and *non*-created existence. But because we are included in the former, we may find we have no context for the latter. So when I read the words of Saint Gregory of Nazianzus, who encouraged us to retain humility as we explored the mysteries of faith instead of getting sidetracked

13. Gen 1:1 (NASB); the word *ruach* (Spirit) is sometimes translated "breath" as in Gen 7:15 and Job 7:7, or "wind" as in Gen 8:1 and Exod 10:13.

and obsessed with "setting and solving conundrums,"[14] I took those words to heart.

But I did find it meaningful to consider various scholars' reflections on "nothingness," and other concepts of non-created existence from which the created universe may have been formed.[15] And I kept returning to the idea that we can only listen well from our position situated in time and space, therefore anything else we might meaningfully contemplate about non-created existence could not possibly originate with us. Therefore, I concluded it was less helpful to contemplate concepts such as "nothingness" and to place my attention instead on the subject in the opening line of the text where we are offered a name for the being responsible for created existence: *God*.

> In the beginning God created the heavens and the earth . . .
> and the Spirit of God was moving over the surface of the waters.[16]

It occurred to me that this picture of the first moment of creation included two actions: God creating, and the Spirit of God moving. I read that the Hebrew for "Spirit" here is different than the word for "God,"[17] giving rise to the sense of God and the Spirit as two collaborators, here at the beginning of everything. But this is not all; I came to also understand this was the creation story that Jesus and his friends would grow up listening to a few thousand years later, and that at least some in Jesus' inner circle would come to perceive him also as having been present in this story, at the moment of creation:

> In the beginning was the Word, and the Word was with God, and the
> Word was God.
> He was in the beginning with God. All things were made through him,
> and without him was not any thing made that was made.[18]

These words appeared to be suggesting that the *logos* (Word), understood as Jesus or Christ, was also a collaborator in this initial act of creation.[19] And

---

14. Gregory of Nazianzus, *Orat.* 27.2.

15. Aquinas, *Summa Theologica* 1.3.4; Saint Athanasius, *Inc.* 5; Barth, *Church Dogmatics* 3.3; Hume, *Dialogues Concerning Natural Religion* 9.189; LaCugna, *God for Us*, 355; Oord, "Open Theology Doctrine of Creation," 28–52; Zizioulas and Edwards, *One and the Many*, 186.

16. Gen 1:1 (NASB).

17. The name *Elohim* (God) distinguished from *ruach* (Spirit, breath, or wind).

18. John 1:1.

19. The word *logos* (Word) is used to convey "wisdom" or "reasoning" as in Aristotle,

I took note of the words of another early theologian, Saint Paul, who is also recorded as having written about Christ being present at the beginning of our story:

> Christ is the image of the invisible God . . .
> in him all things in heaven and on earth were created.[20]

Paul's knowledge of Jesus, and his practice of listening apparently led him to the conclusion that Jesus was God made visible—the image of the invisible God—and this in turn transformed Paul's understanding of the creation story as well. Paul came to think of Jesus as the image of the invisible God, present at the moment of creation.

From there, I remembered Jesus was also recorded as having said:

> Very truly, I tell you, before Abraham was, I am.[21]

Because Abraham was said to have lived several thousand years before Jesus' birth, this became curious as well. I learned that Jesus' listeners would have recognized this phrase from an ancient story where Moses is said to have asked God, "What if they ask me your name? What shall I say to them?" and God answered, "I Am Who I Am."[22] Therefore, when Jesus answered, "I am," his listeners may have understood him to be explaining, "I am God." In listening to Scripture and some of these early theologians, I came across dozens of little clues like these that seemed to point to the possibility that there were *three* collaborators present in this first moment of creation: Jesus, God, and the Spirit—a "Trinity" of collaborators.[23] So what if God indeed exists as three-in-one?

Rhet. 1.2, as well as Hebrew notions of the "wisdom of God" or the "utterance of God" through which the universe was created, as in Justin Martyr, *Dialogue with Trypho* 61; Philo, *On the Creation of the Cosmos*, §§19–25; for reflection, Hillar, *From Logos to Trinity*, 8.

20. Col 1:15–16.

21. John 8.

22. Exod 3:13; the word `ehyeh` (I am) in the future tense "I will become"; for reflection, discussions of verb tense (past, present, or future) when discussing God reflect an emphasis on God existing outside of time or entering historical time; Anderson et al., *Understanding the Old Testament*, 56–57; email exchange with Steve Bishop, Old Testament scholar, in discussion with the author in July 2020.

23. The word "Trinity" is not found in the Hebrew or Greek Scriptures and represents an understanding of God that developed early in Christian history, and we are encouraged to be humble when speaking about matters that are not explicit in Scripture; for reflection, personal conversation with James Alison on March 2017; Shuster, "Preaching the Trinity," 357–81.

I spent time then trying to imagine a three-in-one existence. I liked a poetic suggestion I came across in the writings of Saint Gregory of Nazianzus, who imagined God as intermingling like the light from three interconnected Suns.[24] For a while, I also contemplated God as a symphony composer, with Jesus as the music, and the Spirit as the breath inside each instrument. On a different day, I imagined God as a playwright, with Jesus as the script, and the Spirit as the movement of the actors bringing the play to life on stage.[25]

Each of these images has its shortfalls, but I found they each offered something helpful as well, and I gained some appreciation for the beauty of the idea that the creative act flowed from an Artist who exists as a *relationship*.[26]

And God said, "Let there be light . . ."
And God said, "Let there be sky . . ."
And God said, "Let dry ground appear . . ."
And God said, "Let the earth produce . . ."
And God said, "Let there be lights in the sky . . ."
And God said, "Let the waters bring forth living creatures . . ."
And God said, "Let the earth bring forth living creatures . . ."
And God said, "Let us make humankind in our image, according to our likeness . . ."
And it was so.[27]

When I listened to the unfolding of the ancient story, and imagined God, three-in-one, speaking the universe into existence word-by-holy-word, here is what I saw in my mind's eye:

God the Creator, the One who speaks.
God who is Jesus, the spoken Word
God the Spirit, the movement and breath of life

24. Gregory of Nazianzus, *Orat.* 31.14; Tertullian, *Apol.* 21, offered a similar picture.

25. Early Christian scholars (e.g., Irenaeus of Lyons; Theophilus of Antioch) imagined the *Logos* and Spirit as creative extensions of God like the "hand of God" or the "finger of God"; Irenaeus, *Haer.* 4.4.463; Theophilus, *Autol.* 5; for reflection, Lashier, *Irenaeus on the Trinity*, 28.

26. For reflection, Aquinas, *Summa Theologica* 1.3.3; Athanasius, *Ep. Aeg. Lib.* 2.1; Hooker, *Laws of Ecclesiastical Polity* 1.2.2; Maximus the Confessor, *Op.* 7, 76A–80A; Tanner, *Jesus, Humanity, and the Trinity*, 36, 54; Zizioulas, *Being as Communion*, 83–89.

27. From Gen 1:1–30.

What do we make of this notion of God as three-in-one, bringing the universe into existence through the creative act of speaking? When I considered this, I felt a sense of tenderness at the relationship between speaker, word, and breath that is intimate; the word and breath arise from the speaker's own body. I also felt energized when I thought about how the spoken word is a generative tool; the act of speaking—moving air molecules through breath to generate sound waves—creates vibrations in the inner ear of a listener. On the part of the listener, words also have the power to impact our fleshly organs, altering our heart rate, breathing, the frequency of our own brain waves. And this in turn shapes the speech that becomes our creative (or destructive) response.

It's been said that without language for naming and articulating "what is," it becomes difficult for us to perceive reality and relate to it.[28] And reflecting on that, in connection with the creation narrative, brought to mind something Helen Keller once said. As a child, Keller grew up without words, having lost her ability to see and hear prior to developing language. Keller has likened a wordless world to being at sea in a dense fog, tense and anxious, with no compass and no way of knowing how near the shore is. "'Light! Give me light!' was the wordless cry of my soul," she said.[29] One afternoon when Keller was around seven years old, her teacher Miss Sullivan took her to the garden and placed one of the child's hands under a water faucet while signing the word "water" into the other. Keller has called this moment "my soul's awakening." It was the first helpful link her brain ever made between a word and the expansive reality that the word symbolized. "That living word awakened my soul, gave it light, hope, joy, set it free."[30] After words were introduced, it was as if the world had been created anew.

As the creation story goes, the word was spoken, and the universe was created. I spent some time contemplating this word-by-word, and something fresh popped into my mind. It was not just energy, mass, and matter that were being created in this scene. Something else, other than the heavens and earth, was also created: *time.* Time didn't exist, and now it did; because now there is a *now.* And this sparked more curiosity for me about the meaning of God, three-in-one, engaged in the creative act of speaking everything into existence, but not all at once—*a little* at a time.

28. For reflection, see Tippett, "Shaping Grief with Language"; Williams, *Truce of God,* 56.

29. Keller, *Story of My Life,* 23.

30. Keller, *Story of My Life,* 25.

Time, Why?

Why was time necessary? What is time's purpose and relationship to God and the rest of creation? One afternoon I was driving and Matt Salyer came on the radio.[31] Matt's daughter Rosie was around nine years old, and going through a phase where she asked her dad a lot of questions. Salyer was busy so he told her, "Make a list of your questions and when I'm done, I'll answer them." So she did; Matt says he expected them to be simple but they weren't. She wrote three single-spaced pages of effectively unanswerable questions. Here are a few that made it onto Rosie's list:

> *What is life?*
> *Where do we go when we die?*
> *How do we know what's true?*
> *Time? Why? Explain.*

That last one—yes; explain indeed. What is time's purpose? As I spent time contemplating this, I found it helpful to circle back to those images of the moment when time is said to have first come into existence. Here is an image I stayed with for quite a while: a three-in-one Artist—poised and ready to paint the universe into being:

> *God the Artist, imagining the painting.*
> *God who is Jesus, the paint.*
> *God the Spirit, the movement of the brushstrokes*

And I began to notice that we can conceive of a divine Painter in non-created timeless existence *prior* to the first brushstroke, but everything after that occurs in time. So why the brushstrokes? Why did creation require time and movement through it? Why not simply project *everything* onto the canvas of created existence all at once? My practice of contemplating the need for brushstrokes led me to wonder about God's reason for painting the universe to begin with. So I then pictured God the Painter, bursting with inspiration, giddy at this idea: "We'll create a self-portrait!" Or another way of expressing it may be this: the created universe may be a vehicle for making God *perceptible*.

But I saw a problem with this notion. If the universe exists as a way of making God perceptible, then time occurred to me to be a fly in the ointment. That is to say, if the reason for creating the universe is to paint

31. Matt Salyer. Interview by Foo, "Rosie's Paradox."

a self-portrait, the first noticeable discrepancy between the Painter and painting would appear to be *time*, because time would appear to correspond *imperfectly* with God, who exists in timelessness.

So, as delightful as the idea of painting a self-portrait might be, something would be slightly discrepant in the painting as soon as time was created. The moment a "now" arises, which is perceptibly different from a "then," the universe now lacks a perfect 1:1 correspondence with its Creator. And so I started to wonder if we might feel that discrepancy in every molecule of our being. Which is to say, I wondered if the invention of time inevitably gave rise to stress. Was it possible that simply existing within time—rather than timelessness—introduced stress into the picture?

From there, I began to wonder why time may have been necessary. Could God have painted a self-portrait, all in one stroke? Could the whole image of God have been projected onto the canvas of the universe in an instant? I began to think, no; it seemed a slight discrepancy between the Creator and the creation would be desirable—necessary, even—if the hope was for the Creator and the creation to *perceive* one another. This thought emerged after contemplating what a timeless creation would have achieved. For instance, it occurred to me that if the painting and the Painter enjoyed a perfect 1:1 correspondence, this would render them effectively indistinguishable from each other, essentially resulting in a clone of God—two timeless Gods, relating each One to One's own self. And this did not seem to me to have been the idea that filled the Painter with delight. Which is to say, it appeared to me that the creative inspiration had been—not to render a *second* God—but to render God *perceptible*. Therefore, in order for the painting to perceive the Painter, it seemed there must be some perceptible distinction between the two. And then a thought occurred to me that was larger than anything I had thought so far: perhaps creation reflects God— without becoming God—by unfolding *as a story*. Or put another way, perhaps "story" is *the* vehicle by which God makes God's self perceptible. If so, then the invention of time seemed necessary, and stress perhaps a byproduct.

Reflecting God

When I thought about the notion of the universe and us as perhaps existing as a self-portrait of God—time and stress notwithstanding—I remembered this line from the creation story in Genesis:

Let us make humankind in our image, according to our likeness.[32]

I began to wonder then, what parts of us might reflect God's image? And where were the points of correspondence and divergence? Because if the reason for creating the universe was to render God "able to be perceived" by us, then it occurred to me we might experience ourselves to be at our best when we are perceiving God and making God perceptible. I wondered then if we reflected God with as much clarity as we are able when we are under the "just right" amount of stress, but whether perhaps we do not reflect God's image as clearly when we are under too much stress or too little.

A while back I became interested in the techniques involved in photographing reflections on the surface of bodies of water. Under calm conditions, ponds, lakes, and even the ocean may reflect the image of whatever is above them. And yet, under choppy conditions or after an oil spill or disaster, the water will cease to reflect the sky. So we might say the reflective properties of water exist on a continuum.

Are we also that way?

Is it possible that under "just right" conditions we reflect the image of God, and under extreme conditions the image of God in us becomes distorted, or even obscured altogether? When this thought occurred to me, I recalled how, from a neurobiological perspective, a little stress is good for us. We function optimally under "just right" stress conditions—not too little, not too much. This led me to wonder, "Are these perhaps the conditions under which we reflect God's image?" This appeared to me to be a potentially important link between brain science and theology, so I took out a piece of paper and wrote down the words that I thought corresponded with God and with us when we are functioning at our best. I started with the words that I thought corresponded with the image of God, three-in-one, as described in Genesis, at the beginning of the story of everything. Here is what I wrote:

God is life . . . exists.
God is relational . . . three-in-one.
God is kind . . . tender with God's own self.[33]

32. Gen 1:1; for reflection on "image" and likeness," Aquinas, *Summa Theologica* 1.4.3 and 1.35.1; Saint Augustine of Hippo, *Conf.* 13.22.32; Saint Augustine of Hippo, *Civ.* 15.21; Justin Martyr, *Dial.* 62; Ricoeur, "'Image of God,'" 37–50; Volf, *After Our Likeness*, 183.

33. The word "kind" reflects my understanding of the notion that God as *three-in-one* exists as a kind, collaborative, noncompetitive relationship; for reflection, Tanner, *Jesus, Humanity, and the Trinity*, 90.

God is creative . . . brings new creation into existence.
God is joy . . . appears to create for the joy and delight of it.

Then I considered how we human beings function when we are at our best—when we have access to our upper neocortical networks and their capacities for compassion, self-awareness, creativity, patience, empathy, and all of the qualities we exhibit under "just right" conditions. Here is what I wrote:

We show signs of life.
We relate well to others.
We exhibit kindness.
We are creative.
We feel joy and delight.

I noticed that we might find an almost perfect 1:1 correspondence between the qualities we might observe in God, three-in-one, from the very beginning, and human beings and how we relate to one another under "just right" stress conditions. I wondered then if this might mean that when our stress is just right, we may reflect God's image with greater clarity. From there, I wrote down words that we might consider to be the opposite of those qualities; this is what we experience when we are underwhelmed or overwhelmed, neurobiologically speaking—particularly when our stress is too high and our upper neocortical networks begin to shut down, and our lower threat networks are active and somewhat hijacking the rest of our brain. Here is what that list looked like:

We inflict death.
We are isolated.
We experience cruelty.
We are destructive.
We feel agony and torment.

I thought about my own life and seasons where I have functioned better and reflected some of the qualities on the former list, and times when I have been under extreme stress and displayed some of the qualities of the latter. The more our threat networks are activated, the harder it becomes to make choices, set intentions, and follow through with them. And the more our upper networks are engaged, the easier we may find it to be the relational, kind, creative, enjoyable people we aspire to be.

That led me to two thoughts. First, it occurred to me that, when it comes to the networks in our brain that are activated in any given moment, it would appear that we have a window of choice within which we can influence the direction that activity is headed.[34] That is to say, *choice* also appears to exist along a continuum. Once our lower threat networks take over, activity in our upper networks tends to slow down, and our ability to choose how to respond to a person or situation is diminished. But in that moment just before "system override"—when our threat networks are only partially activated and not yet in full-blown reaction mode—there is a window within which our upper networks can conceivably influence how our body responds to a situation. Within that window, we may find our upper networks capable of soothing and regulating our lower networks; we may be capable of choosing to slow our heart rate through breathing, scan our environment, engage our upper networks, analyze our options, and behave and speak in ways which consistent with our values.

So what factors expand or collapse that window for us? Through neuroscience we are discovering daily practices that over time can help to keep us in that "just right" zone of stress and retain access to our upper networks. But there is also a lot of learning to be achieved through "trial and error," as our brains each respond to stress and regulation practices differently. So as we are learning, we are almost certainly going to experience moments when our stress exceeds our window of tolerance and our choices are limited. In those moments, we can expect to find it difficult or impossible to regulate ourselves. When that happens, speaking theologically, perhaps we also cease to reflect the image of God. That thought led to a second one: if God is made perceptible as a story—rather than a single moment—then how we respond after a moment of difficulty, once our upper networks come back "online," adds something new to the story that may change the meaning of what came before it.

I found this second thought hopeful. When the image of God reflected in us seems cracked or fractured, we may feel tempted to succumb to the stress and allow the fracture to remain unattended to. Perhaps what matters is that we learn instead to "keep the story moving," by practicing ways of dialing down our stress so that our upper networks can come back "online," and we can continue adding to the story. In this way, even moments where our lack of correspondence with God is most noticeable, we may understand God is still capable of being rendered perceptible through us as a story unfolding over time.

Here then is a summary of this first chapter:

34. Siegel, *Developing Mind*, 283.

The Story of Creation

God the three-in-one Artist imagined a way to make non-created existence
able to be perceived . . .
by creating the universe, including time, space, and all of life
to reflect all of God as a story of:

life
relationship
kindness
creativity
and joy

By existing in time, created existence contains within it
a degree of stress.

When stress is just right—
not too high or low
God's image is reflected in us.

A Prayer to God the Creator

Holy Imaginator,
You are Light invisible,
by which all else may be seen.

Artistic Inventor,
You move us grain by grain,
as the wind chisels the cliffside.

Mystical Creator,
You are an explosion of color,
a prism of every possibility.
Like dry canvases, we wait;
May Your brushstrokes come quick
to enliven us.

In the name of God the Artist,
Christ, the creative Word,
and the Spirit, our breath of life,
Amen

A Blessing for One Who Is Creative

May God the Artist,
who imagined oceans and diamonds,
imagine inside you
what now lives in nothingness
waiting to be called into being.

May Christ,
who entered creation
as a dream embodied,
sustain you now
as you endeavor to embody your dreams.

May the Spirit be in you
who animates the stars,
and the redwoods, and jellyfish,
and your own
creative process.

And may God
midwife through you
a new reality,
a glimpse of the universe
the likes of which no eye has ever seen.

In the name of God the Creator,
Christ the visionary,
and the Spirit of inspiration,
Amen

Theological Anthropology

Monday

I ate a strawberry today.
Fingertip to folded leaf,
skin pierced,
teardrop plucked,
crunched.

Two fingers circled a soft globe,
honeycomb
rolled to the light,
organs squished,
stem sucked.

Peaks were summited today;
blood was spilled,
wars were stoked,
enemies were invented,
and today
I ate a strawberry.

2

A Trustworthy Compass

But now to the hard question:
Have we grounds for thinking God trustworthy?

—ROWAN WILLIAMS[1]

ACCORDING TO BESSEL VAN der Kolk, too much stress can cause our inner timekeeper to collapse. Here is how he puts it: "Knowing that whatever is happening is finite and will sooner or later come to an end makes most experiences tolerable. The opposite is also true—situations feel intolerable if they seem interminable. Most of us know from a sad personal experience that terrible grief is typically accompanied by the sense that this wretched state will last forever, and that we will never get over our loss. Agony is the ultimate experience of 'this will last forever.'"[2] What I understand van der Kolk to be saying is that when our stress is too high we may lose sight of the "story" we are living and feel unable to "keep the story moving." Losing sight of the story may further dial up our stress to the point of physiological agony. And when stress turns to agony, we typically lose access to our upper brain networks and their ability to regulate our nervous system; we then become less relational, kind, creative, or joyful. If our stress continues to rise, then we may find ourselves slipping into isolation, cruelty, and destructive behavior leading to further agony.

1. Williams, *Tokens of Trust*, 7.
2. van der Kolk, *Body Keeps the Score*, 69–70.

In the previous chapter, we considered how "just right" stress helps brain networks link up; and when distressing networks link up with more compassionate ones, that is what we call "healing." Therefore, we may understand "just right" stress to be an essential ingredient in learning, healing, and growth; stress has been called the "spice of life."[3] We also observed that stress exists on a continuum—too much and we are overwhelmed and agonizing; too little and we are underwhelmed and stagnant. And we noted that the degree of stress we experience depends less on the cues in our environment and more on our *perception* of them. Which is to say, the same situation can produce either distress or *eustress* (good stress) in our body, depending on the unique networks already established in our brain.[4] In turn, the stress we are already experiencing when we encounter a new situation will shape our perception of it; therefore a recursive relationship exists between stress and our perception of reality. The more helpful the linkages are between networks in our brain, the more trustworthy our perception of reality—our inner compass—may become.

So if much of what we experience in life—whether we are inclined toward relationality, kindness, creativity, and joy or toward isolation, cruelty, destructivity, and agony—depends largely on our perception of reality, which is in turn influenced by our stress, perhaps a helpful question for us is this: what can we do to expand our window of tolerance for stress, thereby enabling us to perceive reality more clearly?

Regulating the Brain

In considering that question, we might find it helpful to understand a little more about how the brain regulates itself. The human brain has a distinct anatomical architecture with networks running through upper, central, and lower regions.[5] Dan Siegel uses his hand to explain this,[6] with his thumb tucked inside his fist. Palm forward, the lower arm represents the spinal cord, and the wrist, the base of the skull. The fleshy part of the palm represents the lower subcortical region. The thumb tucked inside represents the central region. And the fingers represent the upper neocortical region.

Here is the information we may find most helpful for our purposes. Our lower subcortical networks are "threat" reaction networks. These lower

3. Selye, *Stress without Distress*, 85.

4. Lazarus, "From Psychological Stress to the Emotions," 8–17; Milsum, "Model of the Eustress System," 179–86.

5. Clowry, "Renewed Focus," 276–88; MacLean, *Triune Brain*, 9.

6. Siegel, *Developing Mind*, 20.

networks fire to keep us alive when we are facing an actual threat. They may speed up our heart, pumping more blood to our limbs so we can act more quickly; they may also decrease activity in our upper neocortical region because when we are facing an actual threat, we do not necessarily need to analyze it philosophically—we sometimes just need to act. We can feel thankful for our lower subcortical networks because when we are not actually safe, they serve us well. They help us react quickly to avoid or cope with a true threat. But when these lower networks over-function in the absence of an actual threat, this can be problematic for us. When our lower subcortical networks are engaged, it is highly taxing to our system.[7] Our body tenses up in "threat mode," though we may appear perfectly calm on the outside; our insides are on high alert and this extracts a toll on our internal resources, like software draining our CPU power. And the feelings and sensations we experience when our lower circuitry is revved up further increases our stress, creating a recursive relationship between stress and our reaction to it.

In contrast, our upper neocortical networks are "safety" response networks. These upper networks help us navigate reality with thoughtfulness, relationality, attunement to ourselves and others, kindness, compassion, creativity, and emotional regulation. When stress is just right and we feel safe enough, we may find our upper networks active and humming and we may feel like we are being the best version of ourselves. Our upper networks can soothe and calm activity in our lower networks, helping to regulate our emotions, decrease our stress, and increase our awareness of being "safe enough" when we are so indeed, which in turn keeps our upper circuitry engaged.

I am reminded of the way in which my brain processed the stress of labor during unanesthetized childbirth. During most of the intense pain, my upper neocortical networks were still engaged. I felt distress and discomfort, but I was also relational, kind to myself and those around me, creative about what to try next to keep the labor moving, and relatively calm and able to access moments of joy. This tells me my upper neocortical networks were mostly successful at calming the threat-reactions of my lower networks. But there was a brief flash during each of my childbirth experiences when everything changed. With the first, it was a moment when I rolled onto my back for a medical intervention. In the second, was the moment I sensed the baby was coming. Both moments felt agonizing, and then subsided quickly.

So what was happening in my brain during those moments of agony?

---

7. Feldman Barrett, *How Emotions Are Made*, 204–14.

The panic I remember tells me that my lower subcortical networks had hijacked the rest of my brain. Stress was "too high," and when that occurs, the lower brain will often take over. I perceived there to be an actual threat and I felt under-resourced and under-supported to cope with it. In those moments, I became tunnel-visioned; my only goal was ending the agony. With my upper networks "offline," my brain had few possible responses to choose from. I could not have chosen a relational, kind, creative, or joyful response in that moment because that would have required my upper networks to have been engaged. But as soon as I perceived my safety to increase—meaning an increase in resources and support—my upper brain came back "online" and I returned to being "myself."

We can tolerate high levels of stress without our upper neocortical networks going "offline," of course; but to so, requires at least two things. First, our brain must perceives the resources and support available to us to be sufficient for navigating the threat. Second, enough linkages must exist between our upper and lower networks. When these two conditions are met, our upper networks may remain engaged even when our stress and pain is intense, and our upper networks can then calm and soothe our lower ones, helping us to regulate the rest of our body. We then become part of the trustworthy environment to which we are responding. Under the reverse conditions, our brain perceives ourselves and our environment to be untrustworthy so that our lower networks hijack the rest of our brain, and we experience a crisis of *trust*.

The Brain on Trust

"Trust" is a word we have assigned to a series of neurobiological phenomena in the brain; when we experience trust, our brain fires in a pattern that lowers our stress, regulates our heart rate and breathing, lowers the level of distress-related chemicals in the brain, and increases the level of pleasant-feeling neurotransmitters in the brain.[8] We might call this a "trust-response" and it is both a function of our upper networks and helpful for self-maintaining activity in our upper networks—even when we are under intense pain or facing an actual threat. That is to say, when trust is high, our upper networks may remain active and available to us regardless of the circumstances. And the more time we spend in this helpful brain state, the more benefits we receive from it, in the form of boosts to our immune

8. Norman et al., "Social Neuroscience," 18–29.

system, support with moral decision-making, and an increased capacity to relate kindly and creatively with others.[9]

We might say then that the neurobiological phenomenon of trust functions somewhat like a thermostat for the rest of the brain. Trust raises and lowers activity in particular regions of our brain in response to cues in the environment. Without trust, we typically access our upper circuitry only when feeling quite safe, and when we feel threatened, our lower circuitry tends to take over. With trust, we are enabled to access both our upper and lower circuitry simultaneously, even in the face of an actual threat. This is extraordinarily helpful. With trust, we may access information from our lower and upper networks at the same time, expanding the range of responses available for us to choose from. When this happens, we might find ourselves able to respond to a threatening person or situation more creatively, compassionately, and confidently than we can when our upper networks are shut down.

So what or whom are we trusting, in this scenario? It is probably not the threatening person or situation; that would be dangerous and unwise. And yet we find that our brain has the capacity to distrust a dangerous person or situation, while *also* trusting something or someone else who is trustworthy—perhaps God, ourselves, and our sense that the resources and support available to us are sufficient. When this happens, we may find we are capable of accessing both our lower distrusting threat networks and our upper trusting safety networks *at the same time*. And then we will find that trust functions like a thermostat—dialing our stress down to the level that is helpful and appropriate for navigating the situation in front of us. And trust also helps our upper networks remain engaged, so that we can access the support and resources that are available to us. This means there is a recursive relationship between the neurobiological phenomenon of trust and our ability to access trustworthy resources and support in our environment.

Yet when we speak of trust, we are referring to less of a cognitive choice and more of a phenomenon that occurs inside our brain more or less involuntarily.[10] That is to say, when we encounter something or someone we perceive to be trustworthy, we can expect our brain will produce a trust-response automatically. Brené Brown has distilled seven trustworthy qualities that, when perceived in person, may spark trust: respect for boundaries, reliability,

9. Cardoso, "Stress-Induced Negative Mood," 2800–2804; Mankarious et al., "Pro-Social Neurohormone Oxytocin," 1805–14; Onaka et al., "Roles of Oxytocin Neurones," 587–98; Onaka and Takayanagi, "Roles of Oxytocin," 1–20; Zak et al., "Neurobiology of Trust," 224–27.

10. Mureriwa, "Common Factors in Psychotherapy," 1–12; Riedl and Javor, "Biology of Trust," 63–91.

personal accountability, commitment to maintaining confidences, integrity, a nonjudgmental posture, and generosity.[11] When we encounter a person who displays these qualities, we can expect our brain to respond automatically by producing a trust-response; that response helps us to regulate our stress and engage our upper networks, so that we may be capable of being trustworthy in return. But in order for a trustworthy person to spark trust within us, we must perceive that person's trustworthiness accurately. Therefore, the degree of trust—and the degree of stress—we experience depends less on circumstances and more on our *perception* of them; which may be less rooted in reality than we prefer to think.

The Trust Compass

When our brain scans our environment for cues about the trustworthiness of a person or a situation, our brain is often making split-second decisions based on limited information. And much of our brain's response will be shaped by how the present environment activates memory networks established in our brain through previous encounters. When environmental cues remind us of an untrustworthy situation from our past, we are likely to respond in the same way we did in the past, and this response may or may not be appropriate to the current situation. Therefore, we may think of our brain's response to our environment as a "trust compass" with four different options:

Untrustworthy *misperceived*	*Exploring (risky)*	*Trusting (helpful)*	**Trustworthy** *perceived*
Trustworthy *misperceived*	*Sounding a false alarm (unhelpful)*	*Threat reacting (taxing)*	**Untrustworthy** *perceived*

The Trust Compass

11. Brown, *Rising Strong*, 199–200.

When our compass points top-left, we encounter an *untrustworthy* person or situation, but we unfortunately misperceive it, mistaking an actual threat for something trustworthy. Our brain responds by manufacturing a trust-response in our upper networks; we are flooded with pleasant-feeling neurotransmitters and our lower networks remain calm. But this is not the appropriate response for which the environment calls, and an actual threat is going undetected by our lower networks. We feel safe enough to explore, but because the environment is genuinely threatening, this is risky and could be dangerous.[12] Thinking of this reminds me of a day when I was out gardening with our daughter who was six years old, and she tugged my sleeve and said she was thirsty. I instructed her to go inside and find a cup by the bathroom sink and get herself a drink. A few minutes later, she came back outside, said she had drunk something "yucky," and immediately began vomiting. I raced to the bathroom and saw that a family member had left hydrogen peroxide in a cup after disinfecting something. Our daughter picked up the cup, and because the peroxide looked like water, she had taken a large gulp. We spoke on the phone to poison control who reassured us that the next few hours would not be fun but she would recover okay. I read books to her while her system purged itself and felt regret for having sent her trusting into that untrustworthy situation.

The opposite is occurring when our trust compass points bottom-right; in this case, our lower, subcortical networks are engaged, and we are responding to an actual threat with an appropriate threat-reaction. Under these conditions, we will typically feel unsafe to explore, and that is probably a good thing. We have perceived an *untrustworthy* situation accurately. I am reminded of an example from the following year when our daughter was seven years old; she and I were home alone one night and heard a commotion in the backyard. We looked and saw a man trying to climb onto our porch. "Run inside and lock all the doors," I told our daughter. I stood by the back door and called 911 on my cellphone. The police arrived quickly and after speaking with the man, it became clear he was experiencing psychiatric needs. We did not press charges and the police transported him safely to a hospital. Once everyone had left, I knocked on the back door for our daughter to let me in; there was no response. I circled the perimeter of the house, knocking on the windows, and calling to our daughter that it was safe to unlock the doors. Finally, she cracked open the front door, and I saw that she was "armored up," having put on every winter coat, hat, scarf, and gloves she could find to protect her. And she was wielding a pocket

---

12. Cruwys, "When Trust Goes Wrong," 1–27; for reflection, Bader-Saye, *Following Jesus in a Culture of Fear*, 44–50.

knife. Until we are faced with an actual threat, we do not know for certain how our lower subcortical networks will respond; in this case, our daughter was prepared to defend herself and her threat networks were responding appropriately to an untrustworthy situation. Afterward, she seemed to feel energized and eager to relay every detail of the story to her father. When our lower networks fire appropriately in response to the occasional actual threat, it can feel empowering and confidence-boosting. If this were to become a nightly pattern, however, it would tax our resources and extract a toll on our health and wellness over time.[13]

A quite different set of circumstances is occurring when our compass points bottom-left; our lower subcortical networks are engaged in a mistrusting response but this time we are wrong. The environment is *trustworthy*, and our brain is sounding a false alarm. We will typically not feel safe enough to explore or engage under these conditions, therefore we will miss out on the benefits of trust and potentially our relationship to a trustworthy person. And sounding a false alarm too often is also taxing to our system; it will deprive us of resources and diminish our quality of life, relationships, kindness, creativity, and joy over time. This brings to mind a time when our son was nursing; we took him to a fireworks show at the park. I began feeding him right as the fireworks began, and the noise startled him. He seemed frightened and stopped nursing and refused to try it again. When we arrived back home, he was still resistant to nursing so I pumped a bottle and fed it to him so he could sleep. The next day, we tried nursing again but he still seemed frightened and refused. I tried many strategies to reassure him there was no actual threat, but his brain was still perceiving the situation as dangerous. On the third day, we tried once more; he eventually relaxed and we were able to resume our feeding routine. I was never quite sure exactly which cues succeeded in restoring his trust but I was relieved.

The most helpful condition for us, perhaps, occurs when our trust compass points top-right; our brain produces a trust-response and this time it is appropriate. There may still be threats in our environment, however, we are perceiving accurately the trustworthiness of those persons and elements outside us and within which are indeed trustworthy, and responding with a trust-response. Whew! With so many options it is a wonder our trust-response and perception of reality ever succeed in syncing up. But when this happens, it is helpful to us. This is the condition under which we receive all the benefits of trust *and* trustworthiness which in turn contributes to our brain functioning, health, and wellness. And because the situation is genuinely trustworthy, we are safe enough to explore, try new things, and

13. Schneiderman, "Stress and Health," 607–28.

create new brain network linkages. Under this condition, trust is high, stress is more manageable, and we tend to feel most alive and free to choose how to respond to people and situations. And the good news is that we do not need to manufacture this experience; it simply happens automatically when we encounter a trustworthy person or situation and perceive this trustworthiness accurately.

So here is a summary of this second earpiece:

The Neuroscience of Trust

When trust is high, we access our upper, neocortical networks,
even if we are experiencing intense pain, and emotion;
trust helps us regulate our stress.

Trust is released automatically when we encounter
a trustworthy person or situation, rightly perceived.

When we misperceive the trustworthiness of a person or situation,
our trust compass is "off";
our response will likely then be unhelpful
for us and others.

As I developed an ear for listening to indicators of trust from a brain science perspective, I began to pay close attention to the potential role of trust in the Christian story. I wondered how an understanding of the neuroscience of trust might increase or decrease our appreciation for theological notions about humanity and our relationship to ourselves, one another, God, and the planet. So with these questions in mind, I continued the practice of slow listening, as the story of the original couple in Genesis unfolded.

The Garden

God said,
"See, I have given you every plant yielding seed that is upon the face of all the earth, and every tree with seed in its fruit you shall have them for food.

And to every beast of the earth, and to every bird of the air,
and to everything that creeps on the earth, everything that has the breath of life,

I have given every green plant for food."

And it was so.[14]

This is where the opening chapter of Genesis has led us: God created humankind in God's image, and they existed in a garden, with wildlife of all kinds. And then God instructed them in how to keep themselves alive, by nourishing themselves with plants for food. When I read this, I wondered, is it possible the early humans—along with the wild animals—consumed only plants?[15] And if so, how might this have impacted the early humans' brains in terms of the neuroscience of stress and trust?

Many large mammals—elephants, rhinoceroses, hippopotami, horses—subsist on plants alone. And when I imagined the early humans and animals in this story consuming only plants, I began to wonder what impact this might have had on their brains, on the relational environment between them, and on the planet, and here is what occurred to me: the humans and animals may have trusted one another.[16] With the predator-prey dynamic removed, there may have been little reason for fear. Typically, prey animals display nervous systems that are hypersensitive because they are vulnerable; meanwhile predatory animals show instincts toward violence that can be easily aroused. Human beings can display either prey or predatory instincts when our threat networks are activated and our upper neocortical networks are less so. What might then be the ripple effect of removing this dynamic from the equation? How would it change the way our brains function, if no creature ever had to die in order for another to live?

When I imagined life for these early humans, surrounded by food, sleeping under the stars, with wild animals roaming nearby, and with little reason to fear—calm, regulated nervous systems everywhere—I felt something like a grief, a longing to experience this degree of trust. And I was also moved by the stunning elegance of the idea that simply eating plants could be the key to such a reality. But then another detail captured my attention:

And the man and his wife were both naked, and were not ashamed.[17]

14. Gen 1:29–30.

15. For reflection, McFague, *Body of God*, 153–54; Moltman, *God in Creation*, 23–31.

16. The word *radah* (dominion) is used in other scriptures in a non-harsh sense; e.g., Lev 25:43, 46, 53, and Ezek 34:4; for reflection, Clough, *On Animals*, 78–84.

17. Gen 2:25.

Ha! What must *that* be like—to feel so at home in one's own skin? When I read that, I thought, these early humans may have trusted one another as well. It has been said that shame, humiliation, rejection, rape, murder, and racism—these forms of violence have to do with bodies in spaces.[18] What might then be the ripple effect of removing the dynamics of shame and fear from the equation, such that all bodies could feel safe in all spaces? How might that change the way our brains related to each other? I was curious.

One more thing occurred to me as I was reflecting on the couple in the garden. Trust may have been at the core of these early humans' experience of God. Because, as the story goes, all their needs were met. Which to me signaled:

They were alive.
They related well to others.
They exhibited kindness.
They were creative.
They could access joy and delight.

I began to wonder then about the relationship between perceiving all our needs to be met and perceiving God as trustworthy. And because we are dependent on clean water and nutritious food for our basic wellness, I wondered if the perception that there is enough food for all then becomes a key ingredient to unlocking that trust. That idea led me then to wonder about the number of humans on the planet today. Is there enough food for everyone?

From here, I looked at global population size and projected rates of growth. What I read offered predictions of numbers rising to fifty percent more than our current population before stabilizing sometime in the next century.[19] The current global pandemic notwithstanding, based on improved mortality rates around the world, better education, and family sizes leveling to an average of two children per household, I understood the projection was a stable, global population of around twelve billion humans. So then I wondered, could our planet as it exists today feed twelve billion people? Some calculations I found suggested that a quarter to a half of a hectare of land is required to grow enough food for one adult.[20] Then I read

18. Puwar, *Space Invaders*, 4.

19. United Nations, "World Population Prospects 2019." See the first download-able document on this webpage for a detailed breakdown of the projected population increase over the next hundred years or so.

20. According the United Nations, between .25–.50 hectares is needed to feed a person for a year; United Nations, "Fast Facts."

that in the last decade at least, there was an estimated twelve billion hectares of biologically productive land and water on the earth for producing crops, seaweed, and other foods,[21] not including hydroponics. So maybe there is enough capacity on the planet—usable land and water—to grow enough food to feed everyone. Could there be *enough for all?*

This idea led to a second question: if there is enough for all, why then is there so much hunger, scarcity, and fighting over resources? I read that, despite the ample planetary resources, many communities face routine hunger and malnourishment.[22] I wondered, is this merely a distribution problem or is something else going on? I also wondered, for those of us with more than enough to eat, is it possible we also experience the effects of the knowledge of scarcity on our nervous systems? Which is to say, even when all our individual needs are met, could the simple knowledge that this is not the case for everyone nevertheless dial up our collective stress? Is it possible that others' experiences of scarcity may whisper to our own subcortical networks that our situation is still not trustworthy? Even in middle- to high-income countries, we are told many of us will experience mental illness—depression, anxiety, suicidality, or addiction—at some point in our lives.[23] If there is enough for all—and for many of us, all our needs are met—why don't we *feel* as if that is true?

In reflecting on this question, the first thing I noticed is that our brain's response to reality depends largely on our *perception* of it. And how we act is largely governed by our perception of the situation, and the parts of our brain that are engaged[24]—whether that is more our upper neocortical networks or our lower subcortical threat networks. From there, I returned to the idea that we reflect God's image most clearly when our upper networks are engaged, and we are perceiving accurately the trustworthiness of a person or situation, and responding appropriately. These are the conditions in which human beings feel most alive, relate well with others, and exhibit kindness, creativity, and joy! And I noticed in the story of the garden, these conditions appeared to have been present from the beginning.

So what happened?

Knowledge of Evil

You may freely eat of every tree in the garden;

21. Borucke et al., "Accounting for Demand and Supply," 523.
22. World Health Organization, "World Health Statistics Overview, 2019," 14.
23. World Health Organization, "Cross-National Comparisons," 417.
24. For reflection, Schwartz and Sweezy, *Internal Family Systems Therapy*, 66.

> but of the tree of the knowledge of good and evil you shall not eat
> for in the day that you eat of it you shall die.[25]

These are the words that caught my attention; God instructed the early humans in how to keep themselves alive: nourish yourselves with plants for food—except not *this one*; unless you want to die, do not eat of the tree of the knowledge of good and evil. I slowed down here to listen to this phrase, and I wondered, what is "evil?"[26]

In this story, evil appeared to me to be intertwined with death. Or more precisely, I noticed that the *knowledge* of evil appeared to be accompanied by death. I found this intriguing. My prior notions of evil—about which I discussed with colleagues and commented to friends—were chiefly concerned with people's behavior. Here is an example. Last summer, I visited the Legacy Museum in Montgomery, Alabama, which tells the story of slavery in America and the race-based traumatic stress Americans live with today. As I contemplated this, the thought crossed my mind, "Knowledge of the evil of racism is the first step to ending it." But then I thought of this Scripture and wondered why would God caution us then about the dangers of gaining that sort of knowledge? Why would knowledge of evil bring about death? What was I missing?

Then it occurred to me, my original thinking may have been wrong. Knowledge of the evil of racism alone does not appear to reduce racism—at least not *cognitive* knowledge. Knowledge that moves us bodily in the form of intimacy, empathic feeling, and an interpersonal knowing of others— which transforms the neural structures in our brain—appeared to me to be the type of knowledge through which racism might be unlearned. I wondered then if the way I had been thinking about knowledge in this Scripture was also too narrow,[27] and if the form of knowing referenced here was more of an embodied knowledge through a firsthand experience of something from which God had wished to spare us.

That led me to a second idea; I wondered if the way I had been thinking about evil was also too behavioral. What if an embodied knowledge of

---

25. Gen 2:16–17.

26. For reflection, Alison, *Joy of Being Wrong*, 264–65; Aquinas, *Malo* Q1; Cannon, "Wounds of Jesus," 219–26; Cone, *God of the Oppressed*, 150–78; Keller, *Walking with God*, 57–78; Kirk-Duggan, "African-American Spirituals," 158–66; Lewis, *Problem of Pain*, 63–124; Ricoeur, *Symbolism of Evil*, 243–52.

27. The word *yada* (to know) is used in other places in scripture giving the sense of an intimate, embodied or even sexual knowing, as in Gen 4:1, 17, 25; and 19:8; for reflection on the limited influence of cognition on the embodied self, Haidt, *Righteous Mind*, 3–71.

evil starts out first in the brain as a felt experience—a *crisis of trust*—which increases stress and hijacks our nervous system long before it manifests in behavior? What if the knowledge of evil is the embodied experience of misplaced trust plus the neurobiological and behavioral consequences that follow?

From here, I became curious about human perception as it relates to trust and trustworthiness. How is it that we are prone to misperceiving reality—mistaking the trustworthy for untrustworthy, and vice versa—with such regularity? It seemed to me that learning to *unlearn* that knowledge could help the brain link up networks that would then allow us to perceive trustworthiness more accurately and respond to it more regularly with trust. I thought that could be of some theological importance. I also began to wonder this: if there is enough for all, enough food to keep us all alive, enough community, kindness, creativity, and joy to sustain us all living together . . . do we then misperceive reality on a daily basis? I thought no, because the world *is* often dangerous; that is not an illusion. Many of us experience moments of terror from actual threats; those are real. Families are suffering from hunger and poverty and violence; that is unquestionable. So danger is a *functional* reality for many of us on an individual and collective level. And that means aspects of reality are truly untrustworthy; and when we perceive this accurately, we do well to respond by withdrawing our trust.

But what if, theologically speaking, danger is not the *foundational* reality in which we exist? And when danger exists for us *functionally*, what if that is largely the result of our collective and historic *lack of trust*? If that is the case, then I thought learning to perceive accurately the trustworthy aspects of our reality might also hold theological importance. From there, I wondered if this story about the garden and the serpent might offer a few additional insights into how we first came to misperceive reality and mistake the trustworthy for untrustworthy, and whether those insights could shed some light on our potential process of unlearning—*unknowing*—the evil we had come to know by way of a *crisis in trust*.

Here is what I read:

Now the serpent was more crafty
than any other wild animal that the Lord God had made.
He said to the woman,
"Did God say, 'You shall not eat of from any tree in the garden?'"[28]

28. Gen 3:15; the "serpent" has been said to reference Satan or the devil; for reflection, Saint Augustine of Hippo, *Gen. Man.* 2.14.20–15.22; Saint Paul uses similar language in Rom 16:20.

These first words out of the serpent's mouth appeared to hit a false note. And this seemed to me to represent the first conflict we would encounter in this story, the first discrepancy between perceptions, representations, and communications of reality. Simply put, the serpent was the first untrustworthy character in the story, planting a seed of doubt about the trustworthiness of God.

And as the story goes, the woman corrected him:

No, we may eat of all the trees except this one, lest we die.[29]

And the serpent replied with another deception, another misrepresentation of reality:

You will not die . . .
For God knows when you eat your eyes will be opened,
you will be like God, knowing good and evil.[30]

It seemed to me that this falsehood contained within it the suggestion that there was something missing that the couple needed and that God was withholding from them; and up to this point, their trust in God, and their trust that all their needs were being met, had appeared to be high. But false statements like these can erode trust; they plant a seed of suspicion—who is lying to whom? If we were to insert ourselves in this story in place of the woman, we might be able to imagine our lower subcortical networks beginning to engage in a threat-reaction. Who is lying—God or the serpent?

The question is a fair one. It occurred to me that once she became aware that she was being lied to by *someone*, then her lower networks may have already been on high alert.[31] Which is to say, she may have been experiencing a decrease in trust, an increase in stress, and a misperception of her needs as a result.

She took of its fruit and ate;
she also gave some to her husband, who was with her, and he ate.[32]

Did she know evil now? Maybe she did; because her trust had been eroded in God, the animals through the serpent, and perhaps her partner

29. Gen 3:2–3.
30. Gen 3:4–5.
31. For reflection, Thompson, *Anatomy of the Soul*, 207–15.
32. Gen 3:6.

and her own self as well—her ability to perceive reality accurately. Her threat networks were likely activated now, and perhaps to a degree of intensity she had never experienced been before. She would likely have felt the rupture of trust and increase in stress throughout the whole of her embodied self. Once these lower threat networks are activated, there is only one way to *unknow* what is now known—by linking up those networks to more helpful upper networks. And that process of establishing new linkages requires trust, therefore trust would need to be restored somehow. And I was moved by one more thought. When deception is the root of the threat we face, it follows that transparency will play an important in our salvation. But in this story, the couple respond at first with shame, fear, and further deception:

Then the eyes of both were opened, and they knew that they were naked; and they sewed fig leaves together and made loincloths for themselves.[33]

For the first time ever, perhaps, they feel intolerably vulnerable. And so they rush to cover up their soft places with fig leaves. Was this move necessary? Nothing has changed in the environment; the only change was in the couple's *perception* of their environment. The only real change was the level of their *trust*. And had anything changed regarding God's *trustworthiness*? We could argue, no. Nothing foundationally had changed. Food was still available, there was plenty to go around. All their needs were met.

But our brain's response to reality depends largely upon our *perception* of it. And how we act is largely governed by the part of our brain that is engaged—whether those are our upper neocortical networks or our lower threat networks. So from here, I returned to the idea that we reflect God's image most clearly when our upper networks are engaged, and we are perceiving accurately the trustworthiness (or lack thereof) of a person or situation, and responding appropriately. I thought, these are the conditions in which human beings feel alive, relate well with others, and exhibit kindness, creativity, and joy! And I noticed in the story of the garden, these conditions of trust appeared to have been present from the beginning, until they were not.

So here is a summary of this second chapter:

The Story of Humanity

We reflected God's image
as we trusted God

33. Gen 3:7.

and perceived our needs accurately.

Our trust in God
helped us to regulate our stress,
so that we consumed only what we needed
and what was good for us and the planet.

Then we were deceived
into thinking
we needed something
we didn't already have.

Our stress increased
and our trust in God was eroded.

A Prayer to God Who Comes Near to Humanity

Oh Patient God, who walks lonely pathways
in search of those of us who crawl on our knees;

Oh Careful Watcher, who sifts through our ash piles
to help us find something worth keeping;

Loving Homemaker, who shelters us in our shame
and clothes us with unsought protection;

Gentle Companion who beholds us without contempt
and cries with us, the brokenhearted;

Wild Forgiver, whose love is an underground spring,
when we hear Your voice, help us to rise
that we may drink from Your gentle hand.

In the name of God who comes near,
Christ who calls us,
and the Spirit who lifts us up,
Amen

A Blessing for One Who Is Human

When you don't know whether to laugh or cry,
may you find a resting place somewhere in between.

When everything around you flashes "important,"
may you know the eternal significance of you being you.

When you wonder what will go wrong next,
may you take comfort, knowing, whatever it is, you will not be alone
in it.

When you're lied to and disillusioned,
may your compass guide you to those you can trust.

When you lay down to sleep,
may God envelope you in the peace of those who know they're
protected.

In the love of God,
the protection of Christ,
and the comfort of the Holy Spirit,
Amen

THE PROPHET MOSES

Hamartiology

Housekeeping

Change swoops in the side door
unceremoniously;

an efficient cleaner
disturbing the silence;

sweeping corners,
vacuuming up stale particles,
the residue of so much waiting.

Rugs may be beaten.

3

A Cup of Stress; A Cup of Safety

> Why, neither sun nor moon nor heaven nor stars nor water
> nor air altered their course . . . but human beings alone.
>
> —Saint Athanasius (ca. 299–373)[1]

FOR AS LONG AS I can remember, I have wished I felt more confident on my bicycle. Our children seem relaxed and carefree during bike rides, and I have sometimes felt jealous. When our kids were young, we often enjoyed long bike rides as a family on Saturdays, and I liked seeing our children's faces, grinning and confident beneath colorful helmets. I liked the time we spent as a family outdoors together. But I have never liked riding my bicycle. When we arrived back home after a long ride, my hands would be shaking from gripping the handlebars too tightly. I used to wonder, why could I not relax and enjoy myself on bike rides? I thought perhaps my bike was the wrong size, so I tried a smaller frame but that did not seem to make a difference. I adjusted the seat up and down, but that did not help either. As time went on, I began to accept that the problem was me—it was the way the circuits for bike riding were linked up in my brain.

---

1. Saint Athanasius, *Apoll.* 7.43.

48

Teaching the Brain

It does not matter what we are trying to learn—to ride a bike, or to repair a friendship—the learning process does not happen automatically. The conditions for learning have to be "just right" in the brain for new linkages to get established; otherwise either the networks in need of linking will not be activated, or linkages to unhelpful networks will interfere with the linking-up process.

This insight helped me to understand why I do not enjoy riding my bicycle. When I was seven years old, our father was determined to spend time trying to teach me to ride in the evenings after dinner. I can imagine he was exhausted from working all day, and part of him would have preferred to relax in front of the television. But after dinner, he laced up his running shoes and jogged beside my bike, calling out strategies to stop me from riding into parked cars. I do not think I learned much during these sessions; they distressed me and I preferred to avoid them. I have since come to recognize that I was simply not in the correct brain state for the learning task at hand.

When we are learning a new skill, our lower subcortical networks must remain calm enough to allow our upper neocortical networks to form helpful new linkages. When the stakes feel too high, extreme stress will elicit a response from the lower networks that inhibits more complex learning. I was forty years old before I realized the stress I felt on a bicycle was likely because my brain's networks for bike riding were linked up in unhelpful ways. Some networks in my brain associated bike riding with the reason my foster brother Gabriel was given away. This network fired in a pattern that produced an embodied sense in me that the stakes were quite high. That in turn increased my stress, and decreased activity in my upper networks. It is possible to learn a new skill even in a high-stakes environment; however, to create the optimal conditions for learning, safety must be increased to offset the increased stress. Or to put it another way, trust must be high for complex learning to occur.

The Learning Continuum

We might call the optimal conditions for meaningful learning, "safe enough." This is because safety—as a condition perceived by and experienced within the brain—exists on a continuum, just like stress. Too little or too much safety and we stop forming new connections.[2] Therefore, for optimal learning to occur, the balance between safety and stress must be "just right."

2. Badenoch, "Safety Is the Treatment," 85.

Too Much Safety	Safe enough	Too Little Safety

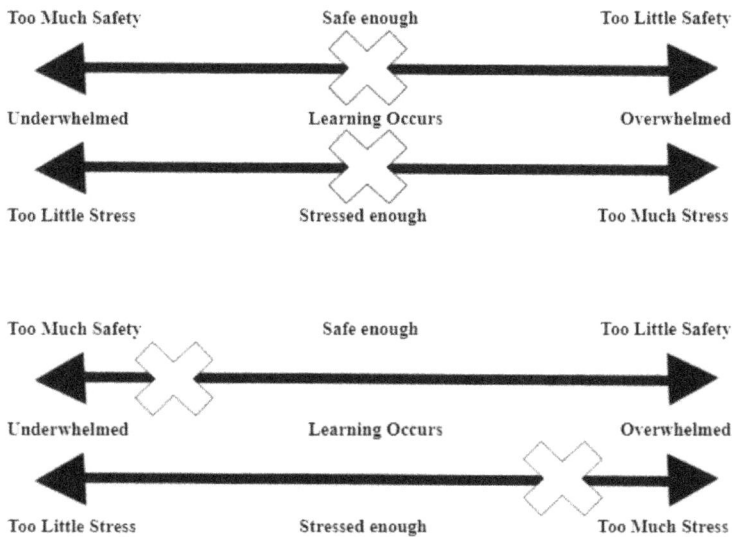

Underwhelmed	Learning Occurs	Overwhelmed

Too Little Stress	Stressed enough	Too Much Stress

Too Much Safety	Safe enough	Too Little Safety

Underwhelmed	Learning Occurs	Overwhelmed

Too Little Stress	Stressed enough	Too Much Stress

The Learning Continuum

This ideal balance between safety and stress can be achieved in one of two ways. Safety and stress can balance each other in more-or-less equal measure, or in opposite proportions. Both of these conditions may create a dynamic, effective learning environment. A good example of the former might be the child who is afraid of falling off the bicycle—a realistic risk. The stress posed by the risk of falling is an important factor that activates the proper networks in the brain necessary for suitable linkage to occur. A child who is not feeling appropriately stressed about falling might never learn to ride a bike, because the brain will fail to activate the appropriate networks, and the proper neurons will be too under-activated to form new linkages. However, as we have said, too much stress can cause the lower subcortical networks to hijack the rest of our body, and then the neocortical networks begin to disengage. Therefore, the addition of training wheels, or a trustworthy parent running alongside, may provide just the right amount of safety needed to counterbalance the stress of the situation.

The Brain on Punishment

Thinking about the neuroscience of learning may begin to spark other curiosities for us. For example, if these are the conditions for optimal learning to occur, then what are the conditions for *unlearning*? How do we change the brain's circuitry for harmful behaviors, like lying, stealing or violence? What are the optimal conditions for *corrective* learning? Corrective learning is perhaps another way to think about "healing," "growth," or "transformation"; what we usually mean by this, from a neurobiological perspective, is that less adaptive networks in the brain link up with a more adaptive ones. That linkage then has the power to change how we feel and the range of behavioral choices we have available to us. And once those networks are linked up, and we begin to use them more frequently, the pathway between these networks becomes slicker and more efficient.

The final piece about learning that we might find helpful for our purposes is that by directing attention and awareness to the networks we wish to link up, we can help them do so. That last point seems particularly relevant to a conversation about how we correct harmful behavior and replace it with more helpful behavior. At the level of individual brains, we can assume all networks are adaptive—or at least they were at the time they were first established. Perhaps a child witnessed a parent or sibling be physically threatened, or perhaps a child was subjected to violence at one time or another; in those instances, the networks that were established to cope with those actual threats were adaptive at the time. It is when those threat networks continue to fire in the absence of an actual threat that they become less adaptive, and in need of being "updated" by linking these networks up with other adaptive networks.

One goal of human development, therefore, is to learn to update our networks. As we grow, we often develop the skills necessary to increase our own safety by seeking out trustworthy environments and developing relationships with trustworthy persons. By linking up our threat-reaction networks with our trust-response networks, we can update our brain circuitry so that we are better able to perceive accurately the trustworthiness of our present environment, and reduce the frequency with which our brain "sounds a false alarm," which is taxing to our system.

Here then is the key element: the linking up of lower and upper networks in our brain occurs only under "just right" conditions—an optimal balance between stress and safety, so that the brain is alert and curious, rather than underwhelmed or engaged in a threat-reaction. Thinking about this led me to be curious about the techniques we often use to intervene in harmful behavior for the purpose of correction. Much of our systems of corrective learning, both in child-rearing and in criminal corrections, rely on punishment which activates a person's lower threat networks. When this happens, neurobiologically speaking, we can expect it to backfire; which is to say punishment that raises a person's stress level too high can be expected to short-circuit the learning process.

James Gilligan once put it this way:

> If we review the past sixty years of research on child-rearing, we
> find that the most solidly confirmed and consistent finding is
> that the more severely children are punished, the more violent
> they become, both during childhood and after they become
> adults. The violent criminals with whom I worked for 25 years
> had been punished by their parents as severely as it is possible to
> punish someone without actually killing him. In fact, the most
> violent among them were those who had been most severely
> punished—the survivors of attempted murder, usually at the
> hands of a parent.[3]

Gilligan has defined punishment as "the deliberate infliction of pain."[4]
Keeping in mind the neuroscience of pain and stress, I thought we might
refine this definition slightly. What if we were to think of punishment as
"the deliberate infliction of stress *to the point of a threat-reaction?*" If so,
then we might begin to see a connection between Gilligan's observations
and the insights we have been exploring from the neuroscience of learning. For the brain science suggests that an act of punishment that solicits a
threat-reaction from the brain of the learner short-circuits higher learning.[5]
In that case, it is the threat networks that get reinforced. That is to say, the
deliberate infliction of stress to the point of a threat-reaction pushes the
learner into the "too much stress and too little safety" zone.

Therefore, the notion that punishment is effective at teaching the brain
any desired behavior—self-awareness, honesty, empathy, critical problem
solving, attachment, creativity, generosity, or emotional regulation—appears to be a false assumption. Those desirable traits and behaviors are
made possible by linkages to and between networks throughout the upper,
neocortical region. For those linkages to occur, those networks must be activated at the same time as the behavior we wish to change, and for that to
occur, we need our threat networks mostly to remain quiet and our stress to
be regulated, through trust.[6]

Before we pivot now to explore theological questions related to this
conversation, we might offer one or two more observations. First, it is possible for two persons to respond to the same corrective intervention in very

3. Gilligan, *Preventing Violence*, 115; for reflection, Jennings et al., "Longitudinal
Assessment," 2147–74; Lereya et al., "Bully/Victims," 1461–71; Siever, "Neurobiology
of Aggression and Violence," 429–42.

4. Gilligan, *Preventing Violence*, 18.

5. Bangasser and Shors, "Critical Brain Circuits," 1223–33.

6. National Scientific Council. "Excessive Stress," 2–3.

different ways, depending on their unique neural circuitry and memory associations. Therefore, if we define punishment as "the deliberate infliction of stress to the point of a threat-reaction," then we are defining punishment less by the method or intention of the punisher, and more by its *impact* on the recipient. And this does complicate things.

I once worked in a middle school where students were placed in small, single-person cubicles within a large detention room, as a punishment for infractions. For one student, this may have been a useful corrective tool; perhaps the stress of missing time with friends and being isolated was "just right," and the relative safety of the small cubicle also "just right." Maybe after a few days of this intervention, the student's brain circuitry would have started to form new linkages, increasing self-awareness, creativity, and emotional regulation as a result. By our definition, then we might say this intervention does *not* qualify as punishment. Rather, we might call this effective correction, because it produced in this student's brain the optimal conditions for learning.

However, for the student in the cubicle next door, the impact of this same intervention might be vastly different, owing to that student's unique brain circuitry. Perhaps the stress of being isolated in a small, enclosed space reminded this student of a time when they were locked in a closet as a young child, frightened and alone. For this student, the stress of being isolated and enclosed may then be "too much," and the safety of the cubicle "too little."

If we peeked into the child's cubicle, we might not observe any sign of stress in the "too high" range, as the child has likely developed circuitry for hiding their vulnerability and emotions from others. However, we can expect that if their brain is producing a threat-reaction to this intervention, then their brain networks will form few if any helpful new linkages. Because their upper neocortical networks are less active, they will likely not be developing any of the qualities we had hoped they might learn. Instead, it is likely this child's threat networks are being reinforced. By our definition then, we could say this intervention is punishing, and is unlikely to serve as an effective tool for correction, as it undermines the optimal conditions for learning in the student's brain.

This perspective on punishment as being different for each person depending on their unique brain circuitry does complicate the matter. I do not know what a system of correction that takes individual brain circuitry into consideration would look like; it is a fascinating thought to consider. Neuroscience is offering us new perspectives on how learning occurs. And if we hope to change harmful, oppressive, and violent behavior patterns in our families, schools, and communities, I suggest we practice slow listening to the brain science and asking thoughtful questions about what is truly required to create the optimal conditions for learning.

So here then is a summary of this third earpiece:

The Neuroscience of Learning

Punishment is defined as the deliberate infliction
of stress to the point of a threat-reaction.

When the brain produces a threat-reaction,
higher learning slows down or shuts down.

Each individual brain responds differently to stress,
depending on prior memories and linkages between brain circuits.

Effective correction of harmful behavior
and teaching of helpful behavior
requires that we prevent a threat-reaction
by counterbalancing stress with safety.

With this in mind, I returned to listen to the stories of Genesis and Exodus through this earpiece of the neuroscience of learning and punishment to find out what I might encounter.

Misperceiving God

Then the eyes of both were opened, and they knew that they were
naked;
and they sewed fig leaves together and made loincloths for themselves.[7]

When I listened to this scene, it seemed to me to be the first moment in the story when these early humans may have misperceived their own needs and consumed something from the planet that they did not in fact need. Borrowing fig leaves would likely not have harmed the fig tree, but it is on the slope toward overconsuming, because it would appear to have been unnecessary. However, under stress, our brain finds it more difficult to perceive our needs accurately, prompting us to overconsume.[8] Did their

7. Gen 3:7.
8. Cartwright et al., "Stress and Dietary Practices in Adolescents," 362–69; Kemp et

overconsumption do anything to lower their stress? Did it raise their trust
in God, themselves, or each other?

> They heard the sound of the Lord God walking in the garden
> at the time of the evening breeze, and the man and his wife hid them-
> selves from the presence of the Lord God among the trees of the garden.

> But the Lord God called to the man, and said to him, "Where are you?"

> He said, "I heard the sound of you in the garden, and I was afraid,
> because I was naked; and I hid myself."

> [God] said, "Who told you that you were naked? Have you eaten from
> the tree of which I commanded you not to eat?"

> The man said, "The woman whom you gave to be with me,
> she gave me fruit from the tree, and I ate."

> Then the Lord God said to the woman, "What is this that you have
> done?"
> The woman said, "The serpent tricked me, and I ate."[9]

When I listened to this conversation, I thought, these two sounded
like they were still feeling hijacked by their threat networks. And not only
was their stress causing them to misperceive their own needs, they also appeared to be misperceiving God as a threat—hiding from God as if God
were untrustworthy. In other words, their nervous systems seemed to be
sounding a *false alarm*.

And this appeared to me to be noteworthy. Is it possible this story
offers us a glimpse into the process by which human beings first began to
misperceive God as *punishing*, inflicting stress to the point of a threat-reaction, contrary to the evidence? For in this story, we encounter God coming near, presumably not to threaten, but rather to teach them something.
We encounter God coming near to *restore their trust*. We do not find God
threatening them in any way that would be expected to further engage their
threat networks. That is to say, God is depicted as *walking* in the garden, not
beating the bushes. God is depicted as calling, "Where are you?" and not

---

al., "Calm before the Storm," 933–45; Sneath et al., "Coping with a Natural Disaster,"
45–60; for reflection, Bader-Saye, *Following Jesus in a Culture of Fear*, 134–38.

    9. Gen 3:8–13.

threatening them with *whoopings*. In fact—and this appeared to me to be extraordinary—throughout this scene God asked only questions and appeared to listen patiently, rather than demanding to be listened to.

When I noticed this, it occurred to me God was *deescalating* the couple's stress and doing it in a brilliant way. Which is to say, if the goal is threefold—to correct harmful behavior, teach helpful behavior, and restore trust—then adding safety to the mix is essential, and this is what it appeared to me that God was doing. When someone is already hijacked by their subcortical networks, loud noises, sudden movements, and threats of punishment are counterproductive—these *escalate* stress, which further short-circuits the learning process. But here we encounter God deescalating their stress: walking calmly, speaking gently, and asking questions—powerful techniques for lowering stress and calling forth from our upper neocortical networks a trust-response. In this scene, then, I thought we encountered God mixing up the "just-right" ingredients for exquisite learning.

From here, I became curious about what God said next.

To the serpent:
"Because you have done this, cursed are you . . ."[10]

When I read this, I noticed that God's first response was directed toward the serpent. The serpent had lied to the couple, and by hinting at the possibility that God could be lying, had succeeded in eroding their trust. Upon being lied to, the couple's stress increased and their perception of their own needs became distorted. This also seemed to me to be noteworthy because much of human wellness and helpful behavior depends upon our ability to perceive reality accurately. When we are lied to—whether it be by conditions appearing different than they are, or people attempting to deceive us out of a private agenda—this diminishes our brain's capacity to distinguish between what is threatening and what is trustworthy. So I became curious about God's approach to correcting the couple's perceptions and beginning to restore their trust.

To the woman:
"I will greatly increase your pangs in childbearing; in pain you shall bring forth children . . ."[11]

10. Gen 3:14–15; "offspring" may be a reference to Jesus; Saint Paul uses similar language in Rom 16:20; "The God of peace will shortly crush Satan under your feet." For reflection, Saint Augustine of Hippo, *Gen. litt.* 10.18.32.

11. Gen 3:16; the word *arbeh* (I will multiply or increase) does appear in English properly translated in first person, imperfect form.

Upon reading this, I thought of my experiences birthing without anesthesia and was reminded of the way in which trust regulates how our body responds to stress and pain. Except for a brief flash both times, the experience of the pain of childbirth—though uncomfortable—was manageable because my trust was high. That is to say, trust in God, myself, and support persons regulated my stress by flooding my brain with neurotransmitters that helped my upper networks remain (usually) engaged and cope creatively with the pain.

From there, I thought then perhaps the pain of childbirth mentioned here was less of a punishment and more of a learning experience. Going through the pain of childbirth taught me important things about my body and stamina, which in turn helped me to prepare for motherhood. When I looked back on those labor experiences, I felt strong and proud of those accomplishments, as I imagined a marathon runner or mountain climber might feel. So then I wondered, how might the pain of childbirth be understood theologically as a corrective intervention—something designed to teach helpful behavior, and restore trust, rather than a punishment designed to induce a threat-reaction? I did not know. But what I observed was that, when trust is high, the pain of childbirth is not necessarily experienced as "the deliberate infliction of stress to the point of a threat-reaction," therefore I thought by our definition of punishment, the pain of childbirth likely fell outside it. And that seemed sensible when I considered that punishment which excessively engages the threat networks erodes trust and short-circuits the learning process, whereas I thought a corrective intervention of God's choosing would likely be designed to teach effectively and restore trust.

To the man:
"... cursed is the ground because of you, in toil you shall eat of it all the days of your life . . ."[12]

Upon reading this, I wondered how the difficulty of working the land and growing food might be understood theologically as a corrective intervention—something designed to teach helpful behavior, and restore trust. I was not sure there, either. But what I observed was that, when trust is high, we tend to be content with only what we need, and we relate, collaborate, and share well with others. Foraging for and gathering food, maintaining sustainable homesteads, community gardens, and small farms for need

12. Gen 3:17.

rather than profit . . . these came to mind when I thought about practices that have sustained human life and the planet from the beginning.

When our kids were young, our family lived on an acre and a half where we experimented with growing fruit, nuts, and vegetables, keeping milk goats, chickens, and bees, and other sustainable forms of feeding ourselves. It sounded romantic at the start, but that quickly wore off—most of the time it was exhausting work. But the rewards were sweet. When I thought of that, here is what I observed. When trust is high, the struggle to feed ourselves is perhaps also not necessarily experienced as a punishment either, meaning it does not have to engage our subcortical threat networks. All conditions equal, I thought that the toil of feeding ourselves likely also falls outside of our definition of punishment as being the "deliberate infliction of stress to the point of a threat-reaction in the brain." And that also seemed sensible when I considered that the ways of feeding ourselves that are healthy for our bodies and the planet also teach us a lot about ourselves, God, and others, and help to restore our trust.

And this seemed to me a pattern worth noting: though the couple, once deceived, began to misperceive God as *punishing*, there appeared to be evidence to the contrary. Which is to say instead of punishing—inflicting stress to the point of a threat-reaction—we encountered God coming near to teach them something. We encountered God coming near to describe the consequences they would now have to bear, living in bodies that now held firsthand "knowledge" of what it feels like to be lied to, threatened, and have our brains sound a false-alarm—a trust crisis. From now on, the couple's brains would have laid down new circuitry—the awareness that deception is possible. This awareness—the knowledge of evil, perhaps—would have added a layer of delicateness to trust that had been less shakable before.

So when we experience a crisis of trust, how is trust restored? It occurred to me that punishment that solicits a threat-reaction will likely backfire. However, an encounter with a trustworthy person or situation can generate a release of trust—those pleasant neurotransmitters—in the brain. And that is what aids the learning process; that is what helps us learn more helpful behaviors. And in this story, God appeared to be exceedingly trustworthy; which is to say, God appeared interested in deescalating the couple's stress, doing them no harm, teaching them helpful behaviors, and restoring them once more to life, community, kindness, creativity, and joy. All and good, however, the difficulty is this: it is not enough to merely encounter a trustworthy person; we must also *accurately perceive* that person's trustworthiness. And that often requires repeated encounters, under "just right" conditions, for new learning to occur.

When this thought occurred to me, I began to wonder if we might find something of this pattern throughout the rest of the stories of Genesis, and perhaps throughout the Scriptures: humankind continuously misperceiving our needs, and misperceiving God as punishing in response, and God repeatedly intervening to correct our misperceptions and restore our trust. If this is so, then it might give rise to something of a rhythm I wondered if we might detect in the Scriptures, wherein God is sometimes misperceived as punishing, and then God intervenes and corrects this misperception and restores trust once more.

With that thought in mind, I turned the page to listen to the next story, wondering if a similar pattern might emerge:

Now Abel was a keeper of sheep, and Cain a tiller of the ground.
In the course of time Cain brought to the Lord an offering of the fruit of the ground,
and Abel for his part brought of the firstlings of his flock, their fat portions.[13]

And the Lord had regard for Abel and his offering,
but for Cain and his offering he had no regard.[14]

When I imagined this scene, I pictured Abel sorting through his flock, and selecting the best cuts of meat, and then . . . giving some away. And I noticed that a brain under stress finds it exceedingly difficult to do that—to be open-handed and generous. But here we find Abel engaged in a practice that likely required a high degree of trust and a sense that there is enough for all. And when we practice acts of trust such as these, our brains release warm, pleasant neurotransmitters[15] that nurture our health and our relationships.

Then I considered his brother Cain, who grew crops and gave some away as well. When I read that God had no regard for Cain's gift, I wondered if the difference had to do with the degree of trust with which Cain was functioning. Perhaps Cain's practice was, in part, superstitious, like an insurance policy against crop failure. Perhaps God was challenging Cain's practice—not because the gift was not good enough—but because God was concerned that Cain's stress was too high, and his trust too low, and his act of generosity was only reinforcing his threat networks and inhibiting the restoration of trust between himself and God.

13. Gen 4:2–4.
14. Gen 4:4–5.
15. Zak et al., "Neurobiology of Trust," 224–27.

I wondered then if God wished to restore Cain's trust and Cain's sense that there is enough for all. I wondered if God wished to nudge Cain to practice acts of greater trust and come to more accurately perceive God's trustworthiness.

> So Cain was very angry, and his countenance fell.
> The Lord said to Cain, "Why are you angry, and why has your counte-
> nance fallen?
> If you do well, will you not be accepted?
> And if you do not do well, sin is lurking at the door;
> its desire is for you, but you must master it.[16]

When I pictured Cain's face, I imagined the expression on my own face when I am overly stressed and perceiving there to be threats nearby. My jaw clenches; my muscles tense up. If this is how Cain felt, I thought his lower threat networks were likely activated and his window of tolerance may already have been closing. The upper neocortical networks—which can help Cain perceive his needs and options more clearly—may have been shutting down.

> And when they were in the field,
> Cain rose up against his brother Abel, and killed him.[17]

And so we have encountered the first murder in this story. What is God going to do? How will God respond?

> Then the Lord said to Cain, "Where is your brother Abel?"[18]

> And the Lord said, "What have you done?"[19]

When I read this, I felt intrigued. If there was ever a time for punishment—capital punishment—we might think it is now. But once again, we encountered God, not threatening Cain's life, but asking, "Where's your brother?" In this scene too, God asks questions and listens, rather than demanding to be listened to. This occurred to me as another example of God *deescalating* Cain's stress, but not for the purpose of going easy on him; rather

16. Gen 4:6–7.
17. Gen 4:8.
18. Gen 4:9.
19. Gen 4:10.

because if the goal is to correct harmful behavior, teach helpful behavior, and restore trust, then adding safety to the mix is essential. Again, when someone is hijacked by their subcortical threat networks, loud noises, sudden movements, and threats of punishment *escalate* stress, which further short-circuits the learning process.

Here we encounter God doing the opposite; we find God speaking gently, asking questions, and responding to Cain—someone who just murdered his own brother—by increasing safety and addressing his concerns.

> "My punishment is greater than I can bear. . .
> I shall be a fugitive and a wanderer on the earth,
> and anyone who meets me may kill me."

> Then the Lord said to him, "Not so!
> Whoever kills Cain will suffer a sevenfold vengeance."
> And the Lord put a mark on Cain, so that no one who came upon him
> would kill him.[20]

And here, again, I thought God was mixing up the "just-right" ingredients for exquisite learning. Once more, I thought, the misperception of God as punishing, from a neurobiological perspective, is being corrected. From there, I wanted to venture a few chapters further, to see if the pattern continued to hold or something different might emerge. We read that Cain eventually married and had children; some of those children built cities; others lived in tents and kept livestock. They created musical instruments, and forged tools of bronze and iron.[21] I began to imagine how the descendants of Cain—those who ventured even farther away from the cradle of the Fertile Crescent—may have developed rituals to help them remember the story of what had happened to their ancestors Adam, Eve, Cain, and Abel. I wondered if they sat around the fire pit under the stars and reenacted the story of the serpent and the couple and God's tender response. I wondered if they reenacted the story of Cain killing Abel, and how God's gentleness and protection restored Cain's trust. The telling and retelling of stories can be a powerful ritual for helping generations remember times when perceptions were corrected, trust was restored, and new learning occurred.

But when stress increases, our brains often fall back into old patterns again.

---

20. Gen 4:13–15.
21. Gen 4:17–22.

A few chapters later, I read about a curious encounter between Abraham and God.[22] By counting the generations recorded in Genesis, we are told that a couple millennia have passed; this dialogue between Abraham and God is recorded as having taken place around 2000 BC. Before going further, I wanted to understand more about the archeological record of the people living near the Fertile Crescent during that era. I read that there is some debate among archeologists about the timing and spread of agriculture during this period; but at some point the Fertile Crescent began showing signs of environmental degradation, possibly as a result of climate change helped along by over-farming and expanded animal husbandry.[23] As resources in the land became depleted, disparity in the distribution of food and supplies between people groups grew, and violence along with it.[24]

I also became curious what types of food and supplies people groups around the world had decided they needed in this era. I read that around 2000 BC the people living in the Middle East were making glass vessels[25] and brewing beer;[26] those living in northern Asia were weaving and trading silk;[27] those living in prehistoric Britain had likely erected the rings of Stonehenge;[28] those living in what would become the southeastern United States—now South Carolina, Georgia, Florida, Alabama, and Mississippi—built monument-sized rings of shells suggestive of permanent camps of families surviving by consuming seafood;[29] those living in the Southern Hemisphere had built homes with hearths, terraces, and private rooms, as well as large amphitheaters for community gatherings.[30]

Against this backdrop of global history, I turned to listen to this dialogue between Abraham and God. In the scene, Abraham looked up and saw three strangers; he and his family washed the strangers' feet, baked them bread, and gave up choice portions of their crops and meat so as to offer cakes, cheese, milk, and beef to their guests. When I read this, I thought Abraham was showing a lot of trust; his stress during this season seemed manageable, and his upper networks seemed well-engaged. God informed

22. Gen 18:1–33.

23. Henry et al., "Blame It on the Goats?," 625–37; Kohler et al., "Greater Post-Neolithic Wealth Disparities," 619–22; Maeda et al., "Narrowing the Harvest," 226–37.

24. Ferguson, "Violence and War in Prehistory," 321–55.

25. Henderson, *Ancient Glass*, 12.

26. Damerow, "Sumerian Beer," 1–20.

27. Ming and Liao, "Influence of Adlai Silk," 934–40.

28. Darvill and Wainwright, "Stonehenge Excavations," 1–19.

29. Russo and Heide, "Shell Rings of the Southeast US," 491–92.

30. Solis et al., "Dating Caral," 723–26.

Abraham the purpose of the visit was to check on the city of Sodom and see
"how grave their sins are."[31] The prophet Ezekiel would later call Sodom a
city of "pride, excess of food, and prosperous ease" that nevertheless "did
not aid the poor and needy."[32] In fact, the night of this conversation between God and Abraham, the men of Sodom would come out to humiliate
these three visitors with the intention of raping them in an apparent show of
dominance through violence.[33] So when Abraham heard that God intended
to visit Sodom, it would appear that Abraham assumed the Lord was plan-
ning to "sweep away" the city.[34]

But I found no indication in the text that this was God's intention. And
when Abraham, whose relatives lived in the city, involved God in a series of
negotiations to forgive the city, each time God responded, "I will forgive."[35]
In this story, God also appeared interested in intervening, teaching helpful behavior, and restoring trust—but not by punishing. Something tragic,
however, did occur. The region of Sodom was rich in petroleum, which the
residents of the city had been mining for profit; some geologists hold that a
shift in tectonic plates in the region could have triggered an earthquake or
lava event, catching the oil and asphalt on fire, and burying the city beneath
salt water, leaving behind "pillars of salt."[36] When I read that, I wondered
about the difference between *prescribed* versus *predicted* outcomes. In
misperceiving their needs and exploiting their resources, could the Sod-
omites have rendered their city predictably vulnerable to disaster?

At this point, I began to wonder if we were perhaps beginning to circle
a helpful definition of "sin." I noticed that the Hebrew word often translated
"evil" [37] was distinct from the word for "sin," [38] indicating two different processes.[39] I noticed that the Hebrew word for "evil" referenced many things:
sometimes a person's mind, temperament, mood, or way of thinking.[40] It

31. Gen 18:20–21.

32. Ezek 16:49.

33. Grypeou and Spurling, "Abraham's Angels," 181–203; for reflection on "sin of
Sodom," see Loader, "Homosexuality and the Bible," 23.

34. Gen 18:23.

35. Gen 18:23–33.

36. Bergoeing, "Sodom and Gomorrah and Plates Tectonic," 1–8; Nissenbaum,
"Utilization of Dead Sea Asphalt," 365–83; Park, "Brief History of Asphalt," 14–17.

37. The word *ra* (evil), e.g., Gen 2:9; 37:20; 2 Kgs 4:41; Prov 25:20.

38. The word *chata* (sin) as in Gen 20:6, "it was I who kept you from sinning against
me."

39. E.g., Gen 13:13; 39:9; 50:17.

40. E.g., Prov 25:20; 26:23.

was also occasionally used to describe a wild animal,[41] poisonous plant,[42] or infected wound. And later in the Hebrew writings of the law, this word for "evil" was also sometimes used in reference to something being "unclean."[43] I noticed the Hebrew word for "sin" appeared to carry in its root the sense of doing something wrong or perhaps "missing the target" as with a sling-shot.[44] I noticed that the Greek word for "sin"[45] appeared to give a similar connotation, and that this word would appear later in Scripture in reference to Jesus:

> She will bear a son, and you are to name him Jesus,
> for he will save his people from their sins.[46]

I wondered then if we might find it helpful to think of "evil" as the condition under which our brain misperceives the trustworthy as untrust-worthy, which increases our stress and induces a crisis a trust. And I won-dered if we might find it helpful to think of "sin" as the harmful things we do as a result of our brain misperceiving our needs during a crisis of trust.[47] There may be other ways to look at it; for my part I thought the distinc-tion between these two words was likely less critical than our understand-ing properly that there are conditions under that our brain function is less helpful, leading us to behaviors which may inflict death, isolation, cruelty, destructivity, and agony on ourselves and others. And I thought it helpful to acknowledge that under such conditions, we may not be able to self-correct. Which is to say, we are in need of helpful intervention.

From there, I looked into Hebrew references to "punishment" for evil or sin, and I discovered something interesting; the Hebrew word often translated "punish" carries a sense of "attending to," "visiting," or "taking notice of."[48] I found this sense used frequently throughout the Hebrew

41. Gen 37:20.

42. 1 Kgs 4:41.

43. E.g., Lev 27:10, 12, 14, 33.

44. E.g., Judg 20:16.

45. The word *hamartia* (sin) as in Matt 1:21, from "missing the mark" in archery; for reflection, *dikaiosyne* (righteousness) as the corrective for "sin" in the New Testa-ment gives the sense of being in right relationship with God and neighbor, and getting "out of right relationship" was commonly understood as happening collectively as a social group; email exchange with Jane Patterson, New Testament scholar, in discussion with the author in July 2020.

46. Matt 1:21.

47. For reflection, Baldwin, *Trauma-Sensitive Theology*, 117–18.

48. The word *paqad* (visit, attend to) as in Exod 32:34, sometimes translated

texts, which appeared to me consistent with the stories of God's response to the original couple, to Cain, and to Abraham regarding the residents of Sodom—drawing near to teach them something, attending to them, visiting them, and taking notice of them with care—presumably to restore trust. So I began to wonder, when did the notion emerge that sin must be punished by God with an intervention likely to elicit a threat-reaction?

God and the Law

My reflection on that question took me into the story of Moses.

> At the end of four hundred thirty years, on that very day,
> all the companies of the Lord went out from the land of Egypt.[49]

It is a stunning story; we are told that 600,000 men followed Moses out of slavery, along with probably one to two million women and children. I tried to imagine traveling in a group that size; for the first several weeks it appeared they were thirsty, hungry, frightened, attacked by strangers, and often quarreling.[50] Their threat networks indeed appeared to be activated and on high alert.

> Moses sat as judge for the people,
> while the people stood around him from morning until evening.[51]

For a while, Moses is said to have attempted to arbitrate all their complaints himself.

> Moses' father-in-law said to him,
> "What you are doing is not good. You will surely wear yourself out,
> both you and these people with you.
> For the task is too heavy for you; you cannot do it alone."[52]

"punish," is used in other places in Scriptures to give the sense of God "visiting" or "taking note of" someone, as in Gen 21:1, Exod 3:16 and 4:31.

49. Exod 12:41.

50. Exod 15:22—17:16.

51. Exod 18:13.

52. Exod 18:17–18.

Moses' father-in-law eventually convinced him to establish statutes and instructions—rules—for the people, and delegate judges to help them settle their disputes:

Teach them the statutes and instructions and make known to them
the way they are to go and the things they are to do.[53]

You should also look for able men among all the people,
men who fear God,
are trustworthy, and hate dishonest gain;
set such men over them as officers over thousands, hundreds,
fifties, and tens.[54]

So in the story, Moses did this second part quickly; he selected leaders whom he and the people could trust to intervene when something needed correction. But the first part—the rules—that appeared to take a bit longer. After three months in the desert, we are told that Moses initiated a series of conversations between God and the people.

Now therefore, if you obey my voice and keep my covenant,
you shall be my treasured possession out of all the peoples.[55]

And the people responded:

Everything that the Lord has spoken we will do.[56]

Three days later, we read that Moses embarked on a series of ascents and descents from the mountain, delivering instructions from God to the people, and for the longest stretch, he disappeared on the mountain for forty days.[57] When I read the statutes and instructions Moses delivered the people, I felt quite moved because they appeared to me an effective tool for increasing safety and decreasing stress. I considered the instructions as

53. Exod 18:20.
54. Exod 18:21.
55. Exod 19:5.
56. Exod 19:8.
57. Exod 24:18.

more or less falling into three categories: 1) relating well to one another;[58] 2) creating art;[59] and 3) performing rituals.[60]

It occurred to me, this is perhaps precisely what a group of a few million people under extreme stress need in order to keep their upper neocortical networks engaged. The social and hygiene laws may have helped to ensure that the people under Moses' care survived disease, and settled disputes more peacefully, without violence rippling through the community. The architectural and artistic laws may have helped to ensure the people had creative pursuits to joyfully occupy their time. And the ritual laws may have helped to ensure the people were regularly coming together as a community, attending to their spirit, asking for and receiving forgiveness, and contemplating aspects of God.

This appeared to me to be a brilliant plan for helping to restore trust among the people, and between the people and God, for as long as they might have to live in the desert. Laws are also a complexity reducer; these rules likely introduced a greater degree of safety to offset the higher degree of stress the people might have been experiencing. And if so, then these rules may have helped to keep the people's brains in the optimal zone for learning and functioning at their best. One more observation occurred to me about these laws; when the people followed them, they were likely to:

. . . feel alive.
. . . relate well to others.
. . . exhibit kindness.
. . . be creative.
. . . access joy.

When I noticed that, I thought, isn't that something? The law may have helped human beings *reflect God* more clearly. Which is to say, neurobiologically speaking, the law may have helped to decrease their stress, and restore their trust. I felt stunned by this gift and what it may have accomplished. I also felt curious about its relationship to notions of punishment. The original couple misperceived God as punishing, and were frightened in a way that was not helpful or necessary. Cain misperceived God as punishing, until he discovered God was protecting him rather than punishing him. Abraham too misperceived God as punishing, though God expressed only

58. Exod 20:1—23:13.
59. Exod 25:1—28:42.
60. Exod 29:1—31:11.

a desire to forgive. I began to wonder, is it possible a misperception of God may appear in the story of Moses and the law as well?

The Triangle of Punishment

I was curious if we might find in the law something of this pattern reflecting a misperception that God requires punishment as a tool for teaching; and then I read this:

Whoever strikes a person mortally shall be put to death . . .[61]

Whoever curses their father or mother shall be put to death.[62]

When people who are fighting injure a pregnant woman so that there is a
miscarriage, and . . .
any harm follows, then you shall give life for life, eye for eye,
tooth for tooth, hand for hand, foot for foot, burn for burn,
wound for wound, stripe for stripe.[63]

If a man commits adultery with the wife of his neighbor,
both the adulterer and the adulteress shall be put to death.[64]

Anyone who kills a human being shall be put to death.[65]

Anyone who maims another shall suffer the same injury in return:
fracture for fracture, eye for eye, tooth for tooth;
the injury inflicted is the injury to be suffered.[66]

When I read this, I reflected for some time on Moses and the stress he was likely under; I contemplated the story of his own childhood, as one of few survivors of an infant massacre.[67] As the story goes, Moses grew up estranged from his family, in the palace of the ruler who would have

61. Exod 21:12.
62. Exod 21:15.
63. Exod 21:22–25.
64. Lev 24:10.
65. Lev 24:17.
66. Lev 24:19.
67. Exod 1:15—2:10.

slaughtered him, perhaps terrified every day. I imagined the stress Moses may have endured and how his threat networks may have been frequently activated.

> One day, after Moses had grown up,
> he went out to his people and saw their forced labor.
> He saw an Egyptian beating a Hebrew, one of his kinsfolk.
> He looked this way and that, and seeing no one
> he killed the Egyptian and hid him in the sand.[68]

From there, we read the Egyptian ruler sought to kill Moses as a punishment, so Moses fled to the desert. And there, in the desert, we read that Moses encountered God in a burning bush:

> God called to him out of the bush, "Moses, Moses!"[69]

> And Moses hid his face, for he was afraid to look at God.[70]

> "I will send you to Pharaoh to bring my people, the Israelites, out of Egypt."[71]

> But Moses said to God, "Who am I . . . ?"[72]

> [God] said, "I will be with you . . ."[73]

Once more, the same surprising pattern emerged that we observed in the story of Cain who killed Abel. God appeared, *attended* to him, visited him, and took notice of him with care rather than punishment, in an attempt to restore his trust. And now in this story of Moses, we also encountered no indication that God was punishing toward Moses who had killed someone. And here we find God, not beating the bushes, but burning inside one; calling to Moses by name, not threatening him with *whoopings*.

When I noticed this, it occurred to me as one more brilliant scene in which God *deescalated* Moses' stress and increased his safety. Which is to

68. Exod 2:11–12.
69. Exod 3:4.
70. Exod 3:6.
71. Exod 3:10.
72. Exod 3:11.
73. Exod 3:12.

say, if the goal is threefold: to correct harmful behavior, teach helpful behavior, and restore trust, then once more we find God mixing up the "just-right" ingredients for exquisite learning. So I was back to my original question: when did the notion emerge that sin must be punished by God—and with an intervention likely to cause a threat-reaction in the brain of the one receiving it? What came to mind was a dynamic[74] I encountered years ago to depict a phenomenon of human behavior that neuroscience supports:

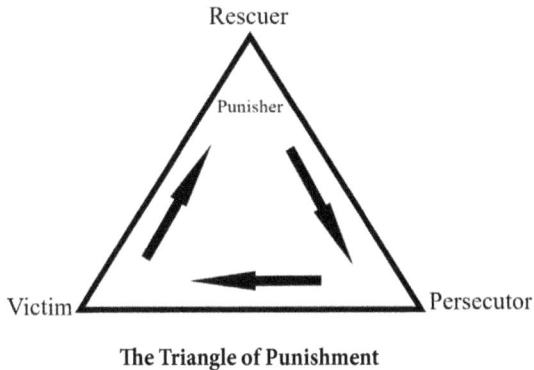

Rescuer

Punisher

Victim   Persecutor

The Triangle of Punishment

This dynamic involves three characters or groups of people; initially, the drama starts out between a Persecutor and a Victim. The Persecutor inflicts stress on the Victim, to the point of threat-reaction which is taxing to the nervous system, and represents a true threat to survival—either physical, emotional, or relational.

Next, the Victim retaliates, becoming a New Persecutor, and they swap roles.

Or a third-party Rescuer steps in. Now if the Rescuer attempts to use punishment as a strategy for "teaching the Persecutor a lesson" this will likely backfire. Keeping with our definition of punishment as an infliction of stress to the point of threat-reaction—regardless of whether the threat is actual or just a false alarm—the Persecutor will now experience themselves to be a New Victim. It occurred to me that when punishment is added to the mechanism, this reinforces every position on the triangle, therefore I began to the think about this dynamic as the "Triangle of Punishment."

I noticed that as the various roles move around the triangle, each position feels justified in playing their part and taking their turn in the

---

74. Adaptation of the Drama Triangle, from Karpman, "Fairy Tales and Script Drama Analysis," 39–43. I understand Alison, *Joy of Being Wrong*, 169, to be reflecting on a similar dynamic between rivals, victims, and heroes.

Punisher-Rescuer position. This makes the Triangle of Punishment very difficult to escape from. In fact, the Triangle of Punishment functions somewhat like an algebra problem; the variables may swap places on either side of the equal sign but they never add up to more than the sum of their parts. When would-be Rescuers encounter this dynamic, it's usually in a single "freeze-frame," meaning they perceive only the most recent Persecutor and Victim positions and assume they are unilateral and fixed. But essentially, we might say that "every stone thrown hits a Victim." If the Rescuer attempts to use punishment as a means of trying to teach someone a lesson or break the cycle of victimization, the Rescuer merely slides into the Persecutor role, and the cycle continues.

It occurred to me at this point, that the brain of the Persecutor—the one who has victimized someone else—will likely sound a false alarm when God draws near, particularly if the Persecutor misperceives God as punishing. And in response, the Persecutor will then move positions around the Triangle of Punishment, learning nothing, and perpetuating the cycle of violence—even if there is no actual threat or need to do so.

When I thought about the law this way, two things occurred to me.

First, I noticed that the law was helpful as a system of naming "what is." That is to say, it appeared helpful for naming what victimization looks like. The law in this way introduced a degree of safety to offset the higher degree of stress that the people were experiencing. The law was also likely helpful for naming what "relating well to others" looks like, along with kindness, creativity, and the peaceful conditions necessary for joy. In this way, the law may have helped the people *reflect God*, or create the optimal conditions for their brain in which reflecting God becomes more possible—by decreasing their stress, and helping to increase their safety.

Second, I noticed, the part of the law that seemed to backfire was the "Triangle of Punishment" part—or more precisely, what the Triangle of Punishment appeared to be suggesting about God demanding a punishment. This also seemed to be noteworthy, considering that human wellness and helpful behavior depends largely upon our ability to perceive reality accurately. From there, I became curious about God's approach to correcting humankind's misperceptions about God, and restoring our trust on a *foundational* level. And I wondered if, as God did so, we might also find ourselves helped to escape the Triangle of Punishment. If it were possible to escape the Triangle of Punishment, neurobiologically speaking, it seemed to me this might help us then to create the optimal learning conditions for our brain, on an individual and societal level. But collapsing the triangle would not be easy; a triangle is one of the most stable structures in the universe and it is difficult to collapse a triangle from the outside.

I thought that the Triangle of Punishment would likely have to be undone *from within.*

Here is then a summary of this third chapter:

The Story of Sin

We worried God might punish us
for consuming something we didn't need.

Instead God came near,
decreasing our stress, increasing our safety.

Our trust was restored,
in part;
then our stress rose again.

We began to
victimize one another.
and worried again
that God was punishing.

Our stress rose further,
and we were deceived
into thinking
reality must
be so.

A Prayer to God, Our Teacher

God of wisdom,
teach us to listen,
willing to hear an unexpected word
which did not originate in us.

Christ our companion,
help us peer bravely
into the mirror
of self-reflection.

Spirit within us,
teach us to be humble
about everything imperfect without and within,
and may we recoil from nothing
which your touch would transform.

In the name of God our Teacher,
Christ, the living Word,
and the Spirit who guides us into all wisdom,
Amen

A Blessing for One Who Is Learning

May God grant you the patience of a learner,
to sit in the tension between
what is known and not known yet—
the tediousness of unlearning and relearning
what was understood before the plates shifted
and the continents settled.

May Christ grant you stamina as you walk the labyrinth of a learner,
until the way opens up inside you.
For the road is long,
therefore we will companion you—
thrilled to explore the interior of your mind
where the landscape is always changing.

And may the Spirit grant you courage as you risk
stepping out on limbs which have not yet been tested.
For to learn is to be vulnerable
and a drop of cynicism can poison the body;
therefore, we'll be the anti-venom which makes you bold,
for learning is always a sacred act, and failure need never be fatal.

In the name of God our Teacher,
Christ our Companion,
and the Spirit of all wisdom,
Amen

Christology

Desire

Hungry for a bite of existence,
it finds an empty lot inside us
and claims squatters rights,
and our effort to place distance between us only
draws us closer.

Eager to dig,
it takes up residence inside us
and what's this?
The desire to be rid of desire
is a fountain of desire.

And what of this?
The groundwater is sweet!
A singsong of refreshment:
"I make things grow!"

So if this sweetness is not the enemy, then what is?
(An enemy must exist or else we would not be in torment.)
It flutters our heart;
it circles our brain chanting,
"Give up the ghost; give up the ghost."

Is it keeping us alive?

Find out; give it breath.
Give it body—your body.
Cut it from your belly with your own two hands;
hold it over your head,
the cord pulses with life!

And all that can be
will be snatched from the cradle
and flung across time—
all that is,
from all that is not.

4

A Borrowed Body

Without the knowledge of God that comes through divine fellowship, the
oppressed would not know that what the world says about them is a lie.

—JAMES CONE[1]

SOON AFTER STARTING SEVENTH grade, I met a girl who would one day
become one of my closest friends. I noticed her first during tryouts for
our school's talent show. I had prepared a mime routine that I thought was
pretty special. Mine was a solo routine since I was new to the school and
had not yet found a friend group; I was hoping the talent show would help
me start to meet people. This girl was well-established in a group of friends
with whom she had grown up, plus she had an older sister, and they had
prepared a pop dance routine. Watching them in rehearsal, I thought they
seemed energetic and fun, and I felt a little embarrassed about how much I
had liked my mime routine.

In the weeks that followed, other details about the girl, like her preferences in clothes and music, caught my attention. I learned her name: Cheryl.
I noticed she wore brown leather ankle boots. And that Christmas, I asked
my grandmother for the same type of boots. Cheryl and I were in history
class together, and one day I overheard her saying some things about our
teacher she found annoying; soon after, I began drawing cartoons of our
teacher and passing them to Cheryl during class. We began chatting more

1. Cone, *God of the Oppressed*, 132.

77

after that, and Cheryl disclosed the name of a boy in our science class on whom she had a crush; I soon developed a crush on his best friend.

Over time, the desires with which I had entered school slowly began to resemble the desires of Cheryl and her friends. This was not a conscious decision, and it did not feel inauthentic; I genuinely enjoyed these friends and the objects of their desire brought me pleasure too. In addition, our common interests became a topic of conversation around which we could connect. Cheryl's social life was embedded in a group of friends with trust built over several years. My situation was a little different; I was new in school and recovering from a stressful transition after my parent's separation and our subsequent move across state. I was starting over in a new environment and not sure who I should trust; but I began developing a connection with Cheryl and her friends that would eventually come to feel quite trustworthy. And this connection was facilitated, in part, by an intriguing system in the brain which produces a "mirroring" dynamic.

Mirroring the Brain

Our brains tend to be highly aware of the brains of others, and we have the capacity to effectively "sync up" with other brains in terms of wave frequency and neural activity, such that our networks may even begin to fire in a similar pattern. "Mirror neurons" is the name Giacomo Rizzolatti initially assigned to the neurobiology involved in this phenomenon;[2] in reality, there are likely many networks and regions of the brain involved when we find ourselves "mirroring" another person. Certain networks may become activated when we imitate another's motor movements, or feel a sensation or emotion similar to the one we imagine another is feeling in their body.[3] The act of witnessing that you desire something, move toward it, and experience pleasure, pain, relief, or healing as result, can effectively produce a mirrored response within my own body.[4]

The mirror function of our brains may help explain why, when I watched Cheryl and her sister's dance routine, I felt—for a brief flash—a sense of the freedom and fun I imagine they were feeling in their own bodies. Cheryl and I eventually grew close, and when two people are in close proximity and attentive to one another, their neurons can begin to fire "in

2. Rizzolatti and Sinigaglia, *Les Neurones Miroirs*, 10; for reflection, Banks and Hirschman, *Four Ways to Click*, 4–8; Iacoboni, *Mirroring People*, 21–27; Oughourlian, *Mimetic Brain*, 25–29.

3. Sapolsky, *Behave*, 522.

4. Siegel, *Developing Mind*, 164.

concert." When one friend smiles, the other may smile automatically. Observing, through sight, sound, or touch, the sensation of pain in one friend's body may in turn produce signals of hurt felt in the other friend's body, though perhaps to a lesser degree. When the mirror systems of two brains are synchronized, the two people may find their breathing, heart rate, and even frequency of brain waves begin to look identical in scans. And that is intriguing, considering that the brain of one friend may be responding to an external cue while the brain of the other is simply responding to *the friend.* This mirroring function in the brain likely contributes to our experiences of empathy and resonance, where we find ourselves capable of feeling in our body what may be happening in someone else's.

The first time I remember hearing about the brain's mirror systems, I was listening to a colleague describe experiments with patients recovering from the amputation of a hand, arm, leg, or foot. Patients after an amputation are often plagued by false signals in the brain that misfire and produce excruciating sensations of pain or tingling where the limb was once located. This is because, though the limb is gone, the brain circuitry for that limb still exists and can still be activated. Because it is a misperception on the part of the brain, the signals of discomfort and pain can be quite difficult to soothe.

Neuroscientist Vilayanur Subramanian Ramachandran discovered an elegant solution.[5] Ramachandran and his student built a mirror box; a patient with an amputated arm could place their intact arm in the box, alongside a mirror. By looking into the mirror, the patient's brain would *perceive* there to be the missing arm reflected in the mirror! Once a patient gained the sense again of having two arms, it was discovered that much could be done to alleviate the pain in the phantom arm—movement, massage, etc. When a soothing technique was applied to the patient's existing arm, the brain, observing this happening in the mirror, experienced relief *as if* the missing arm were being soothed.

There is likely more going on in this remarkable phenomenon than what can be explained by our current understanding of the brain's mirroring mechanisms; however, there is another part of the story I find even more fascinating. Researchers have since discovered the physical mirror is unnecessary to produce the effect; simply witnessing *another person's* arm being massaged can produce relief in the brain of the amputee.[6] I was discussing the implications of this with a friend one day who made a comment that has always stayed with me; he said, "So we are not just similes for each other, as in 'your body is like my body' . . . we can be metaphors for one another,

5. Ramachandran, *Tell-Tale Brain.*
6. Tung et al., "Observation of Limb Movements," 633–38.

as in 'your arm can be my arm.'" This seemed a poetic way of putting it; the brain's mirror systems effectively allow you to "borrow" my body, and me to "borrow" yours, giving rise to the potential for us to become healing agents for one another.

The Brain on Desire

There is one more interesting thing I find noteworthy about the research on the mirroring mechanisms in our brain. It has been hypothesized that the phenomenon through which we learn to desire certain things by imitating the desires of others is also facilitated, in part, by our brain's mirror systems.[7] And that notion leads us into some interesting territory, because we may find that the helpfulness of our "borrowed" desires then exists on a continuum. That is to say, when we imitate the desires of others, this can help to facilitate connection and introduce us to new pleasurable experiences we would not have encountered otherwise, all of which may be helpful to us as we are learning and growing. But we may also find there is a tipping point at which our imitation of the desires of others becomes less helpful to us.

Here is one way we might think about that tipping point. Whether with seventh-grade girls or leaders of nations, our organic bodily needs may be fairly universal. Our human bodies need enough food, shelter, clean water, creative outlets, and social support to be physically well. When any of those are in short supply—or when there is the perception of scarcity—we may perceive a need to increase our social and economic capital, so we can more reliably meet our needs and the needs of our loved ones. One way of increasing our capital is by imitating the material and cultural desires of others, similar to how I began to imitate the music and fashion preferences of Cheryl and her friends. According to Marco Iacoboni,[8] the mirror systems in our brain include both less and more complex circuitry, and the complex mirror circuitry can inhibit simpler circuitry and vice versa. My understanding of this inhibitory function is that it helps to regulate our mirroring instincts—to promote imitation when it is helpful to us and inhibit imitation when it is not.

Here is where I think stress comes into play in this process. Under stress, our brain is prone to misperceive our needs; when this happens, we may be prone to imitate the desires of others and misperceive those desires to be organic needs essential for our own survival. When our stress is in the "just right" zone, we may find our complex mirror systems working properly

---

7. Oughourlian, *Mimetic Brain*, 25–29.

8. Iacoboni, *Mirroring People*, 200–213.

to inhibit mirroring when it is not useful or necessary. But when our stress is dialed up too high, we may find our brain is prone to imitating the nervous systems of others, even when this is not helpful to us. Consider, for instance, the way panic may sweep through a crowd in the absence of an actual threat, or the way anxiety or stockpiling behavior appears "contagious."

Under stress, our brain may mirror the nervous system and subsequent behavior of others unnecessarily, and we may also begin to desire whatever we perceive others to consider desirable. And taken one step further, if the object of our "borrowed" desire is perceived to be in scarce supply, then we may come to view the person whose desire we are imitating to be a potential *rival*. It has been said that the mirror systems in our brain give rise to three possible options for relating to one another: as models, rivals, or obstacles.[9] When trust is high and we are exploring territory related to our organic needs, the mirror systems in our brain may point us toward helpful models to imitate. Consider, for instance, how infants learn which foods to try and which objects to play with by imitating others. Imitation of trustworthy models can be helpful and not necessarily lead to conflict or rivalry on its own.

However, when trust is diminished and stress increases, we may come to misperceive the desires of others as organic needs that we must also seek. And then if the object of our mutual desire is perceived to be in scarce supply, we can expect to find ourselves relating to others as if they were threats.[10] We may then feel compelled to pursue social and economic capital we do not actually need and in larger quantities than we need. This can produce a downward spiral, wherein our brain increasingly perceives our authentic needs less accurately, and increasingly and indiscriminately consumes whatever is perceived to be both desirable *and* in short supply.

So how then do two or more rivals, whose brains are in a dance of escalating desires and misperceived needs, negotiate their way out of this fight? This can be particularly tricky, especially when the circumstances that led to the fight—the perception of scarcity, coupled with the imitation of desire—have not changed. When rivals perceive one another to be in competition over resources that are in limited supply, this is the recipe for a zero-sum game. As our trust diminishes and our stress increases, we can expect our brain will be prone to threat-reactions; at the slightest provocation, a fight between us may break out and escalate until we destroy one another unless we find a third party to mediate between us.

9. Oughourlian, *Mimetic Brain*, 57.

10. Oughourlian, *Genesis of Desire*, 115; for reflection, Jennings, *Liturgy and Theology*, 69; Williams, *Truce of God*, 111–23.

So here is now a summary of this fourth earpiece:

The Neuroscience of Desire

The mirror systems in our brain help us to feel one another's pain.

*The mirror systems in our brain also sometimes
lead us to imitate one another's desire.*

*Under stress, we may misperceive the thing which we both desire
to be both needed and in scarce supply,
and we may then perceive one another as rivals.*

*When we perceive each other as rivals,
our stress further increases and we become prone to threat-reactions.*

*If a fight breaks out between us under these conditions,
we may destroy one another, unless we find a third party to mediate between
us.*

With the neuroscience of desire and rivalry in mind, then, I began
listening to the stories of the Scriptures and noticing places where a third
party was enlisted as a mediator to help establish peace between rivals.

The Scapegoat Mechanism

When I listened to the story of Jesus unfolding slowly in the book of Matthew, I paused at this part:

Go and learn what this means, "I desire mercy, not sacrifice."
For I have come to call not the righteous but sinners.[11]

The author of the book of Matthew recorded these words of Jesus in a
conversation with the religious teachers of the day. And in this story it appeared to me that Jesus was defending and protecting Matthew from them.
When I read this, I wondered, why did Matthew need protecting? To place
this scene in context, we read that two thousand or so years have passed
since Abraham, and nearly fifteen hundred years since Moses. In those

11. Matt 9:13.

generations, many stories were recorded in the Hebrew Scriptures about the descendants of Abraham and their encounters with God. Reading through the accounts of Moses, Joshua, Samuel, Saul, David, Esther, Job, Solomon, Isaiah, and the prophets, I gained a sense of the rise and fall of trust in God experienced by individuals and societal leaders of each generation, and collectively by the people as a whole. And I noticed that the rise and fall of stress, along with misperception that God was punishing—deliberately inflicting stress to the point of a threat-reaction as a tool for correction and teaching—appeared to correspond with this pattern of the rise and fall of trust. That is to say, during times of high trust, and regulated stress, it appeared to me that God was frequently perceived and recorded in Scripture as being forgiving and merciful and deciding not to punish.[12] During times when God was perceived to be punishing, it appeared to me that the individual authors or groups of people were often exhibiting signs of high stress and low trust.[13]

Occasionally an author would attribute a distressing event to God and write about it as if it had been a punishment by God.[14] More frequently however when punishment was mentioned, I found it to be in the form of warnings about the future: "God *will* do this . . ."[15] along with subsequent comments noting that God actually did not follow through on the punishment that had been expected.[16] I read in the story of Job, for instance, a back-and-forth dialogue between Job's friends who perceived God as punishing—"you got what you deserve"—and Job who insisted his suffering was not a punishment from God.[17] I thought that Job's perception of God as not punishing seemed to me to be an example of Job's brain producing a trust-response, even in the midst of high levels of pain. Which is to say, Job was under extreme stress, and yet his upper networks appeared to be engaged so that he remained thoughtful, intentional, prayerful, and creative in his responses toward his own suffering, his friends, and God. I imagined his lower networks were reacting to his pain and suffering—which were a true

12. E.g., Exod 34: 6–7, directly following a stressful scene where Moses breaks the stone tablets, the Lord is said to have passed before him, and proclaimed, "The Lord, the Lord, a God merciful and gracious, slow to anger, and abounding in steadfast love and faithfulness, keeping steadfast love for the thousandth generation, forgiving iniquity and transgression and sin . . ."

13. The word `ebrah` (wrath) is attributed to God in Ezek 21:31, for instance, during the Babylonian captivity, a time of likely high stress; Block, *Book of Ezekiel*, 8.

14. E.g., Isa 9:19; Lam 4:11.

15. E.g., Ps 2:5.

16. E.g., 2 Chr 12:12.

17. For reflection, Greenstein, *Job*, 44.

threat to his wellbeing—and yet, surprisingly, his upper networks remained engaged and appeared to help him to further regulate his stress through trust.

After reflecting on this, I began to wonder if the Scriptures could be understood as a narrative of the rise and fall of humanity's trust and how our perception of God as punishing perhaps rises and falls with it.[18] Under times of extreme stress, are we more likely to misperceive threats, sound a false alarm, and expect punishment? I wondered also if, under high stress, we might misattribute actual threats to God rather than perceiving accurately the source of the threat. Each of these conditions may be understood as an example of our brain mistrusting the trustworthy and vice versa. If this was a helpful way to describe the pattern of human history over time, then it appeared to me that, time and again, God entered our story in one form or another to correct our misperceptions. Throughout the Scriptures, generation after generation, this pattern seemed to be replicated, beginning in the garden when the seed of deception was first planted, sparking a crisis of trust:

We sinned by misplacing our trust and misperceiving God as punishing.
Our stress increased.
God entered our story and corrected our misperceptions.
Our trust was restored, and our stress decreased.
We misplaced our trust again, and misperceived God as punishing.
Our stress increased.
God entered our story and corrected our misperceptions.
Our trust was restored, and our stress decreased.
We misplaced our trust again . . .

And then Jesus was born.

18. Where God's wrath is mentioned in the Greek Scriptures, we find no mention of associated punishment, torment, or distress inflicted as a result; Saint Paul in Rom 1:18 maintains God is not punishing, and in Eph 5:6, speaks of God's wrath with no mention of punishment; in Rom 12:19, Paul speaks of wrath and the English translation inserts God after it—however, this attribution is absent in Paul's reference, also in Rom 2:4–8 and 1 Thess 1:10, and in John the Baptist's reference in Luke 3:7, and Saint John's reference in Rev 14:10; in Rev 19, God's wrath is associated not with punishment but with the spoken word, also in Eph 6:17 and Heb 4:12. In John 3:36, Jesus is recorded as saying, "the one not believing the Son will not see life, but the wrath of God remains on him." Mention of punishment is absent, and we might reflect on whether the difference between "seeing" or "perceiving life," or "perceiving God's wrath" is a matter of belief or *trust*.

When I arrived at this part of the story, I became curious about the timing of it. Why now? What was it about the first century BCE which made it the "just right" time for God to enter the story, as Christian tradition holds, in a body like ours? As I reflected on this question, I thought about the descendants of those original people of the Fertile Crescent who returned to Palestine, and who had so carefully preserved, recorded, and repeated the stories of their ancestors' encounters with God. By the first century BCE, Rome had amassed unprecedented civil and military strength,[19] and placed Herod, described as tyrannical,[20] in charge of the Hebrew people. When I read this, I noticed that as an occupied people, with their homeland and sacred temple facing risk of destruction (the Romans eventually would destroy it in 70 CE), the Hebrew people were perhaps living under conditions of unusually high stress.

I initially dismissed this as inconsequential, however, because the Hebrew Scriptures reflected many similar moments in history and these eras were typically followed by an encounter with God that restored trust, calmed stress, and clarified the people's perception of God as non-punishing and trustworthy. So why would this era be any different? Or to put it another way, what necessitated God entering our story at this point in an unprecedented way, as the story of Jesus would indicate?

I wondered if it was possible that the threat in this era was even more extreme than it had been before. I began to wonder if the Roman occupation represented a risk of near genocide for the Hebrew people, and if there was also the risk that Rome might decide to destroy every Hebrew document and scroll as well. And if that were to happen, I wondered if the entire story of God's trustworthiness—the carefully preserved narrative beginning with the creation account, and continuing through the accounts of Abraham, Moses, David, and the prophets that traced God's encounters with this group of people over four thousand years—was possibly at risk in the first century BCE of being lost to antiquity.

During this time, I had been reading about the Indus Valley Civilization whose stories about themselves and their perceptions of life, reality, and God were largely unpreserved or destroyed when war, drought, or natural disaster wiped out their history.[21] I wondered if the stories of the Hebrew people faced a similar risk of being lost in the first century BCE, and if this moment in history represented the moment right before a massive oil spill

---

19. Avi-Yonah, "Development of the Roman Road," 54–60; Goodman, *Rome and Jerusalem*, 29–47; Hitchner, "Roads, Integration, Connectivity," 222–34.

20. Josephus, *Ant.* 16.1.

21. Parpola, "Study of the Indus Script," 31; Possehl, *Indus Civilization*, 237–46.

renders the sky's image unrecognizable in the sea. When I thought about the first century BCE this way, it appeared to me as a potential moment of unprecedented crisis, when the individual and collective stress of the Hebrew people may have been rising in response to an actual threat that called for an intervention of such magnitude on God's part.

In times of crisis, I thought the law may have helped to decrease the people's stress and increase their trust. But I also thought that in times of extreme stress the law may have backfired, producing the opposite effect. Were there ways in which the law may have already been backfiring as the story neared the first century BCE? The system of sacrifice—an eye for an eye[22]—appeared to me to be a potential example of the backfiring of the law, possibly negating its benefits for teaching helpful behavior. According to these rules, a Rescuer or Punisher attempted to correct an offense that made a Victim of one person by making a Victim of another. And when the first round failed to settle the score, we could expect the fight to continue, with the roles being swapped around the triangle. When thinking of the mirror systems in our brain that, under stress, give rise to rivalries between us, we may understand then how the Triangle of Punishment escalates and entraps all parties in a zero-sum game.

There may appear to be no way out of the Triangle of Punishment, and from a neurobiological perspective it is a trap from which we may be unable to consistently release ourselves. This is because, when a Rescuer enters the Triangle of Punishment as a "third-party mediator" who punishes someone, this perpetuates the swapping of roles around the triangle. Rivals may, however, purchase temporary peace by agreeing on a Scapegoat to sacrifice.[23] The Scapegoat then becomes a New Victim, whose sacrifice becomes the object of mutual desire between rivals, bringing them into peaceful alliance—at least for the time being.

22. Lev 24:19.

23. For reflection, Alison, *Joy of Being Wrong*, 139–61; Bartlett, *Theology Beyond Metaphysics*, 125; Cone, *God of the Oppressed*, 132; Flood, *Healing the Gospel*, 69–75; Girard, *Scapegoat*, 110; Girard, *Violence and the Sacred*, 254–73.

Scapegoat

The Scapegoat Mechanism

We may think of this as the "scapegoat mechanism," and it does suc-ceed in stabilizing the triangle in a new way. Which is to say, the scapegoat mechanism recreates the Triangle of Punishment in such a way that peace is purchased between Persecutors through the punishment of the Scape-goat. However, a few complexities exist, the first being that the Scapegoat enters the triangle as one who is not a Persecutor, according to the roles of the triangle. In fact, Scapegoats are typically selected because they are not perceived by the Persecutors to be rivals. Which is to say, Scapegoats are typically targeted for their perceived *vulnerability*—their nonthreatening position.[24]

But there is a complication: the rules of the Triangle of Punishment dictate that violence is sanctioned only as a means of punishment for a perceived offense—to correct harmful behavior or teach helpful behavior (its ineffectiveness to do either notwithstanding).[25] Targeting a Victim, therefore, who has not victimized anyone violates the rules of the triangle. If the public witnesses a nonthreatening Victim being sacrificed, they can be expected to rise up to prevent it. Even a people operating under the misperception that punishment is necessary for the correction of an actual offense will insist on evidence of the offense; and when it becomes clear that a non-offending Victim is scheduled for punishment, a critical mass of clear-minded people will rise up to stop it.

Therefore, a false story is needed.

Persecutors succeed in purchasing peace through the victimization of a Scapegoat by inventing a story about the Scapegoat's "badness." In some

24. For reflection, Kirk-Duggan, "African-American Spirituals," 153.

25. DuBois Gilliard, *Rethinking Incarceration*, 177; Figueiredo, "Effect of Punish-ment," 1017–97; Hoffman, "Mass Incarceration's Second Generation," 247–74; Mulch, "Crime and Punishment in Private Prisons," 70–94.

cases, new laws may get written that the Scapegoats will be said to have already broken.[26] The story of the "badness" of the Scapegoat will therefore transform the unsanctioned violence of the Persecutors into sanctioned and even demanded punishment, and the Persecutors then become heroic Rescuers. When this happens, not only does the Scapegoat's sacrifice succeed in stabilizing the triangle and purchasing peace between Persecutors, the violence against the Scapegoat may be celebrated and rewarded by the people who now misperceive themselves to have been rescued from a threat that never even existed.

It may be worth noting that peace purchased through the scapegoat mechanism is always temporary; as quickly as one Scapegoat is sacrificed, the next one must be chosen. And to ensure that the vulnerability of the Scapegoat and the arbitrariness of the selection remains hidden from view, new laws may be written, stories invented, and categories of Scapegoats created *ex nihilo*—spoken into existence. Because Scapegoats by definition are less of a true threat—and *any of us* could be scapegoated if we become vulnerable—we can imagine that everyone's nervous system is perpetually sounding a false alarm that is neurobiologically taxing. But because our lower networks are reacting to this threat, our upper networks may not be fully engaged in order to perceive the source of the threat accurately or respond to it creatively, making this trap very difficult for us to release ourselves from. Therefore, Persecutors and Scapegoats remain bound up in the trap of the triangle together, with the Persecutors' peace and in many cases survival dependent upon the Scapegoat's perpetual existence.

If the public ever begins to suspect that they are being lied to about the Scapegoat's "badness," there is always the risk they will mobilize into the Rescuer role to punish the Persecutor and "free" the Scapegoat. However, we may quickly recognize this as simply a return to the classic Triangle of Punishment, which succeeds only in creating a new generation of Victims. Therefore, we may understand the scapegoat mechanism to be both self-maintaining and self-reinforcing.

If the public ever begins to suspect that punishment is not in fact necessary or helpful—even if there has been an actual offense—there is always the risk they will mobilize to dismantle the triangle and deal with the Scapegoat and the Persecutor in a different way. Therefore, the scapegoat mechanism also maintains itself by ensuring that the usefulness of punishment will not be questioned by the people. The misperception of God as a punisher who demands that offenses be punished thus may fulfill this function; if the Scapegoat is perceived no longer to be the arbitrary choice of the

26. Girard, *Scapegoat*, 102.

Persecutors but rather chosen by God, we may find this renders the triangle virtually non-collapsible by the people trapped inside it. And the people, aware that any of us could be scapegoated for any one of our actual offenses if punishment is necessary, therefore may find ourselves, with low trust and high stress, participating in the scapegoat mechanism simply because we naturally desire to avoid becoming the next scapegoat ourselves. In facing this actual threat—albeit one of our own collective making—we may find ourselves then navigating daily life with our stress perpetually dialed up too high, leading us to misperceive our needs, engage in unnecessary rivalries, victimize the vulnerable, and overconsume from the planet.

And the ocean ceases to reflect the sky.

When I considered this, the initial scene in the garden came to mind. I thought about the story of the serpent who first planted the seed of mistrust in the couple's brain. The articulation of that first deception seemed to me to be something like "God is untrustworthy." I also thought this lie suggested to the couple, "You need something you don't already have." When I thought about the ripple effects of this initial deception, I noticed that this lie appeared to set the stage for persecution between rivals, the Triangle of Punishment, and the scapegoat mechanism which followed. And this initial crisis of trust may have been what gave humanity our first felt experience of being hijacked by our lower threat networks—the *knowledge of evil*—which succeeded, as the story goes, in keeping our threat networks engaged unnecessarily. Under those neurobiological conditions, our stress is too high, our brain misfires, and we misperceive our own needs and the trustworthiness—or lack thereof—of persons and situations. From here, I looked back at this initial scene in the garden to remind myself how God had responded to this original crisis of trust. Once the couple's trust had been broken, they appeared to feel ashamed and afraid for the first time, and they misperceived God as a punisher from whom they withdrew.

And then God came near.
God deescalated their stress, and increased their safety.
God mixed up the "just right" ingredients for optimal learning.
And God began to restore their trust face-to-face.

I wondered then if the story of Jesus was perhaps a culminating example of God coming near, deescalating our stress, increasing our safety, correcting our misperceptions of God, and restoring our trust face-to-face.

Jesus Christ

> . . . the Word was God . . . and the Word became flesh and lived among us . . .[27]

As the story goes, God entered our human story as Jesus, in a body like ours.[28] This might be like the Painter entering the painting, and becoming one of the painted ones—not a simile, but a metaphor. If God became a human being with a brain like ours—an upper neocortical region and a lower subcortical region—then God became a walking, talking nervous system, God with soft parts—God vulnerable, God woundable, God able to be victimized and scapegoated.

When I reflected on this, I thought, if God were to enter our story in any other way—which is to say, to attempt to collapse the trap of the Triangle of Punishment from the *outside*—we would likely have continued to mistake God for a Persecutor, a punisher, or a threat. What we needed was for God to collapse our trap *from within*. We needed God to expose the lie upon which the scapegoat mechanism is founded, once and for all. We needed help to perceive God more accurately, so that our trust could be restored on a foundational level.

So now that God was on the inside of our story, I wondered how God would accomplish this.

> He committed no sin,
> and no deceit was found in his mouth.
> When he was abused, he did not return abuse;
> when he suffered, he did not threaten
> but he entrusted himself to the one who judges justly.[29]

From there, I reflected on the observation of those closest to Jesus that he never *sinned*;[30] and when I read that, I understood it, neurobiologically speaking, to mean that Jesus consistently responded to threats appropriately. Which is to say, Jesus appeared to accurately perceive the trustworthiness of

27. John 1:1–14.

28. The early church worked out this understanding together, e.g., Alexander of Alexandria, "Letter to Alexander of Thessalonica," 33–37; Saint Athanasius, *Inc.* 11.19; Saint Gregory of Nazianzus, *Orat.* 31.14; Justin Martyr, *Dial.* 63; Tertullian, *Apol.* 21.

29. 1 Pet 2:22–23.

30. John 8:29; 19:4; 2 Cor 5:21; 1 John 3:5; 1 Pet 1:18–29; 2:22–23; for reflection, Alison, *Raising Abel*, 25–28; Baker, *Diagonal Advance*, 298.

God and trustworthiness or lack thereof of others,[31] and respond either way with his upper networks engaged, regardless of the circumstances. Trust regulates our nervous system, which means Jesus' brain was likely flooded with beneficial neurotransmitters. That sense of safety with God would then have balanced out any escalated stress in his body. Under these conditions, Jesus could have accurately perceived threats and, trusting God *in toto*, responded with his upper, neocortical networks rather than his subcortical networks alone. In this case, Jesus' response to each person and situation would possibly then have been a clear reflection of *who God is*—a calm ocean reflecting the sky.[32] That is to say, regardless of the stress or pain he was experiencing, Jesus' response—made possible by trust—may have reflected, and preserved for others, life, relationality, kindness, creativity, and access to joy.

I wondered then how Jesus responded to sinners. If punishment was necessary, and if God was punishing, and if Jesus was God, then we would expect to find Jesus punishing as well—inflicting stress to the point of a threat-reaction in the brain of his enemies, in order to give them a lesson, correct harmful behaviors, or teach helpful ones. But I did not find this to be the pattern; rather, when Jesus encountered Persecutors or victimizers of others, I found him to be forgiving. Finally we had arrived at the cornerstone of my curiosity.

Forgiveness

From here, I wondered about the relationship between forgiveness and the Triangle of Punishment. I listened to the words Jesus is said to have spoken to those with social and economic capital—those who presumed to tell the people who God was and what God required them to do; and I noticed that Jesus supported the law.

> Woe to you, scribes and Pharisees, hypocrites!
> For you tithe mint, dill, and cumin,
> and have neglected the weightier matters of the law:
> justice and mercy and faith.
> It is these you ought to have practiced without neglecting the others.[33]

Jesus was recorded as having advocated for matters of the law, while also calling for justice, mercy, faith, and perhaps trust. The word translated

31. E.g., John 2:24.
32. John 10:30; 14:7, 10.
33. Matt 23:23.

as "faith" appears elsewhere in verb form as "to trust";[34] when I noticed that, I thought of the neuroscience of trust, and the neurotransmitters that are released when we encounter a trustworthy person or situation, perceived accurately. It also occurred to me that justice, mercy, and trust appeared to be the necessary ingredients for forgiveness. The word translated "to forgive" holds a sense of "to release or let go."[35] I thought then that justice might involve the ability to perceive accurately an untrustworthy person or situation so that we can respond appropriately. And mercy might be understood as the compassion we may find for an untrustworthy person who is likely experiencing extreme stress, which is taxing to their system. And I thought then that we might understand trust to be the mechanism that regulates our own nervous system and keeps our upper neocortical networks engaged, permitting us to set aside the lie that says punishment is necessary, and respond with forgiveness and interventions that support life, relationality, kindness, creativity, and access to joy.

It seemed to me these three together—justice, mercy, and trust—formed the key ingredients, the optimal neural conditions, to allow us to forgive. And forgiveness, in turn, created perhaps the optimal conditions for learning. It is under the conditions of forgiveness then that the brain of a Persecutor may also learn and grow. And this seemed to be the potential logic of the pattern I saw in Jesus' forgiving response toward Persecutors; which is to say, he appeared to take issue with the practice of punishing those who broke the law.

Let anyone among you who is without sin be the first to throw
a stone at her.[36]

You have heard that it was said, "An eye for an eye
and a tooth for a tooth."
But I say to you, "Do not resist an evildoer."[37]

34. The word *pistis* (faith) as in Matt 23:23 may also convey a sense of trust, as in John 2:24; for reflection, in Greek there is no distinction between faith and faithfulness; these are not two different words—in the sense of the original Greek, we can't "have faith" without us also acting faithfully, which fits the notion that trust occurs automatically upon encountering a trustworthy person and in turn makes us more trustworthy; email exchange with Jane Patterson, New Testament scholar, in discussion with the author in July 2020.

35. The word *aphiemi* (to forgive) as in Luke 23:34 may convey a sense of "leaving, dropping, or releasing," as in Matt 4:20 "they left their nets and followed him".

36. John 8:7.

37. Matt 5:38–39.

I say to you, "Love your enemies
and pray for those who persecute you . . ."[38]

And when I thought about punishment as we have been defining it—
the deliberate infliction of stress to the point of a threat-reaction—I thought
this made sense. Jesus would likely not attempt to interrupt a pattern of
persecution using punishment that backfires and short-circuits the learning
process. And two things occurred to me then: by taking issue with the practice of punishment, Jesus was also interrupting the scapegoat mechanism
and in doing so, correcting the misperception that God is punishing.

Christ is the image of the invisible God . . .[39]

For in him the whole fullness of deity dwells bodily . . .[40]

From here, I became curious what these two interventions—the inter-
ruption of scapegoating and the revelation that God is forgiving rather than
punishing—may have accomplished.

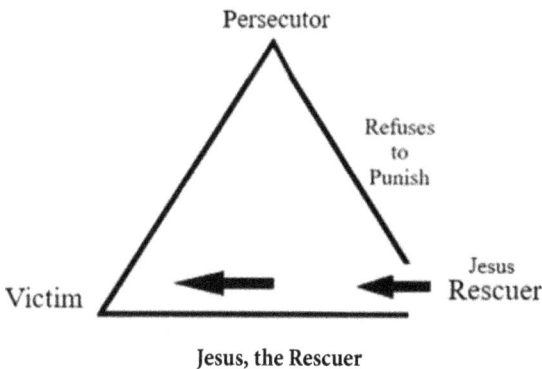

Jesus, the Rescuer

I thought about the ripple effects of God entering the Triangle of Punishment in the Rescuer position but refusing to punish anyone. In the original triangle, the Rescuer enters to defend and protect a Victim by punishing
a Persecutor.[41] I noticed that Jesus instead entered and advocated for justice
for the scapegoated—calling out the Persecutors who were victimizing the

38. Matt 5:43–44.
39. Col 1.
40. Col 2:9.
41. As in John 6:15 when Jesus' followers were said to have attempted to force him
to be their king who might lead them in battle.

vulnerable—but refusing to punish the Persecutors. In this way, I thought Jesus transformed the Rescuer position on the triangle, paving the way for a more effective form of rescue.

Next I noticed that Jesus often restored to health the sick, injured, and marginalized—those scapegoated because they were vulnerable. In this way, Jesus was also exposing the story of the Scapegoat's "badness" to be a misperception.[42]

> And just then some people were carrying
> a paralyzed man lying on a bed.
> When Jesus saw their faith, he said to the paralytic,
> "Take heart, son; your sins are forgiven."[43]

By refusing to play along with the invented story of the "badness" of the Scapegoats—the sick, injured, and marginalized in the community—Jesus exposed the deception that the scapegoat mechanism requires in order to maintain itself. And it occurred to me that by tugging on this one thread, Jesus appeared to be unraveling the whole tapestry.

> When they came to the place that is called The Skull,
> they crucified Jesus there with the criminals.[44]

So then Jesus became the next Scapegoat.

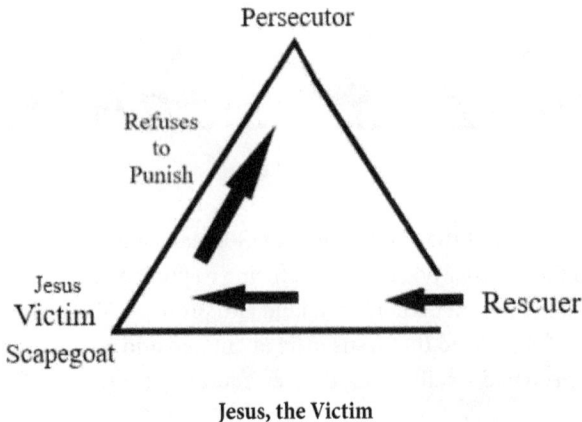

Jesus, the Victim

42. Alison, *Raising Abel*, 23–24.
43. Matt 9:2.
44. Luke 23:33.

Except none of the stories of Jesus' "badness" would stick. So when Jesus was sacrificed as an innocent Victim, this may have succeeded in unraveling the final thread.[45] The lie upon which the scapegoat mechanism is founded was exposed once and for all.

As said, when people begin to suspect they are being lied to about a Scapegoat's "badness," there's always the risk they will rise up to punish the Persecutor—particularly if they misperceive God as a punisher who demands it. But this only multiplies the problem, leaving the triangle fixed in place. At this point, it occurred to me that the solution represented in this story may have been the *only* way to collapse the trap from within, through *forgiveness*:

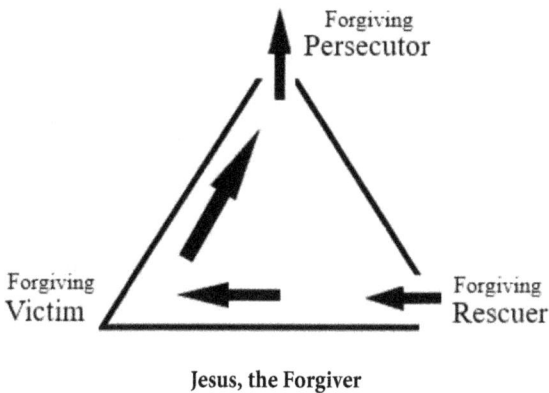

Forgiving
Persecutor

Forgiving
Victim

Forgiving
Rescuer

Jesus, the Forgiver

God became a human being—a potential Persecutor
who refused to victimize anyone.
God became a Rescuer
who refused to punish anyone.
God became a Victim, an innocent Scapegoat
whose "badness" was exposed as a lie.
And in doing so, God transformed every position on the Triangle of
Punishment
through forgiveness—revealing to us the way out.

Jesus being God—and forgiving rather than punishing—revealed God to be, not punishing, but forgiving. And in doing so, Jesus corrected our misperception about God, a misperception that had been both the cause and result of our threat networks being engaged unnecessarily. Our brain's

45. Alison, *Joy of Being Wrong*, 168–75; Girard, *Scapegoat*, 102.

response to reality depends largely upon our *perception* of it, and how we act is largely governed by the part of our brain that is engaged—whether that is our upper neocortical networks or our lower subcortical networks. Punishment that elicits a threat-reaction tends to backfire because it erodes trust, increasing stress, and deactivating our upper networks. But an encounter with a trustworthy person or situation—accurately perceived—generates a release of those warm, pleasant trust neurotransmitters in the brain. And that is what aids the learning process, helping us access our upper circuitry and learn more helpful responses to reality.

From here, I wondered again whether we might reflect God's image most clearly when our trust is high, and our stress is regulated. I thought this seemed to be the conditions in which human beings feel most alive, relate well with others, and exhibit kindness, creativity, and joy! And in Jesus, it seemed God had revealed the Triangle of Punishment to be the very mechanism preventing us from experiencing life in this way. And Jesus had revealed the triangle to be an invention of our own making, born out of a misperception of our own needs and God's trustworthiness. To correct our misperception, it appeared to me that God had come near, in a body like ours, deescalated our stress, and increased our safety. And in doing so, God had mixed up the "just right" ingredients for optimal learning. God had solved the Triangle of Punishment through forgiveness, by saying to Persecutors, "If you mistakenly think that one of us must die, *let it be me.*" And in doing so, God had demonstrated God's willingness to sacrifice God's own self in order to demonstrate that God is not punishing and to restore our trust in God's trustworthiness once and for all time.

Here then is a summary of this fourth chapter:

The Story of Jesus

In our stress,
we misperceived punishment as necessary
and trapped ourselves
in a triangle of victimization and scapegoating
from which we could not release ourselves.

God came near,
in a body like ours;
and entered our story—
a Rescuer who refused to punish;

a Scapegoat whose "badness" was false;
a Persecutor who declined the part.

By dying as he did, Jesus revealed God
to be non-punishing, forgiving, and trustworthy,
And in doing so, God transformed every position
on the Triangle of Punishment
through forgiveness—revealing to us the way out.

A Prayer to God Who Frees Us

Oh God, we trust You,
for You are trustworthy;

You would drain the whole ocean to unmask us,
You would breathe mercy into our lungs,

You would expose our lies and let us shiver,
only to be warmed by Your insistence on our forgiveability.

You would pick the lock on cages we cannot see,
You would restore to us our unclipped wings.

And when we refused to rise,
You would open up a hole in the floor,

that we may free fall the distance
into Your cupped hands.

In the name of God,
the trustworthiness of Christ,
and the freedom of the Spirit,
Amen

A Blessing for One Who Is Free

May you know in your bones
a belonging that is yours
because you are "you" and no one else.

May your body rest
in a welcome that encircles
all that is in you, both seen and unseen.

May you inhale and exhale
particles of love;
may you laugh with the aspens,
as your word bubbles up inside you.

May you whisper it first to the moon,
and then bury it with the worms,
and then, when it breaks through to the light,
cradle it to your chest.

And then sing it from the roof
so brightly, it shatters the universe.
And now listen, as the stars echo it back.

Your sacred word,
in the language of all who are free:
"You are loved and unrepeatable."

In the name of God,
the freedom of Christ,
and the life of Spirit,
Amen

Soteriology

a twist

a
slow
grief
broke
me
open
. . .
there
I
found
my
soul

5

A Healing Story

It is the access to the truth of God-beyond-death made manifest
in the self-giving of Jesus . . . which permits the reordering
of the whole of a person's life.

—James Alison[1]

I CALLED UP MY friend Laura the other day; we have known each other since
we were kids. There was a memory I had been trying to sort through and I
hoped Laura could help. The phone call was illuminating and the outcome
made me laugh. Here is how our conversation went:

"I'm hoping you can help me with the details of an event that happened in first grade," I said. "We've never talked about this because when we
were growing up, I was always afraid to ask you about it."

Laura said she had difficulty remembering things, but would try to
help.

"Did we sit next to each other in first grade?" I asked.

Laura thought it was possible.

"Do you remember a day when the teacher told us to make our own
snack, and passed out bananas and plastic knives? She said to be careful because though they were plastic, the knives could still injure someone. Right
then, the girl next to me turned around and my knife caught her in the
eye! I was horrified! I didn't know if her eye was okay or if I had seriously

1. Alison, *Joy of Being Wrong*, 191.

injured her. I always worried about the girl's parents being upset and holding it against me. Is it possible that was you?"

Laura said she had no memory of the "knife incident," though she remembered us being friends in the years that followed. She recalled some sleepovers at another friend's house.

I remembered that, too. "I always wanted us to be closer, but I was scared. I tried to avoid any situation where I might have to go to *your* house or meet your parents. I felt certain they would remember that I had done this awful thing to your eye and they would want to talk to me about it." I apologized again for never having brought it up.

Laura said her parents never mentioned anything about an eye injury, but she would ask them about it. We chatted more about friends and birthday parties we remembered all those years ago.

"Then you moved away. . . right?" I asked.

Laura confirmed in middle school, her family had moved across state.

"I'll confess, I felt relieved. And then, my family moved, to your new city" I said, "and we ended up in the same school again!"

This matched Laura's memory as well.

"You were so kind then to invite me to your new house," I said. "But I was still scared to meet your parents. I worried they had been angry over the knife all this time!" I told Laura my next memory was of going to her house and meeting her parents, and that her father had been kind and welcoming to me. "Then my fears disappeared; I decided either your parents were very forgiving, or maybe the injury hadn't been as serious as I had feared. Either way, I was finally able to put the whole thing out of mind after that. And I regretted having let my fears get in the way of our friendship."

A few days later I received the following text from Laura. "An update: my parents have zero recollection of the plastic knife incident. More helpfully perhaps, I didn't start at that first school school until third grade!"

I had either misremembered who I sat next to in first grade, or the year of the dreaded "knife incident," or both. And regardless, the memory had haunted me throughout my childhood and interfered in my friendship with Laura whom I liked spending time with and whose parents had been exceedingly nice to me. My way of coping with the distress over what I thought I had done was to avoid discussing it with anyone, especially Laura. If I had simply broached the matter sooner, the story could have found a new ending much earlier. And I could have enjoyed an even closer friendship with someone I have always enjoyed.

Healing the Brain

The central and upper circuitry of the brain plays an important role in the processing and storage of our memories.[2] The way in which we remember events is impacted by a number of factors: our emotional state at the time of the event, the responses of others toward us immediately during and after it, our sleep, dream, and REM states, the ways in which we recall, reflect upon, and speak about the event to others, and their responses toward us in return. All of these factors impact our narrative memory about an event and the meaning we assigned to it. And two people can have two very different memories of the same event. The question then becomes, how accurate or helpful are our memories to us?

When our brain experiences a stressful event that shoves us, neurobiologically, into a threat-reaction, the brain will store this event in a particular way. We may remember certain details—sights, smells—and forget others that our brain determines are not essential to remember. The brain is trying to ensure that it can recall the details necessary to survive a similar event, should one ever occur again in the future.

Some stressful events are chronic, like systemic poverty, war, or long-term child abuse or neglect. But most events are temporary, like an accident, injury, or disaster; we are threatened, and then the danger passes. However, our brain does not always perceive accurately that the danger has passed. This helps to explain how when soldiers return from war, they may find their brain producing vivid flashbacks even though they are now safely home. That is an extreme example, but many times our brain stores the memory of an event, along with associated details or "cues," in a way that links up with feelings of stress, to keep the body vigilant *as if* the danger was still ongoing.

When the danger has passed, therefore, it becomes important that we find a way to update our brain. Otherwise the constant sounding of a "false alarm" takes a toll on the body. Researchers describe the process of updating our brain as bringing resolution to the "unresolved narrative," or providing a new ending to the story so that the brain now remembers the event as a narrative with a beginning, middle, and hopeful end.[3] Narrative is another word for a pattern into which the brain organizes memories and sequences of events, and we experience—and eventually articulate these patterns—as *stories*.

2. Siegel, *Developing Mind*, 86.

3. Porges, "Polyvagal Theory," 67; Schore, *Affect Regulation and the Repair of the Self*, 53; Siegel, *Developing Mind*, 137 and 330–65.

The Brain on a Story

It has been said that the capacity to construct a cohesive and coherent autobiographical narrative is one of the most robust predictors of resilience.[4] When our brain experiences an event that overwhelms our ability to cope, meaning our stress was too high and our system overwhelmed, our unresolved story of the event might sound something like this:

This horrible thing happened (or I did something horrible),
and I didn't know what to do, and no one supported me with it.

A story like this violates the two conditions that the human brain needs for wellness: to feel 1) resourced enough; and 2) supported enough. When the brain codes a memory as an unresolved story like this, the hopeful ending is missing. Human beings are amazingly resilient and can survive horrific things and come out the other side stronger, more resilient, wiser, and more compassionate because of it. We often call this post-traumatic growth or post-traumatic transformation; but for this to be the outcome, our brain must be able to tell a coherent, meaningful story about the thing that happened. And that story needs to include a beginning, middle, and hopeful ending.

A resolved story might sound something like this:

This horrible thing happened (or I did something horrible),
but I learned what to do, and others supported me through it.

The beginning of the story may be horrific, but it has a hopeful ending. When we can tell a story like this about an event, it is an indicator that our brain is aware the immediate danger is in the past, not the present. This does not mean there is not still the possibility of *future* danger. But the resolved story is an indicator that, for the time being, we have determined conditions are *safe enough* to engage the upper neocortical networks. A resolved story, therefore, corrects for the two major violations of the original event by linking the memory network of the event up with the networks which hold the awareness that "I learned what to do" and "I am no longer alone."

When we speak of "healing" from something, we are referring to the process by which we come to be able to tell a resolved story about it. We can recall the memory of the event, and speak about it, without our threat

4. Fosha, "Emotion, True Self, True Other," 523.

networks hijacking us, meaning, we may still feel some distress over the memory without slipping back into the illusion that the original danger is still present today. The process by which we come to tell a resolved story necessitates three things: that 1) the original danger has indeed passed; 2) we gained the resources to learn what to do to increase our safety and decrease our stress; and 3) we accessed the support of others to take the steps to do so.

As we take steps to address our unresolved stories, we may find the most helpful ingredient to our own healing is often added by *someone else*.[5] Though I know now that the "knife incident" may never have involved Laura or her family to begin with—and the person I need to make amends to may still be out there somewhere—going over to Laura's home and meeting her father did alleviate my distress. Meeting her father and receiving his forgiveness, even if the original threat was all in my head, gave my unresolved story a hopeful ending. But I probably would not have arranged that resolution myself, had it been up to me. The stress was too high; Laura's invitation was a gift and her father's kindness an ingredient that changed my brain in a way I would not have known then to ask for.

When Laura texted me to say that the knife incident probably hadn't involved her, I answered, "Ha! I must have conflated two memories."

She replied, "Perhaps that was part of the healing that your mind arranged for you."

Living with unresolved stories produces conditions that can agonize and torment us; and resolving these stories through compassion, creativity, resources, and support can change our brain. We experience these changes in our brain as "healing." Once new linkages between the networks that hold the distressing memory and the networks that hold awareness of our resources and support are established, we may find ourselves suddenly capacitated to be more compassionate, creative, and supportive toward others.[6]

So here is a summary of this fifth earpiece.

The Neuroscience of Healing

For optimal wellness, the human brain needs to be
sufficiently resourced and supported.

An unresolved story is one where something distressing took place
and we felt under-resourced and under-supported.

5. Thompson, *Anatomy of the Soul*, 137.

6. For reflection, Bader-Saye, *Following Jesus in a Culture of Fear*, 80.

A story is given a new ending
when we re-experience the distress relived
but this time, with sufficient resources and support.

When this occurs, the brain forms new linkages that we experience as
healing;
this in turn reduces stress and increases our capacity
to experience life, relationship, kindness, creativity, and joy.

With this mind, I turned my attention to listening to the story of Jesus, and what it might be communicating to us about our own healing and salvation, by providing a new ending to our own story of misplaced trust and victimization.

Saved from What?

Indeed, God did not send the Son into the world to condemn the world, but in order that the world might be saved through him.[7]

When I thought about those words attributed to Jesus, I wondered, "Saved from what?" Throughout the stories of Jesus, I noticed he often spoke about saving human beings from something;[8] what was it? From what did we need saving?

If Jesus *was* God, then God did not seem to be the answer,[9] because as the story goes, Jesus was non-punishing toward sinners. Which is to say, in the story of Jesus' life, he forgave his enemies rather than punishing them. And by refusing to punish anyone, the misperception that God is a threat to sinners had been corrected; God had come near, in a body like ours, to say, "This is who I am," and restore our trust face-to-face. Therefore, it did not seem accurate to think that we needed to be saved from God; this seemed in fact to resemble both the falsehood told by the serpent in the garden, as well as the falsehood upon which the punishment trap was constructed. And Jesus' refusal to punish anyone appeared to unravel that falsehood. Which is

7. John 3:17.

8. For instance Matt 10:22; 16:25; Luke 7:50; 8:12; 19:10; John 5:34; 10:9; 12:47.

9. Here I find I part company with Edwards, "Sinners in the Hands of an Angry God," 15; Piper, *Desiring God*, 53; and others who might maintain that we need to be saved "from God," as I understand the incarnation to be communicating that Jesus reveals the fullness of who God is.

to say, Jesus' unconditional kindness[10] gave the story of our own victimization, punishment, and scapegoating a new ending, which might transform our understanding of its beginning.

I thought this new ending sounded something like this: we experienced a crisis of trust, misperceived God as a threat, and God came near; we made God a victim, we killed God, and were still shown kindness and forgiveness. And this new ending indeed seemed capable of transforming our understanding of what came before it: if God was never punishing to begin with, then perhaps punishment—and the misperception of its necessity—was an invention of *our own* making. I wondered then if the threat from which we needed to be saved might be *ourselves.*

Yet, when I traced the story back to the beginning, that answer also did not seem quite right. In the story of the original couple in the garden, trust appeared to be high, at least it was at first. And under those conditions, I thought:

> *They were alive.*
> *They related well to others.*
> *They experienced intimacy.*
> *They were creative.*
> *They could access joy and delight.*

In the story of the garden, it appeared to me that the threat was not so much the couple themselves, but the lie to which they were introduced. And when deception is at the heart of our difficulties, it follows that learning to perceive the truth of reality more accurately will be important then for our salvation.

> *. . . and you will know the truth, and the truth will make you free.*[11]

We might say the goal of human growth and maturity is to come to perceive accurately the difference between that which is trustworthy and that which is not. Then our brain will respond to the trustworthy with trust, and to the untrustworthy with a response still guided by our upper neocortical networks—a response that increases safety and decreases stress, so that helpful learning can occur.

Otherwise, we will continually misperceive reality, sounding false alarms when there are no true threats, which taxes our nervous system.

10. Sanders, "Jesus and the Sinners," 5–36; also Saint Paul in Rom 2:4 and 5:8.
11. John 8:32.

And we will mistakenly trust that which is inherently untrustworthy, as we trusted those who told us Scapegoats needed punishment. Here then is the pattern we might find emerging over time, when we exist too long in a state of nervous-system hijack, with stress too high and trust too low:

> *We inflict death.*
> *We are isolated.*
> *We experience cruelty.*
> *We are destructive.*
> *We exist in agony and torment.*

The more our threat networks are activated, the harder it becomes to make choices and live our values; the more violent we become toward ourselves, others, and the planet. When that occurs, we inflict death, and experience isolation, cruelty, and destructiveness; we feel agony and torment in our bodies. Our trust continues to decrease, and our stress rises further. And the ocean ceases to reflect the sky.

> . . . it is better for you to enter life maimed than to have two hands and to go to hell.[12]

From here, I wondered about the places in Scripture where Jesus was recorded as warning us about "hell." Jesus' descriptions of hell seemed consistent with the consequences of a crisis of trust: death, isolation, cruelty, destructiveness, agony, torment—the felt experiences of human bodies hijacked by our brain's threat networks.[13] Could *hell* possibly then be the answer to the question, "saved from what?" Was hell what we needed saving from?

That thought sparked my curiosity about Jesus' teaching about the possibility of experiencing hell—not just in life, but after death also.

> And these will go away into eternal punishment,
> but the righteous into eternal life.[14]

---

12. Mark 9:43.

13. For instance, in Matt 5:22–30; 10:28; 23:33; 25:31–46; Mark 9:42–48; and Luke 12:4–5.

14. Matt 25:46.

As the story goes, three days after Jesus was crucified, he appeared alive again to his friends in a series of emotional scenes.[15] In the story, Jesus allowed his friends to touch him; he ate food.[16] And surprisingly he was a body once again, with a human brain, and visible injuries—not healed nor perfected—resembling his body as it had been before death. When I read this, I wondered about the possibility of our own human body—brain included—living beyond death. I noticed the places in Scripture where Jesus spoke as if our bodies would be resurrected as well,[17] and I wondered if the distinction between *heaven* and *hell* could conceivably be related to the functioning of our bodies, particularly our brains. Could a brain prone to misperception and mistrust in life remain so also after death? If so, then it occurred to me that a brain that has not learned to perceive reality accurately enough in life might conceivably be resurrected in heaven and yet *misperceive* it to be hell.[18] Which is to say, as in life, when we have a crisis of trust, our brain sounds a false alarm, which produces in our bodies the felt experience of death, isolation, cruelty, destruction, agony and torment. Could this possibly occur after death as well?

What if the factor that distinguished *hell* from *heaven* was our brain's perception of it? If so, then I thought a good definition of hell might be "our brain's continued misperception of our own needs and God's trustworthiness, such that our stress remains too high and we experience death, isolation, cruelty, destruction, agony and torment unnecessarily, even beyond death." I sat with this definition for some time, and after reflecting on the other elements of the story, it seemed to me consistent in two key ways: God is not punishing, but our felt experience of punishment persists nevertheless—certainly in life, when our trust is too low and stress too high—and perhaps also after death, given Jesus' warnings about hell. I noticed too that Jesus identified *hell* as something from which we can be *saved*, translated elsewhere "cured" or "healed."[19] I wondered then if the process of being saved perhaps meant developing the ability of our brain to perceive God in a more accurate way so that our nervous system could respond with *trust*. That seemed to me in keeping with how Jesus appeared to respond to reality—trusting God and himself, so that he was capable of also responding to

15. Matthew 28; Mark 16; Luke 24; John 20.

16. Luke 24:39.

17. Matt 19:16–22; Luke 10:25–28; John 3:16; 10:27–28; 17:1–3.

18. For reflection, Lewis, *Great Divorce*, 68–69.

19. The word *sozo* (saved) is translated in other places in Scripture as "cured or healed" as in Matt 9:21; 10:22; Mark 5:56; 10:52; Luke 7:50; 8:48; John 11:12.

untrustworthy people with his upper circuitry engaged, which is to say with nonviolence and forgiveness.

In this way, Jesus' responses toward his enemies also reflected trust—the conviction that punishment was not necessary, even to the point of saying, "if you mistakenly think one of us must die, *let it be me*." Jesus' responses in this way reflected an intention to preserve his enemy's life; he invited his enemies into relationship, intimacy, creativity, and access to joy, by offering forgiveness and showing the way out of the trap of punishment. When Jesus was met with a threat, his responses deescalated the situation—decreasing stress and increasing safety for all. As the story goes, some of Jesus' enemies responded with trust, and as a result, their brain began to perceive reality more accurately.[20] Others continued to misperceive the trustworthy as untrustworthy, and their brain responded with continued rivalry and scapegoating.

I wondered then if trust was the key—the key—to unlocking it all, "trust" being the ability to perceive accurately that which is trustworthy and respond with trust. Looking back through Jesus' teachings and the example of how he responded to others, a pattern emerged that appeared to me to echo God's response to the couple in the garden:

> *God came near to restore trust face-to-face*
> *God reassured them, you have what you need.*
> *God was forgiving.*
> *God revealed that punishment wasn't necessary.*
> *God restored their trust, which helped them to regulate their stress.*

I began to write down the teachings and stories of Jesus, to see how they fit with this pattern; five themes emerged and I did not encounter a teaching or response from Jesus that appeared to fall outside one of these themes. Here are a few of the notes I took on these five themes, along with some examples of teachings or stories of Jesus that I thought were a good representation of each theme:

God has come near.

The kingdom of heaven has come near . . .[21]

20. E.g., Luke 19:1–9; 24:37; Matt 8:5–13.
21. Mark 1:15.

Flesh and blood has not revealed this to you, but my Father in
heaven . . .[22]
Where two or three are gathered in my name,
I am there among them . . .[23]
He showed them his hands and his side . . .[24]
Remember I am with you always . . .[25]

You'll have what you need.

Don't worry about what you'll eat or drink;
ask and it will be given to you . . .[26]
Give freely; practice fasting; the Sabbath was made for you . . .[27]
The measure you give will be the measure you get,
and still more will be given you . . .[28]
Don't store up treasures on earth; you cannot serve God and
money . . .[29]
Take no bread, no bag, no money in your belts . . .[30]
All ate and were filled . . .[31]
Consider the ravens: they neither sow nor reap,
and yet God feeds them . . .[32]
Sell your possessions and give to the poor . . .[33]
Take, eat, this is my body . . . drink, this is my blood . . .[34]

God is forgiving.

Forgive . . . even seventy-seven times . . .[35]

22. Matt 16:17.
23. Matt 18:20.
24. Matt 27:9.
25. John 20:20; Luke 24:40.
26. Matt 6:25.
27. Mark 2:27.
28. Mark 4:24.
29. Matt 15:19–20.
30. Mark 6:8.
31. Matt 15:37; Luke 9:17.
32. Luke 12:24.
33. Luke 12:33.
34. Luke 22:19–20; Matt 26:26–28; Mark 14:22–24.
35. Matt 18:21–22.

He went about curing disease and sickness . . .[36]
What did David and his companions do when in need of food?[37]
He will leave the ninety-nine and go in search of the one . . .[38]
He said, "Friend, your sins are forgiven you . . ."[39]
They spat in his face, struck him, slapped him; after mocking him, they
stripped him; then Jesus breathed his last . . .[40]

Punishment isn't necessary

Don't be cruel to your partner; turn the other cheek; love your
enemy . . .[41]
Do to others as you would have done to you . . .[42]
I desire mercy, not sacrifice . . .[43]
Put your sword back into its place . . .[44]
He touched his ear and healed him . . .[45]
Let anyone among you who is without sin be the first to throw a
stone . . .[46]
And Jesus said, "Neither do I condemn you . . ."[47]

Trust will help you to regulate your stress.

Why are you afraid, you of little faith? Do not fear, only believe . . .[48]
Come to me, I will give you rest; my yoke is easy, my burden is light . . .[49]
You of little faith, why did you doubt?[50]

36. Mark 1:32.
37. Mark 2:25.
38. Matt 18:12.
39. Luke 5:20.
40. Matt 26:67—27:50.
41. Matt 5:31–45.
42. Luke 6:31.
43. Matt 9:13.
44. John 18:11.
45. Luke 22:51.
46. John 8:7.
47. John 8:11.
48. Mark 4:40; 5:36.
49. Matt 11:28.
50. Matt 14:31.

Have faith the size of a mustard seed . . .[51]
Not my will, but yours be done . . .[52]
Friend, do what you came here to do . . .[53]

Having identified these patterns in the stories of Jesus, I now wondered if we were perhaps drawing near to the heart of the first question,
"saved from what?" and beginning to circle a second. To the first question,
hell seemed to me to be a good candidate, with hell being defined as what we
experience bodily when our brain is hijacked by a crisis of trust, misperceiving our own needs and God's trustworthiness, such that our stress remains
too high and we experience and often inflict death, isolation, cruelty, destruction, agony and torment unnecessarily.

So if it was true that hell was the threat from which we needed saving,
the next question became "how?" How were we saved? What was accomplished by God coming near, in a body like ours, living the life Jesus lived,
dying the death Jesus died, and, as the story goes, appearing again?[54] What
did that loving, nonviolent, forgiving death actually make possible?

A Transformative Story

I reflected on that question for some time. I thought, if it is true that what
distinguishes *hell* from *heaven* is our brain's capacity to perceive accurately
that which is trustworthy and respond with trust, then I thought salvation
might involve some neurobiological change in the brain—a linking up of
new neural networks such that we perceived reality and God more clearly,
and responded with trust, unlocking other possibilities for neurobiological
healing and transformation. That is to say, I wondered if salvation might be

---

51. Matt 17:20.

52. Luke 22:39–46; Matt 26:39; Mark 14:36.

53. Matt 26:50.

54. For reflection, Tanner, *Jesus, Humanity, and the Trinity*, 29, appears to empha-
size the incarnation—along with Saint Gregory of Nazianzus, Clement of Alexandria,
and others, as the mechanism of salvation—suggesting that human nature was healed
by virtue of the incarnation; I am inclined to say we are transformed as we come to
understand that Jesus—who died in such a nonviolent, forgiving way—was also God
and survived the ordeal. Said a different way, it is by coming to understand the relationship between the incarnation, crucifixion, and resurrection that our perception of
God's trustworthiness may be transformed. And it is the trust then sparked within us
that unlocks the key to our salvation—regulating our stress and supporting the estab-
lishment of new linkages between networks in our brain that we refer to as "healing,"
"growth," or "maturity."

understood as everything that follows a *correction* of our misperceptions, about ourselves, others, and God's trustworthiness.

When this thought occurred to me, I recalled how we function optimally under "just right" stress conditions—not too little, not too much. I understood it to be these "just right" conditions under which we reflected God's image more clearly:

> *God is life . . . we feel alive.*
> *God is relational . . . we thrive in relationships.*
> *God is kind . . . we exhibit kindness toward each other.*
> *God is creative . . . we are creative.*
> *God is joy . . . we can access joy.*

And trust seemed key to unlocking this capacity within us. At this point, it occurred to me that God coming near, in a body like ours, living the life Jesus lived, dying the death Jesus died, and appearing again—the Christ story—may have been the *only* way to correct our misperceptions of God. I thought also that it may have been the only way to ensure the corrective story would be recorded, taught, and handed down through the generations, such that trust might be restored on a scale so great that we could say, "God so loved the world . . ."[55] It appeared to me to be a stunning solution to an otherwise unsolvable problem of the trap of the Triangle of Punishment from which, neurobiologically speaking, we do not seem able to release ourselves. So I sat down to make an attempt at articulating this as a cohesive story:

Transforming the Triangle

55. John 3:16.

We misperceived God to be a Persecutor.
God entered our story as a Rescuer
who refused to punish anyone.
We killed God as a Victim—
a scapegoat whose "badness" was a lie.
God rose from the dead, and forgave us.
Through this story, we encounter God's trustworthiness.
As we listen to it,
our trust may increase;
our stress may be regulated;
and we may perceive our needs more accurately;
in all of this, we may be enabled to forgive,
heal, grow, and mature,
and come to reflect God's image more clearly.

An encounter with a trustworthy person—accurately perceived—generates a release of those warm, pleasant trust neurotransmitters in the brain. And that is what aids the learning process for human beings, helping us access our upper neocortical networks and learn more helpful responses to reality as it presents itself. Pain may still exist, but our stress will be dialed down to a manageable level, and we may find that . . . we can cope. We may find that we have the sense of being resourced and supported by God and by trustworthy others; we are not alone. And under these conditions, we can practice kindness with greater ease; we surprise ourselves with bursts of creativity. And joy is more accessible.

I wondered now if we were perhaps drawing near to the heart of the second question, "saved how?" If God came near, in a body like ours, lived the life Jesus lived, died the death Jesus died, and appeared again, what had been accomplished? It occurred to me that perhaps everything that came before had been pointing to this:

We're saved from hell
as we come to perceive
that the story of Jesus
reveals God to be wholly trustworthy,
which increases our trust.[56]

56. This is what I understand Jesus to have been communicating in Matt 8:10; 17:20; 21:21; Mark 10:52; 11:22; Luke 5:20; 7:9, and that *pistis* (faith or trust) may cure or heal a person as in Matt 9:22; Mark 5:34; and Luke 8:48; to my mind, we might find this squares with a *sola fide* (faith alone) or *sola confidere* (trust alone), and *sola gratia* (grace alone) understanding of salvation.

If so, then I wondered, as we reflected on the story of Jesus, and came to perceive God and ourselves more accurately through it, if the story itself would
spark a "trust release" within our brain that may in turn save us. Could an
encounter with the story of Jesus that corrected our perception of God have
the power to link up networks within our brain, sparking trust and regulating our stress, and making us well—in all the many ways in which we need
to be made well?[57]

Get up and go on your way; your faith has made you well.[58]

From here, I had a new question—could faith and trust be the same
thing neurobiologically? If so, then I thought "saved by faith" appeared less
as a cognitive decision to believe, and more the response of a nervous system
to an authentic face-to-face encounter with a trustworthy person perceived
accurately. And if that is the key to unlocking everything, then it seemed to
me that having an accurate understanding of the story of Jesus, and what it
revealed about God, would be paramount.

I reflected then on the implications of the notion that trust might be
sparked upon an encounter with the story of Jesus that transforms and corrects our misperceptions about God. It occurred to me that, as we continued
to reflect on and contemplate this story, our trust might grow stronger over
time, and I wondered if that might allow us also to heal, grow, and learn to
access our upper neocortical networks, such that we too might be enabled
to respond to our enemies with forgiveness rather than punishment. And as
these new neural linkages in our brain began to help us respond creatively
to threats, increasing our safety, and decreasing our stress over time, I wondered if we might collectively perceive our needs more accurately, and learn
to do less harm to one another, our own bodies, and the planet. Might we
then have the brain capacity to create entire communities that make available to others the "just right" mix of stress and safety necessary for optimal
learning and wellness? And under those conditions, could it be possible for
humanity collectively to reflect God's image more clearly?

If so, I wondered if we could come to understand ourselves then as being saved in life before death, as well as after. I thought, as we practiced perceiving God's trustworthiness more accurately, and our bodies responded
with trust, this just might change the way in which our brain functioned

---

57. The word *sozo* (to save) appears elsewhere in instances when Jesus cures or heals
a person who is suffering, as in Luke 7:50; Mark 6:56; Luke 8:36; John 11; and Acts 4:9.
I understand Alison, *Joy of Being Wrong*, 168–75; Flood, *Healing the Gospel*, 69–75; and
Thompson, *Anatomy of the Soul*, 233, to be reflecting on a similar notion.

58. Luke 17:19.

over time—returning us to that condition of trust we once felt as children prior to that trust being broken. And from there, I wondered if the resurrection story was an indicator that it was possible for our brain to retain that capacity beyond death,[59] so that if heaven exists, we might perceive God's trustworthiness there as well, and respond with the same trust we had come to experience on earth.

If so, then this seemed to hold implications for how we might understand ourselves then as being saved in life before death, and life after as well. Perhaps salvation, then, involves a healing process that includes a linking up of neural networks in the brain during the course of our life, and these linkages become both the product of and catalyst for our ability to perceive accurately that which is trustworthy and respond with trust. And then the process of establishing new neural networks—facilitated by trust—might turn out to be what we mean when we speak of things like "healing," "growth," "transformation," and perhaps salvation.

Here then is a summary of this fifth chapter:

The Story of Salvation

In reflecting on
Jesus' death
we came to understand
God was not punishing,
but forgiving.

This revelation
decreased our stress,
restored our trust,
making it possible for us also to forgive others.

In reflecting on Jesus' resurrection
we came to understand
life extends beyond death,
therefore, we may also say to our enemy,
"If you mistakenly think one of us must die, let it be me."

---

59. For reflection, Lewis, *Great Divorce*, 68–69; Williams, *Tokens of Trust*, 141.

As our trust increased, we were healed;
we came to perceive reality more clearly,
and experienced ourselves
to be saved in this life
and after.

A Prayer to God Who Heals Us

Holy One,
recite for us the old and beautiful story.

Give us strength to stand attentively
and listen as it's read out loud.

Remind us not to lock our knees,
lest we faint before the good part.

And ring a bell to wake us up
when our chapter arrives.

Steady our hand now, as we take the quill;
bless us with clear vision.

O! Inventor of love stories,
our hand is slipping.
Before the quill drops,
write it, write it!

Write upon us the story of healing
You have intimated could be ours.
We offer our words for Yours,
our words for Yours.

In the name of God the Author,
Christ the living Word,
and the Spirit who heals us,
Amen

A Blessing for One Who Is Waiting

When the path is dark ahead,
the light behind,
and the shadow before you,

still your feet.

The sun finds it no bother
to traverse an entire sky to find your face.

In the name of God above,
Christ beside,
and the Spirit within you,
Amen

Pneumatology

Welcome Home

There are roads in this world
with many stones,
and there are roads
that are lined with trees.

There are roads
that follow the river,
and roads
that lead to the sea.

But whatever road
you choose, My child,
wherever you
may roam,

You will always have
My love to hold,
and you are
always welcome home.

6

Integration

Who can tell the Spirit's story? Who, indeed, would dare to attempt to?

—Phyllis Tickle[1]

During my third-grade year, the tension in our house grew, until one night our parents called us into the living room. I was eight years old; my brother and sister were three and four years younger. Our parents sat us down, three in a row, on the brick fireplace. Our mom began to explain that our dad was moving out of the house and into a new apartment.

"Are you getting a divorce?" I wanted to know.

"Not yet; but we're taking a time-out."

I started crying.

Our father said, "No matter what happens, I'll always be your dad and your mom will always be your mom."

Later that night, I searched the house for our mom. I found her in the bathroom brushing her teeth. She seemed—not happy—but not sad either.

"Why aren't you crying?" I asked her.

"I cried my tears already," she said.

I understood by these words that, for our mother, this was an ending to a story in which the middle had been the sad part. For me, this time felt very much like the middle of a story and I did not know when or how it might end.

---

1. Tickle, *Age of the Spirit*, 145.

In order for the brain to heal through the formation of a coherent story, processes in the right hemisphere must be integrated with those on the left. Or as Dan Siegel puts it, coherent narratives are created through *interhemispheric* integration.[2] This is because the left and right hemispheres each play a different role in helping us process and make sense of the world, ourselves, and the story of humanity, into which our story fits.

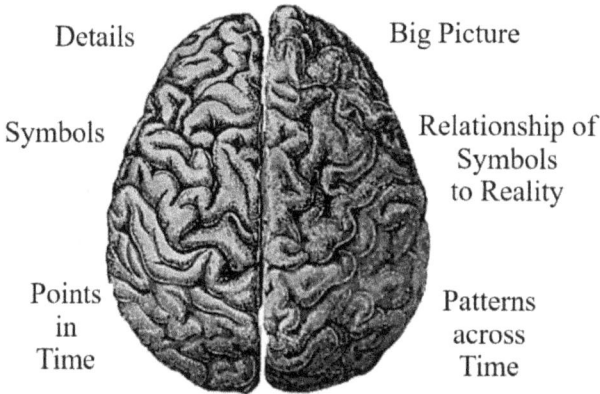

Details Big Picture

Symbols Relationship of
Symbols
to Reality

Points
in
Time Patterns
across
Time

Right and Left Brain Hemispheres

It is generally understood that networks in our right hemisphere give us a sense of the big picture; our right-side networks recognize patterns across time and draw connections. Our right networks help us zoom out, in an attempt to grasp reality as it "really is." We might say our right networks add complexity to our experience. In contrast, the networks in our left hemisphere help us to notice the details and specifics of reality. Our left-side networks help us to think in terms of units of time. Our left networks are constantly zooming in and trying to interpret reality as simply and concretely as possible. The left networks help us to create an understanding of life that can be pinned-down. We might say our left networks are trying to reduce complexities in our experience.

Both the left and right networks contribute essential tools for our survival and wellness. Psychiatrist Iain McGilchrist has speculated that the dominance of one hemisphere over the other may help to explain differences between personality types, cultural groups, and civilizations.[3] He has wondered, for instance, whether in early European civilization there was perhaps more balanced support for both hemispheres. Over time, however, modern Western civilization has seemed to invest more heavily in the left

2. Siegel, *Developing Mind*, 371.
3. McGilchrist, *Master and His Emissary*, xxii.

hemisphere, which may over time cause our picture of reality to become "fragmented."

As neuroscience advances, we may better understand how our left and right networks are differentiated and what helps them to integrate. Neuroanatomist Jill Bolte Taylor has documented her observations on brain hemisphericity and her experience as a left-side stroke survivor. Taylor says that when her left-side networks went "offline," during her stroke, she lost control over her ability to speak, interpret details like numbers on the telephone, and plan for the future that requires an awareness of time. But with her right networks still active, she felt extraordinarily alive and attuned to patterns of connection and meaning. After analyzing her experience, she concluded: "the feeling of deep inner peace is neurological circuitry located in our right brain."[4]

I thought about this when my uncle Dave survived a stroke in his left hemisphere. My father and I visited him shortly after the stroke and we sat on his back patio. The right side of Dave's face drooped and he struggled to form words. With his stronger arm he pointed out his favorite plants and indicated he was happy he had gotten them in the garden prior to his stroke. Then he grew quiet, like he wanted to say something. My dad and I leaned in. It took a while to get the words out. "I'm still here . . ." Dave said, gesturing to his head. We nodded but I had the sense we were not following him. "I have . . . love . . . joy . . ." A smile spread across his face; then he laughed heartily like I remembered from childhood. We leaned even closer and Dave struggled to say, "They tell me I'm lucky I still have my right side . . . or I'd be a real articulate asshole."

Integrating the Brain

To make sense of our physical, mental, emotional, relational, and spiritual lives, it appears we need access to both hemispheres. We also need effective connections between our upper and lower networks. Dan Siegel's work centers around helping the brain heal and grow through vertical and horizontal integration.[5] We may understand vertical healing to be what happens when neural linkages increase between the upper, central, and lower regions of our brain—a bottom-to-top or top-to-bottom integration. We can help to create the conditions under which our brain establishes these new linkages by directing attention to distressing memories that activate our lower networks, and holding that awareness together while also activating networks

4. Taylor, *My Stroke of Insight*, 41–62.
5. Siegel and Bryson, *Whole-Brain Child*, 14–65.

in our brain that are trusting, relational, kind, creative, and able to access joy, simultaneously. It is the practice of dual awareness that, in part, helps to create the conditions for vertical integration to occur.

We may think of horizontal healing as what happens when neural linkages increase between the left and right regions of our brain—a crossing-of-the-midline form of integration. We can help to create the conditions under which our brain establishes these horizontal linkages by directing attention to the information we are receiving from each hemisphere. This requires something of a "quieting down" of one side, in order for us to listen to the other, and vice versa.[6] Both hemispheres are making sense of reality in different ways, and each perspective is helpful to us. The right hemisphere attempts to take in the bigger picture and is scanning for patterns and connections that assist us in gaining an emotionally-attuned and intuitive sense of reality. The left hemisphere's perspective is more "zoomed in" and focused on the details, logic, and rules by which the left side organizes and makes sense of the world.[7]

To navigate reality in the most functional, efficient, and relational manner possible requires that we gain the capacity to draw upon all parts of us—the lower and upper networks, as well as the left and right hemispheres. And assisting the brain to establish as many linkages as possible between circuitry takes on a new importance as we come to better understand how being "bottom-heavy" or "left-side-heavy" limits our problem-solving capacities.

I entered third grade "bottom-heavy."

My third grade teacher knew my parents were separating. She and my mom were friends. One afternoon, Ms. Stephens asked if I would stay after class for a minute. "I know what's happening with your folks. I'm here if you want to talk." Ms. Stephens had red hair and freckles, and I already thought she was pretty and kind. But from this moment on, I loved her.

Nevertheless, I did not want to talk. Or more precisely, I could not. At least, not about this—my inner feelings. I could speak about things in the outer world that fascinated me, Madeleine L'Engle books, the space-time continuum, or Morse code, but not my inner world. My left networks were not even close to being well-linked with my right.

My right-side brain circuitry loved Ms. Stephens. Children can typically intuit an adult's intentions toward them, so even if the adult doesn't know the most helpful thing to do or say, their desire to be kind and helpful can spark trust. Being in Ms. Stephen's classroom that year gave me a

6. Badenoch, *Heart of Trauma*, 183.
7. McGilchrist, *Master and His Emissary*, 6.

sense of belonging and comfort. When she took notice of me, my right-side networks registered this as a compassionate response from an adult who was looking out for me. And though I did not have enough access to my left hemisphere to express verbally what my right networks were experiencing, I appreciated her caring response.

One afternoon, we took our seats after recess, and waited for instruction. Ms. Stephens often graded papers when we went to recess, and when we returned to the classroom, she would call upon a student to pass out the papers. I wanted to do anything Ms. Stephens asked, and I liked being trusted with tasks. I also had to go to the bathroom. Instead of visiting the toilet during recess, I had spent my free time digging for earthworms in the mud. That decision meant I was now in a precarious spot. I wanted to be available if Ms. Stephens planned to call upon me, but I also had an urgent need. My lower threat networks were firing quicker, and my upper networks were firing more slowly—the priority (to my lower networks) seemed to be preserving Ms. Stephen's care and trust in me. The care of an attentive adult can mean survival for a child, and a child's lower networks sense this. So my lower networks called the play: I would stay in my seat and wait to see who she called on; if it was another student, then I would raise my hand and ask if I could be excused.

"Gena, would you please pass out these papers?"

Okay, so that was how this would go. I rose solemnly, receiving the attention as a gesture of care I was determined not to jeopardize. More linkages between my upper and lower networks would have enabled me to trust that Ms. Stephens' care was less fragile than I perceived it to be. But my lower networks were firing and I was misperceiving the trustworthy as less than entirely so; I took the stack of papers from Ms. Stephens and began winding a path around the room, passing them out.

Within half a minute, the field had changed—the needs were shifting. I looked up at Ms. Stephens; she was at her desk across the room. I knew I would never make it that many yards to ask her if I could be excused to the restroom. I caught the attention of my friend Casey and made a joke that animated a larger conversation at Casey's table; when the surrounding tables joined in, and my classmates were distracted, I stepped into the corner where I pretended to be sorting papers, stood with my legs crossed, and peed down my tights.

Dissociation is a word for the capacity of the brain to disconnect one part of us from another.[8] In this case, the lower networks in my brain that needed Ms. Stephens and hadn't wanted to disappoint her were disconnected

8. Siegel, *Developing Mind*, 360.

from the upper networks in my brain. Those upper networks were more attuned to my needs and the trustworthiness of Ms. Stephen's care. But there were simply too few linkages to allow the upper networks to communicate with and regulate the lower networks. The moment passed, and then my lower networks determined there was no other option but to proceed with passing out the papers.

A child survives childhood, in part, because of dissociation. A child's brain circuitry is not well-enough established to process all of the complexities that adult life presents, so the child's brain is selective about which parts to attend to. And because the survival stakes are so high during childhood, the child's lower networks are continually running a cost-benefit analysis. The networks and decisions that appear to offer the best chance of helping the child survive are given priority. And when disconnected from the upper networks, the lower networks may drive the child to do things that the upper networks would find objectionable.

Often too, the child's right and left networks may find it difficult to each contribute the helpful information they have to offer. That is to say, in times of stress the right-side networks may be firing in response to the bigger picture. But if there are few linkages across the midline, the left networks may not be able to add the words and details that render that picture able to be articulated. When this happens, the child may be left with an unresolved story about an event. In order to organize our experiences into a coherent story with a resolved ending, we must be able to draw upon and integrate information from both our left and right circuitry. As we grow, there is much we can do to assist our brain with making these top-down, right-left connections; but those linkages necessitate that optimal conditions for learning exist. When a child grows up in a "bottom-heavy" environment, optimal "safe enough" conditions may not be present for complex linkages in the brain to occur.

Later that afternoon, Ms. Stephens rang a bell to get our attention. She gestured to the corner of the room. "Who did this?"

My face warmed.

Classmates rose to survey the puddle and looked around.

A boy next to me pointed to my soiled tights.

I never liked him much.

"I was digging for worms," I told him.

The Brain on Spirituality

When a child's brain is "bottom-heavy," meaning the threat-reaction networks are too engaged too much of the time, complex linkages between brain networks may occur more slowly and less frequently. The child is learning and establishing new brain networks, but those networks may have fewer linkages *between* them. When this is the case, the child's brain functions like a road system with too few intersections—a highway system with too few on and off ramps.

For instance, a distressing memory network may get established primarily in the right hemisphere, with too few linkages across the midline. When the distressing memory is activated, therefore, the child may feel intense emotion, but have difficulty speaking about it—the neural activity may get effectively "stuck" in the right hemisphere. Likewise, a distressing network may get established primarily in the lower subcortical region, with too few linkages to networks in the upper neocortical region. When the lower network is activated, the child may feel hijacked by the brain's fight, flee, or freeze response, and have difficulty accessing the upper networks to calm the body and choose a creative response.

When we use words like "growth," "maturity," or "healing," what we mean is that the brain is complexifying and integrating over time. As more of our brain networks link up, we find ourselves better able to regulate our nervous system, access our upper networks to make creative choices, and draw upon the strengths of both the left and right hemispheres. To function in an integrated fashion, therefore, we need to develop linkages between the left and right hemispheres—across the midline—and between lower and upper circuitry, giving us greater choice over how we respond to people and situations.[9]

Neuroscience has shed some light on what we can do to help our brain networks establish linkages. For instance, linkages between networks associated with memory and emotion may be facilitated by activities wherein our brain waves oscillate in the alpha and theta frequency ranges; this brain state is often associated with receptive learning and memory reconsolidation.[10] Alpha waves may indicate that our brain is calm and alert, whereas theta waves may indicate that we are moving into—or resting in—a therapeutic, meditative state. Theta waves have been found to be associated with activities where our brain is processing emotion or memory while our eyes are moving back and forth, such as in REM sleep or EMDR therapy.

9. Siegel and Bryson, *Whole-Brain Child*, 14–65.

10. Jensen, "Brain Oscillations, Hypnosis, and Hypnotizability," 230–53; Nishida et al., "REM Sleep," 1158–66; Sun et al., "Reports of Empirical Studies," 12–25.

Contemplative prayer and meditation have also been found to be associated
with this receptive, potentially healing brain state.[11]

Spiritual practices which help to facilitate these brain states have been
found to expand neural functioning in regions of the brain associated with
introspection, perspective-taking, and the development of empathy.[12] Experiences of awe—the sense of transcendence we may feel when contemplating God or nature or beauty—have also been found to facilitate expanded
functioning in regions of the brain associated with empathy, compassion,
and prosocial behavior.[13] During times of stress or crisis, spiritual practices
like these have been found to help the brain establish new linkages between
networks which increase meaning-making, connection, and a sense of trust,
which in turn helps to regulate our nervous system.[14]

All of this is to say that we are learning increasingly more about the
daily practices that may contribute to the optimal conditions for brain healing and integration. In order for spiritual practices to help our brain establish helpful linkages between networks in our left and right hemispheres,
and between our lower and upper brain regions, however, the networks in
need of linking must be activated. That is to say, for prayer to "heal" a distressing memory, the networks associated with the painful memory must
be activated; this means we will experience some stress and distress in our
body—hopefully a "just right" amount to provoke those networks to stretch
and potentially link up with other helpful networks. And the distress must
not overwhelm us to the point of a threat-reaction or the practice will likely
backfire.

The networks to which we need the distressing memory to link up
must also be activated, so that the distressing memory networks and the
more helpful networks are active at the same time. This dual awareness is
necessary if we hope to link these networks up.[15] Once a strong enough
linkage is established, then the helpful upper networks can alleviate some
of the intensity we feel when the distressing lower networks are activated
in the future. For instance, we might spend time in a calm, meditative state
recalling a childhood memory that evokes shame, while also reflecting on
Jesus' compassion. If our brain holds both awarenesses simultaneously, under the "just right" conditions for learning, these networks might succeed

11. Amanpreet et al., "Systemic Review of Meditation and Psychophysiology,"
212–19.

12. E.g., Hölzel, "Mindfulness Practice Leads to Increases," 36–43.

13. E.g., Piff et al., "Awe, the Small Self," 883–99.

14. Kohls et al., "Relationship between Spiritual Experiences," 1–23; Pargament et
al., "Brief RCOPE," 51–76.

15. Shapiro, *Getting Past your Past*, 318.

in linking up. If they do, then when the childhood memory is activated in the future, the compassion network will likely also get activated, and we can expect to feel less shame and greater compassion.[16]

The science of how brain networks link up has deepened my understanding of what may be happening when we experience practices—such as contemplative prayer, *lectio divina*, holy silence, meditation, or labyrinth walking perhaps—as "healing," "restorative," or "transformational." It has also helped me understand that it is possible for us to practice these activities *without* our brain networks linking up; that is to say, if the proper networks that need linking up are not being activated during a practice, we cannot expect integration—healing, relief, and transformation of pain—to result from the practice.

Therefore, we may be engaged in any number of helpful practices which are not actually producing any meaningful linkages between networks in our brain. But we cannot fault ourselves for this too much; we may find it very difficult to identify which networks—painful memories, emotions, desires, compulsions—need to be activated at a given time, as these are different for each of us. And it requires self-energy and focused attention on our part, directed toward these brain networks, in order for us to activate them during a time of calm, resting meditation. And it can be quite taxing on our brain to hold that attention and distress while also holding awareness of God's presence or compassion *at the same time*. And if we do, it is challenging for us to hold that dual awareness long enough for new linkages to occur.

That is all to say, though we may understand some of what is happening in the practice, the practice itself is no easy task! And when our brain succeeds in establishing new linkages, I do not think we are able to say that we are the ones responsible for the linking. There is still much we don't know about how linkages between networks are established—when, where, why, and to what degree. For my part, learning about the mechanics of the process has erased none of the mystery. Our healing is a process that doesn't originate with us; we are not the source of it and because our small part in it remains so very difficult for us, even under the best of circumstances, I think we are continuously in need of help with it.

Here now is a summary of this sixth earpiece:

The Neuroscience of Integration

Our left networks contribute details to help us see particularities.

16. Ecker, *Unlocking the Emotional Brain*, 7.

Our right networks contribute the bigger picture
to help us recognize patterns.
We function best when we're able to draw upon both to formulate our
response.

Our lower subcortical networks help us react to threats.
Our upper neocortical networks help us respond with trust.
We function best when we're able to draw upon both to regulate our stress.

Integrating top to bottom, and right to left requires new linkages
to be established.
We can help our brain to establish new linkages
by creating the "just right" conditions.
Practices that engage multiple parts of our brain at the same time while we're
in a receptive brain state may help our networks link up.

With the neuroscience of integration in mind, then, I began listening to the stories of Jesus when he taught about the role of the Spirit and how the Spirit might help us to learn.

The Spirit as Movement

[Jesus] breathed on them and said to them,
"Receive the Holy Spirit . . ."[17]

When I read this, I pictured once more the opening scene from the beginning of this story, with God, three-in-one, the Creator, Word, and Spirit.[18] And I thought again of Saint Gregory of Nazianzus' picture of intermingling light emerging from three mutual Suns.[19] The image of God as a symphony composer, with Jesus as the music, and the Spirit, the breath inside each instrument also came to mind, as did the idea of God as a playwright, with Jesus as the script, and the Spirit as the movement of the actors bringing the play to life on stage.

I noticed that in the opening scene of Genesis, the Spirit is spoken of as being in *motion*.[20] Movement is a perceptible change in the position of

17. John 20:22.

18. From Gen 1:1; Col 1:1.

19. St. Gregory of Nazianzus, *Orat.* 31.14.

20. The word *m`rachefet* (hovering) in Gen 1:2 gives a sense of "moving" or "fluttering" as in the form of the word which appears in Deut 32:11 when the eagle spreads its wings (hovers) over its young.

an object in space over time. A heartbeat, a leaf waving back and forth on a tree, a wave cresting and collapsing, a chest rising and falling—these movements are perceptible only because time exists, and they are also the way in which time is marked. Which is to say, we perceive movement because we compare images in a sequence over time, and we detect a less than 1:1 correspondence between the images. Or to put it another way, movement is how time becomes perceptible. We come to perceive reality only as we trace patterns of movement across time. And the articulation of the pattern of those movements gives rise to a *story*.

When I thought of that, I noticed one more thing: we only perceive movement that has limited directionality, meaning an object that moves pandirectionally—in all directions at once—ceases to be perceptible by us. It occurred to me that if such an object existed, it would be misperceived by us either as existing in complete motionlessness or not existing at all. So when I reflected on the Spirit as being in motion, I thought, if that movement is what makes God perceptible to us, then that movement would have to be perceived by us as movement in a discernible direction.

From there I wondered, in what direction then might the Spirit be moving?

When I listened to the emotional scenes right after Jesus' death in which Jesus appeared again to his friends, I thought he seemed very intent on his friends understanding and speaking to others about the story of his life, death, and reappearance.[21]

> ... the Holy Spirit, whom the Father will send in my name,
> will teach you everything,
> and remind you of all that I have said to you.[22]

And Jesus' words indicated that the Spirit would continue to teach them more about what this story meant, and remind them if they forgot. And when I read that, I thought of our brain's tendency toward misperception, and losing access to our upper neocortical networks, particularly during times of stress. I wondered then if any movement in the direction of helping us to perceive accurately the meaning of the story of Jesus—correcting our misperceptions about God and increasing our trust—might be understood as movement of the Spirit.

In another scene, Jesus was said to have breathed the Spirit into his friends; when I read that, I was reminded of the role of our breath in helping

21. See for instance Matt 28:18–19; Mark 16:15–16; Luke 25:45–47.
22. John 14:26.

our upper circuitry to engage during times of stress.[23] I wondered then if any movement in the direction of helping us to access our upper neocortical networks and regulate our nervous system by sparking trust, might also be understood as movement of the Spirit.

In that same scene, I noticed that Jesus' words drew their attention next to forgiveness.

> [Jesus] breathed on them and said to them,
> "Receive the Holy Spirit.
> If you forgive the sins of any, they are forgiven them;
> if you retain the sins of any, they are retained."[24]

When I read that, I wondered if an encounter with the story of Jesus that corrected our perception of God had the power to link up circuits within our brain, such that we might be enabled to choose forgiveness over punishment. I thought, over time, we might find that increased our collective safety and decreased our stress, so that our brain could come to trust the trustworthy—now and in the life to come—and I wondered if this might be what is meant by salvation. If so, then I thought any movement in the direction of helping us to forgive one another might also be understood as movement of the Spirit.

When I reflected on the conditionality of Jesus' words, "if you forgive . . ." and "if you retain . . ." it occurred to me that our experience of being forgiven or punished is a matter of both perception and relational reality. If we perceive God to be forgiving, we will respond with trust and be better equipped to forgive others. If we perceive God to be punishing, we will respond with stress and be more inclined to punish others. Likewise, if others forgive us, we will be more likely to experience ourselves forgiven by God as well. And if others punish us, we may be more likely to perceive God as punishing as well. I saw then how intertwined our own actions and our perceptions of God are with one another.

I paused then to consider these three potential directions of the movement of the Spirit: 1) correcting our misperceptions about God; 2) sparking trust; 3) and helping us to forgive. And I thought this made sense; as we move in this direction neurobiologically, we can hope to live healthier, relate better with others, and exhibit kindness, creativity, and access to joy. But these are movements that must take place within our brains—linking up circuits that make these outcomes possible. And these are movements that

23. E.g., Doll et al., "Mindful Attention to Breath," 305–13.
24. John 20:22–23.

we cannot reliably manufacture for ourselves, given that the only instrument we have for doing so is the very one in need of assistance to begin with. Therefore, I thought we needed help. We cannot hope to be the ones to correct our own misperceptions; we cannot hope to coerce trust or force ourselves to forgive if we lack the neural network linkages to do so.

Each of these three movements therefore involves a change in the anatomy of our brain that must be sparked by an interaction with someone else—someone who is *not us*. Therefore, I wondered if this was perhaps a helpful way to think about the role of the Spirit in our salvation: assisting us with the process of engaging the interactions and practices we need in order to help us come to perceive God more clearly, trust the trustworthy, and choose forgiveness over punishment. From there, I was curious, if that is the Spirit's role, then what might be ours?

Giving Consent

I wondered if a clue to our role might be found in the phrase Jesus used—"Receive the Holy Spirit"[25]—and I thought about this in terms of consent. I was reminded of the story of Mary, the mother of Jesus, when she was told that the Spirit would come and move inside her. And Mary said:

> . . . let it be with me according to your word.[26]

This response seemed to me to indicate understanding and consent on Mary's part, saying "yes" to something trustworthy happening inside her—a process in which she would participate but not be the source of its outcome. Which is to say, I understood Mary to be receiving the movement of the Spirit inside her, consenting to it, and saying "yes" to being helped by it.

What might it mean then for us to receive the movement of the Spirit—to consent to being helped by it? In reflecting on this question, something occurred that made me smile. I was researching sea turtles for a friend's birthday recently; a group of us adopted one for her as a gift through a rescue organization. With our donation, our friend received a link where she could log onto a website anytime and track her sea turtle's whereabouts in the world. While researching this gift, I noticed some of the sea turtles appeared to migrate thousands of miles across the ocean, and that sparked my curiosity about how sea turtles travel and navigate.

25. John 20:22.
26. Luke 1:38.

My quest to learn about the travels of sea turtles led me to encounter a few things that I did not know about ocean currents. For instance, I learned that the blowing of the wind across the surface of the sea produces currents in the upper 300 feet or so of water; but these weaker currents change direction frequently and are therefore less reliable for navigation. However, at a lower depth, the currents are stronger and consistent and their directionality depends upon the temperature and salinity of the sea water. These deeper currents flow in a particular direction, regardless of whether or not the wind is blowing on the surface.

On its own, a sea turtle would be unable to swim the long distance back to the beach where it was hatched. So swimming is perhaps not the sea turtle's primary role when traveling long distances. But it can do *something*. A sea turtle has wing-like flippers that can propel a turtle into the current's flow; once there, the turtle can receive the help of the current, doing whatever it can to stay within the flow, and beating its flippers every now and then, perhaps, to self-correct when it finds itself drifting out of it.

I wondered if that was perhaps a helpful way for us to think about spiritual consent. We may not be able to do much to rewire our own brains, but perhaps we can do *something*. Perhaps we can receive the support of the Spirit—doing whatever we can to stay inside the current of its movement, and say "yes" to being helped by it, perhaps beating our flippers every now and then when we find ourselves drifting out of its flow. So I wondered then what this might look like in daily life. What are the practices that may help us to say "yes" to the Spirit's healing movement within us?

Breath Prayer

A few years ago I was introduced to a contemplative practice known as breath prayer. St. Teresa of Ávila was a sixteenth-century Spanish theologian who practiced breath prayer; she called it *oración mental* and "the prayer of quiet."[27] Practitioners of breath prayer may find a word or phrase can be helpful for guiding the mind's attention back to God.[28] I understand this to be a way in which our brain might be helped to produce the dual awareness that is so useful for linking up brain circuitry. A word or phrase that is easy enough to think silently, or whisper with the natural rhythm of the breath, may help us to gently focus our attention on God—lighting up the proper

27. Saint Teresa of Avila, "Book of Her Life," 4.7.
28. For reflection, Saint Ignatius of Loyola, *Spiritual Exercises* 4.249–58.

networks in our brain—and indicating a willingness to be helped by the Spirit. The *Jesus Prayer*[29] may be a helpful example of a breath prayer:

Jesus Christ, Son of God
Have mercy on me, a sinner

This prayer begins with a short phrase, "Jesus Christ, Son of God."[30] When I reflected on this phrase, it reminded me that, as the story goes, Jesus was God in a body like ours.

And the phrase, "Have mercy on me, a sinner," may remind us that, as the story goes, God is non-punishing. By asking for mercy, and acknowledging our inclination toward misperception, we are reminded that mercy is available if we perceive it and trust it to be so. And by asking for it, we are giving our consent to receive it—saying "yes" to being forgiven, which is perhaps important for updating the networks in our brain so that we might become aware that we are forgiven indeed.

Short phrases like these that are easy to match with the breath can be extraordinarily helpful in creating the optimal conditions within us for new linkages in our brain to be established. As we practice this form of prayer, our attention on the breath may serve to regulate our nervous system, helping us to generate brain waves in the alpha and theta frequency ranges—the optimal conditions for new brain linkages. In reflecting on that, I wondered then if breath prayer was perhaps helpful to us in times when distressing memories or stress-related networks were also activated in our brain. In this way, our brain might be helped to hold both awarenesses simultaneously, under the "just right" conditions for learning, so that these networks might succeed in linking up. Once they did, then we could expect the distressing networks, when activated in the future, to activate the trusting ones also. If so, then over time we could expect to find our stress dialed down, our sense of safety increased, and our upper networks engaged more frequently.

29. An inscription containing the Jesus Prayer is said to have appeared in the ruins of a cell in the Egyptian desert dating back to the fifth century; Guillaumont, "Esquisse d'une Phénoménologie du Monachisme," 51.

30. The use of the full name, Jesus Christ, may convey an understanding of him as both human and God; discussion with Daniel Joslyn-Siemiatkoski, church history scholar in Septempter of 2018.

The Lord's Prayer

Reflecting on prayer as a form of consent then sparked my curiosity about the prayers of Jesus, so I listened to the story of a time when Jesus' friends asked him how they should pray. Here are the words Jesus is said to have given them: [31]

> *Our Father in heaven,*
> *hallowed be your name.*
> *Your kingdom come.*
> *Your will be done,*
> *on earth as it is in heaven.*

I noticed that Jesus' words referred to God as a trustworthy caregiver; I wondered then if we were to sit in quiet, meditative contemplation of God as a trustworthy caregiver, if we might also find the circuitry in our brain responding with increased trust within us as well. The phrase "your will be done on earth, as it is in heaven" appeared to me to be a communication of consent—a form of saying "yes" to that trustworthy caregiver's help and support.

> *Give us this day our daily bread.*

When I reflected on the phrase, "Give us this day our daily bread," it seemed to me that Jesus' words reflected a trust that we will have what we need. We will be given what we need in order to experience life, relationship, kindness, creativity, and access to joy. I wondered too if this might serve as a helpful reminder to our brain that we can trust there is enough for all, which might help regulate our nervous system. Because our brain tends to misperceive our needs under stress, moving us to consume things we do not need or in larger quantities than we need, I thought this was perhaps also a form of consenting—saying "yes"—to receiving help to perceive our needs more accurately. I wondered then what the ripple effects of that might end up being, in terms of reversing the harm we have done to our planet and one another through overconsumption and the creation of scarcity unnecessarily.

> *And forgive us our debts,*
> *as we also have forgiven our debtors.*

31. Matt 6:9–13; see also Luke 11:1–4.

I noticed the Greek in this phrase in the book of Matthew where Jesus is said to speak of forgiveness of "debts" differs from the word in the book of Luke where Jesus is said to speak of "sins."[32] I thought both words painted a picture of an interaction between us and others thought to require a response in kind—either a punishment or repayment as in "eye for an eye." Therefore, these words of Jesus appeared to me to reflect a trust that God's intention—will—is to forgive rather than punish, along with the assumption that we will practice this too with one another. I wondered what chain reaction could be sparked by that forgiveness practice as our nervous systems regulate and creative ideas for effective correction and intervention surface as attainable possibilities.

> *And do not bring us to the time of trial,*
> *but rescue us from the evil one.*

This phrase gave me pause; the Greek word for "trials"[33] appears in the story of Jesus being led into the wilderness to be tempted by the devil.[34] It appears also in the scene known as the Last Supper, where Jesus looks at his friends and says, "You are those who have stood by me in my trials";[35] and it appears again in the story of the garden of Gethsemane where Jesus twice tells his friends, "Pray that you may not come into the time of trial."[36] I thought these scenes were reminiscent of the setup for the story of Job; as the story goes, an adversary[37] asked permission to test Job and God granted permission. All of these instances appeared to be trials, in which the brain was faced with a stressful challenge, and the outcome could go either way, depending on which networks in our brain were activated and how. So I looked again at the story of the garden of Gethsemane, where Jesus faced this form of trial, seemingly aware that a genuine threat was crouching

32. The word *opheilemata* (obligations or debts) in Matt gives the sense of owing a response in kind in exchange for material debt, or an offense or favor; in Luke the word is *hamartiai* (sins); email exchange with Jane Patterson, New Testament scholar, in discussion with the author in July 2020.

33. The word *peirasmon* (trials) gives the sense of a series of probes or tests, as in Luke 4:13.

34. Luke 4:1–2.

35. Luke 22:28.

36. Luke 22:40 and 46.

37. The word *ha-satan* (the Satan or adversary) is used in other scriptures as a reference to a human adversary as in 1 Sam 29:4 and 1 Kgs 11:14, or an angel as in Num 22:22.

around the corner. And here we find him praying something quite similar to these same words:

Father, if you are willing, remove this cup from me;
yet, not my will but yours be done.[38]

All of these stories of trials appeared to me to paint a picture of reality as we actually encounter it: we will at times experiencing stress quite intensely, and need help continuing to trust and avoiding slipping down into our threat networks and responding in unhelpful ways. The words we are told Jesus prayed—in teaching his friends to pray and in the garden of Gethsemane—appeared to me to be a form of consent. Which is to say they sounded like a "yes" to receiving God's help when we find ourselves in a situation where our stress is too high and we need a greater degree of support in order to continue trusting.

Perhaps practices such as these—prayer, contemplation, meditating on words like these from the stories of Jesus—are what we can do to stay inside the "current." Which is to say, perhaps the Spirit does the work of the current, carrying us to where we need to go, and prayer practices like these are the equivalent of a turtle beating its flippers. When I reflected on this idea, I thought of the Spirit as lifting and moving us in the direction of correcting our misperceptions about God, sparking trust, and helping us to receive forgiveness and forgive one another. And as we practiced consenting to being helped in this way, I thought there seemed to be a chance this might release us from the punishment trap from which we seemed to find it difficult to release ourselves.

And if this were so, then I thought we might understand practices such as prayer, contemplation, and meditation to constitute our role in the whole thing. This type of spiritual practice has the power to generate the optimal neurobiological conditions for learning—the alpha and theta waves that facilitate new neural linkages. And each time we move ourselves to practice this, we may understand ourselves to be giving a form of consent—receiving help from the Spirit to learn what we need to learn. Meaning, these practices may be our way of saying "yes" to the Spirit who facilitates the movements of trust, forgiveness, healing, growth, maturity, and transformation at the level of our neural anatomy, and which—though we see it occurring in brain imaging—remains transcendent and mysterious in the fact that it does.

So here is a summary of this sixth chapter:

---

38. Luke 22:42; for reflection, Garrett, *Stories from the Edge*, 85–88.

The Story of the Spirit

To help us learn
the Spirit moved inside us.

As we practiced consenting to the Spirit,
we learned to regulate our stress.

As our trust increased,
we found we were able
to respond to our enemies
with the forgiveness of Christ.

And we came to understand
that by saying "yes" to being helped
by the Spirit,
God's image was more clearly
reflected in us.

A Prayer to God on the Inside

God above us,
vertical You are, like a star.
The air is thin up there.
Unreachable You seem,
from down here.

God before us,
fantastic You seem, like a dream,
a mysterious fire,
untouchable
from here.

God within us,
confounding You are,
and most tender.
Hold us on the inside,
tickle our ribs.

And when we pray
"Come by here,"
flutter and whisper
"I'm as close as can be,
closer still."

In the name of God above us,
Christ beside us,
and the Spirit within us,
Amen

A Blessing for One Embarking on an Adventure

May your feet be anchored to the sandy floor,
as the tides rise around you.

May you drop everything that would weigh you down,
trusting the ocean can absorb it all.

May the waves which would toss you,
instead, gently carry you forward, weightless like a sea bird.

May you sail out past the breakers,
trusting your compass will point the way.

And may you know the joy of sea-turtles and sailors,
upon returning to the shore and your beloved.

In the name of God who calls you,
Christ who goes with you,
and the Spirit who brings you home,
Amen

Ecclesiology

Sanctuary

Let's circle a room with no doors and grieve.
You've been my teacher; now I'll teach you.
Here's something—a window!
Too high? That's okay.

Let's flap in circles, let's bloody our beaks
and these walls perhaps.
If we do, we do
(if we do, we do).

We'll build a nest in the cobwebs
and be flightless together.

7

Reconnection

We need not be mystified by the crowd or frustrated by their failures to act for the common good; Jesus has acted for them and offers his body as a way out and a way to be together.

—WILLIE JAMES JENNINGS[1]

WHEN OUR DAUGHTER WAS around eight years old, I was tucking her into bed one night and listening to the adventures of her day. I remember feeling almost moved to tears in that quiet time, just the two of us. Then a memory crossed my mind from a few years back when I had been less than trustworthy in handling a situation with her, and I wished to go back and make it right. I leaned over to kiss her goodnight, paused, and said, "Hey there's something I've always wanted to apologize for. . . do you remember the day we went to catch crawdads?"

It had been a hot July afternoon and our daughter was preschool-aged, and her cousins and a couple of the neighborhood kids were at our house. By midday, I found myself with eight children under the age of ten and no air conditioning. I was without our car for the day; so I packed the littlest nephew in the stroller, and gave the older kids bikes and scooters; our daughter walked next to me, and we began to snake through the neighborhood toward a creek we visited frequently.

1. Jennings, *Acts*, 43.

The older kids gained an advantage on me and the younger kids, and eventually disappeared around a corner. I walked more slowly with our daughter, pushing her little cousin in the stroller. The heat was oppressive. When I turned the last corner, I expected to see the rest of the kids—my son included—cooling off in the creek but they were not there. I huffed and puffed, maneuvering the stroller down an embankment to a spot where we usually stopped to drop our bags and remove our shoes. I could find no shoes, no bikes nor scooters—there was no sign of the kids. They had vanished.

Sweat was pouring off my face; I peered to see if perhaps the kids were further along down the creek bed. Our daughter began pulling off her shoes; I stopped her. "We can't stay! We have to find your brother and the rest of the cousins. I don't know where they are!"

When I said this out loud, the seriousness of the situation registered in my body. Where could they be? My heart raced. Could they have turned down a wrong road? Had they kept going further? I hollered for them but there was no response.

"Come on," I said. "We'll have to retrace our steps." I struggled to push the stroller back up the embankment. Back on the sidewalk, the sun felt even hotter. Our daughter protested, but I insisted; I did not know what else to do. I began pushing the stroller back toward our house, swiveling left to right, looking for signs of the kids. I heard our daughter crying behind me, and urged her to keep walking. "We have to find your brother and cousins!"

After a minute or two, I came to realize she was not following me. I looked and saw her several yards back, lying on the grass and crying. I turned the stroller around and pushed it toward her yelling, "Get up!" I pulled two water bottles out; by the redness in her face and the pounding in my head, I thought we were both in danger of overheating. I sat next to her, and gave one bottle to her and the other to her little cousin.

I may have looked calm but I was furious—mostly at myself. And I was terrified. We drank; the seconds ticked by. The sun was scorching. I did not have a cell; my plan was to get to the house and call a friend. And say what? The kids were missing, and I needed a car so I could drive around looking for them. I wanted to throw up.

"I'm tired," our daughter said in a meek voice, and inched toward me. I saw that she meant to crawl in my lap. I stopped her.

"We can't sit here any longer." I stood up. "We have to keep walking." The expression of disappointment on her face still fills me with regret.

Leaning over her bed years later, I kissed her on the cheek and said, "I've always wanted to say sorry for not cuddling you right then." I tucked her in. "You knew what we both needed, and I should have trusted you."

"I don't remember any of that," she said.

"Well, I've always wished I could go back and do it differently."

She wanted to know then how the story ended.

"It's funny!" I said "As soon as we started walking again, you remembered something I'd forgotten—there was a different creek off another road. You suggested we try looking there and we found them!"

She laughed and I snuggled her extra and told her goodnight.

Growing the Brain

The relationships that contribute the most to our growth and wellness are *not* reliably safe—that is to say, two people in an optimal relationship are not perpetually connected, attuned, or happy with each other. This discovery has also shifted our understanding of what makes for a growth-fostering relationship; we now understanding optimal relationships as those that are able to effectively move between *connection, disconnection,* and *reconnection.*[2]

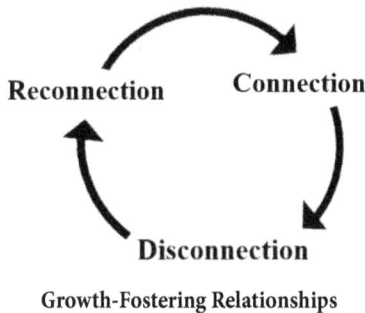

Growth-Fostering Relationships

Attachment research supports this view; when caregivers are relationally connected and attuned to their children *some of the time*, the foundation for a secure attachment may be established.[3] Other times, the caregiver may be disconnected—distracted, confused, frustrated, or simply misperceiving the child's needs; but important learning may also be happening in these moments of disconnection. However, disconnections are stressful, and if they evoke a threat-reaction in the child's brain, then this short-circuits the benefits of the relationship. But when the stress of disconnection is "just right," or when the caregiver manages to reconnect with the child skillfully and effectively, the child's upper networks may remain engaged

2. Jordan, "Recent Developments in Relational-Cultural Therapy," 2–4.

3. Newton, *Attachment Connection*, 3.

and trust restored—strengthened even. A goal of human development then is to learn effective skills for reconnection. And moving between connection, disconnection, and reconnection is how a trusting, growth-fostering relationship is built.

Jean Baker Miller's scholarship on growth-fostering relationships elucidated the cycle of connection, disconnection, and reconnection, and quietly revolutionized the field of psychology. In the 1950s, Miller graduated from Columbia Medical School as one of ten women in her class of one hundred. After graduating, Miller became a practicing psychiatrist, during a time when the prevailing theory of human development claimed that the hallmark of maturity was self-reliance and individuality.

Around 1970, one of Miller's colleagues, Carol Gilligan, was working as a research assistant for Lawrence Kohlberg, perhaps best known for studies on moral development. Gilligan's account of her experience reflects the epistemology of the researchers of that day: students were taught to leave women and minorities out of their studies because they skewed the data.[4] Curious what "skew the data" might mean, Gilligan, Miller, and colleagues like Judith Lewis Herman developed a rhythm of meeting after hours, around living rooms and kitchen tables, and examining the stories from the women with whom they were working. As these researchers verbalized patterns they were seeing in their practices with women and minorities—patterns that did not fit neatly into the theories they had been taught—they began to perceive reality more clearly. As Judith Jordan once put it, they were "listening each other into voice."[5] Miller and her colleagues learned to write down their insights, so that when they returned to their offices and were immersed once more in the prevailing theories of the day, they would not lose the threads of their conversation. As they connected more dots, they expanded their team to include researchers of diverse cultures and backgrounds. Over the next several decades, the scholarship Miller and her colleagues produced would be credited with sparking the *relational revolution* in psychology and a more accurate perspective of the goal of human development: individuality *and* relationality.

The quest now is for parents to learn to foster in children both independence *and* the ability to ask for and receive help, as these are not mutually exclusive. And we now better understand wellness as a byproduct of our ability to move fluidly between separateness *and* intimacy with others. We also hold more appreciation for the fact that differentiation *enhances* our relationships and vice versa. Individuality and relational connection

4. Gilligan, *In a Different Voice*, 1–4; Robb, *This Changes Everything*, 23.
5. Jordan, "Relational-Cultural Model," 102.

are two core needs all human beings share in common, and they work hand-in-hand.

The Brain on Relationship

The relational insights sparked by Miller and her colleagues continue to find validation in neuroscience.[6] Miller coined the term "growth-fostering relationships" to refer to relational contexts that support our individuality and mutuality, and she identified five hallmarks of these types of relationships; they produce in both parties: 1) a sense of zest or vitality; 2) increased ability to take action as empowered individuals; 3) increased clarity about self, other, and the relationship; 4) increased sense of mutual mattering and worth; and 5) expanded capacity for more of these types of relationships.[7] Growth-fostering relationships are those that contribute to our wellness and our maturity, and encourage us to be separate individuals *who are also* kind, relational, and collaborate well with others.

It has been suggested we enjoy optimal wellness when our "top five" relationships—those in which we spend the most time in close proximity—possess these characteristics.[8] Because the primary ecology to which human beings are adapted is one that is rich with other human beings, the presence of others, it has been said that relational networks are a human being's natural biome.[9] When we fail to establish a sufficient number of growth-fostering relationships characterized by mutuality and trust, our health suffers. Social rejection and isolation diminishes the brain's ability to regulate sleep, food intake, and immune responses. In contrast, being near those we love inhibits stress hormones and reduces threat-reactions in our brain, which in turn helps us to better regulate our emotions. When surrounded by growth-fostering relationships, even very young children demonstrate a sophisticated "share-and-care" instinct to support—rather than compete with—one another in times of stress.[10] Adults who enjoy trusting, growth-fostering relationships also display this capacity; the human stress response has typically been characterized as "fight-or-flight," but when trust is present, a third option emerges: "tend-and-befriend."[11]

6. Banks, *Wired to Connect*, 3–13.

7. Miller, "What Do We Mean by Relationships?," 1–13.

8. Banks, *Wired to Connect*, 92.

9. Beckes and Coan, "Social Baseline Theory," 976–88.

10. Warneken et al., "Young Children Share the Spoils," 267–73.

11. Taylor, "Biobehavioral Responses to Stress in Females," 411–29.

The neuroscience of relationships is also causing us to rethink outdated models of addiction. We used to think compulsive drug and alcohol use was strictly related to the brain's pleasure-based dopamine system. But studies of the failure of the "war on drugs," along with surprising successes in sobriety achieved by soldiers upon homecoming, caused us to look more closely at addiction from an interpersonal neurobiology perspective. And what we have determined is that it would appear that the addicted brain is not primarily seeking pleasure, but to numb the pain of relational disconnection.[12]

And the pain of social exclusion may have a physical component; fMRI researchers have noted an overlap in the way in which the brain processes social pain and physical pain.[13] Some neurobiological indicators point to the possibility that social pain and physical pain may share some common underlying networks in the brain. There is much yet to be understood, but an overlap between social pain and physical pain would help to explain the body's intensely stressful reaction to relational rejection and isolation. And we find here too, neurobiologically speaking, trust serves as a buffer against social pain, by sparking the release of neurotransmitters and hormones that reduce stress even during times of relational conflict.[14]

So here is a summary of this seventh earpiece:

The Neuroscience of Relationship

We thrive in growth-fostering relationships.

*The best of all relationships cycle
through phases of connection, disconnection and reconnection.*

*As we develop skills for navigating each of these phases,
we grow in trust.*

*When we experience isolation, exclusion, or rejection
our stress increases,
and our wellness decreases.*

When we experience connection, disconnection, and reconnection

12. Luke et al., "Addiction, Stress, and Relational Disorder," 172–86.

13. Eisenberger et al., "Does Rejection Hurt?," 290–92; Eisenberger and Lieberman, "Why Rejection Hurts," 294–300; Lieberman and Eisenberger, "Pains and Pleasures of Social Life," 890–91.

14. Yanagisawa et al., "Does Higher General Trust Serve," 190–97.

our trust increases
and our wellness along with it.

With the neuroscience of relationships, and the rhythm of connection, disconnection, and reconnection in mind, I began listening to the stories of Jesus' friends following his death and resurrection, as they practiced becoming the "body of Christ" together.

The Body of Christ

As the story goes, forty days after his resurrection, Jesus' friends gathered for an annual festival. The large crowd present that day included travelers from many nations, speaking multiple languages. Early in the morning, the Spirit moved through them and Jesus' friends began narrating the story of his life, death, and resurrection:

> . . . this man [Jesus], handed over to you
> according to the definite plan and foreknowledge of God,
> you crucified and killed by the hands of those outside the law.
> But God raised him up . . .[15]

In this scene, Jesus' friends were attempting to communicate this story to those who spoke other languages, and we're told that with the Spirit's help they were being quite effective. When I reflected on this scene, it appeared to me that a reconnection of sorts may have been happening. Jesus' friends had been connected with him for approximately three years as they traveled with him and learned from him. The crucifixion had been an unexpected and distressing disconnection. After his resurrection, though it seemed to have brought them some comfort to know he was alive, his absence was still a form of disconnection. But now, in this scene and from this point forward, the Spirit appeared to be a felt presence for them: a reconnection.

We are told that around three thousand folks of different backgrounds were present that day and came to trust Jesus' friends and their story, and they soon formed a community.

> All who believed were together and had all things in common;
> they would sell their possessions and goods
> and distribute the proceeds to all, as any had need.
> Day by day, as they spent much time together in the temple,

---

15. Acts 2:23–24.

they broke bread at home and ate their food
with glad and generous hearts,
praising God and having the goodwill of all the people.[16]

When I read about this community, it appeared to me to have been inspired by what Jesus' friends had understood of his life and teachings:

God has come near.

Where two or three are gathered in my name, I am there among them . . .[17]

You'll have what you need.

Sell your possessions and give to the poor . . .[18]

God is forgiving.

He said, "Friend, your sins are forgiven you . . ."[19]

Punishment isn't necessary

Let anyone among you who is without sin be the first to throw a stone . . .[20]

Trust will help you to regulate your stress.

Come to me, I will give you rest; my yoke is easy, my burden is light . . .[21]

We read in the writings of Jesus' followers that they referred to themselves as the "body of Christ."[22] Their vision appeared to be a community that would relate to one another as Jesus had related to them. Part of this vision

16. Acts 2:44–47.
17. Matt 18:20.
18. Luke 12:33.
19. Luke 5:20.
20. John 8:7.
21. Matt 11:28.
22. See Rom 12:4–5; 1 Cor 12:12–27; Eph 1:20–23; 3:6; 4:4–12; 5:23–28; Col 1:17–24.

seemed to be that when individuals from diverse backgrounds, who may not have been expecting to find this a safe-enough community, encountered a belonging that was trustworthy, it would perhaps correct their misperceptions about God and spark trust within them in the same way it would have had they encountered Jesus in the flesh.[23] I imagined then the potential impact of such an encounter on someone for whom belonging had been fragile before. In human communities, belonging is often framed as needing to be earned, and earned belonging has a paradoxical effect on the nervous system. On the one hand, the brain perceives an element of control over the earned situation: "if I continue to behave in the proper way, I can secure my belonging." On the other hand, our capacity to behave in "the proper way" is dependent on many factors—our stress, trust, the trustworthiness of those around us, and the way in which other brains are perceiving and responding to us. The capacity to behave in "the proper way" is something to which we might aspire over an entire lifetime of practice, learning, and growth; but we may find something beautiful is missing in communities overly focused on "proper behavior." That is because "behaving properly" negates the need for forgiveness; and we may find that relationships that never generate any need for forgiveness are stagnant, underwhelming, and not growth-fostering.

We might understand then that the goal of human maturity is not perpetual relational connection, or "proper behavior" necessarily, but rather the ability to move between connection, disconnection, and reconnection with neurobiological resilience and trust. When I thought about it that way, I noticed places where this pattern appeared to be woven into the fabric of created existence. We might recognize this pattern, for instance, in the mini-sermon written in the life, death, and rebirth story of butterflies, oak trees, and stars. We might find this pattern in the changing of the seasons, the turning over of generations, and the rise and fall of civilizations.

And when I read about the relationships within the early body of Christ, I noticed also a similar pattern. This was not a community in perpetual connection with God and one another. Rather, it was a community that cycled through connection, disconnection, and reconnection. This was not a gathering of individuals who were unstressed and perfectly regulated; they faced threats daily.[24] They did not always behave properly.[25] There was friction and conflict, rivalry and disconnection.[26] And yet, by the accounts of these individuals, they appeared to be skillful and effective at one

23. Eph 2:11–16.
24. E.g., Acts 4:3; 5:40; 7:54–59; 8:3; 9:1–2; 12:1–5.
25. E.g., Acts 5:1–11; 6:1–2.
26. E.g., Act 15:36–41.

thing: reconnection. This seemed to me to be an indicator of trust, which in turn would help them to regulate their nervous system and avoid recreating the trap of punishment when an offense had occurred. I noticed, too, that in times of extreme stress and victimization, they appeared to retain the engagement of their upper circuitry. Which is to say, even when they faced martyrdom, Jesus' friends and followers frequently were observed to respond with nonviolence and forgiveness. The story of Stephen may be a helpful example of this:

> Then they dragged [Stephen] out of the city and began to stone him. . .
> While they were stoning Stephen, he prayed,
> "Lord Jesus, receive my spirit."
> Then he knelt down and cried out in a loud voice,
> "Lord, do not hold this sin against them."
> When he had said this, he died.[27]

Two things stood out to me about these accounts of Jesus' followers. First, they were frequently said to have been helped by the Spirit.[28] I understood this to mean that those recording the stories perceived Jesus' followers to be exhibiting signs of trust and responding in a way that I came to think was characteristic of upper neocortical engagement in times of stress. In situations where an "eye for an eye" style of punishment or retaliation would have been expected, Jesus' followers commonly displayed a calm nervous system and an intention toward forgiveness that witnesses often attributed to their having been helped by the Spirit.

Second, I noticed Jesus' followers were said to have begun a rhythm of practices that they shared in common. For instance, they were observed gathering together for meals, storytelling, and rituals. Two of these rituals, baptism and the reenactment of Jesus' Last Supper, were described in detail, which sparked in me curiosity about what they might have meant for these early communities. What was the neurobiological impact of these rituals and how might they have aided Jesus' followers to continue their growing in trust and forgiveness, even in his absence?

---

27. Acts 7:54–60.
28. E.g., Acts 4:8; 7:54; 8:29; 9:31; 10:19, 44; 11:12, 15; 13:2, 4, 9; 19:6; 21:4.

Baptism

When I read that Jesus' followers practiced a ritual of baptism,[29] I looked through the stories of Jesus to remind myself of the narrative of his baptism.[30] I remembered then that it was said that Jesus' friends were also offering baptism to folks while Jesus was still alive in the body.[31] I wondered about the ritual of baptism and the impact it had on those who practiced it. It occurred to me that the ritual of immersion in water as in Jesus' baptism could be perhaps understood as a tiny version of the story of everything, in three movements.

I thought the first movement of the story might be represented by the person at the water's edge—alive, breathing, present to and trusting of those nearby. This reminded me of the garden, the original couple, and the trust that had regulated their nervous system. And it appeared to me to be a picture of *connection*.

The second movement seemed to me to be a picture of *disconnection*. This movement consisted of the person slipping below the water's surface, unable to breathe, at the mercy of those nearby. This reminded me of the moment of disconnection—a crisis of trust—when the serpent first deceived the couple. Depending on how a person's brain responded in this moment, it crossed my mind that one of two outcomes were possible. If the person's brain responded with trust, then the upper networks would remain engaged and the stress of disconnection experienced as tolerable. If however the person experienced a crisis of trust in this moment, this would dial up stress, making it more difficult for the person to receive assistance finding the surface again.

It appeared to me that the third movement of the story occurred when the person was raised out of the water. This reminded me of the moment when God came near to restore the couple's trust once more, decreasing their stress and increasing their safety. There was no threatening punishment inflicted for the couple who slipped below the water's surface—only an offer of kind assistance finding the surface once more. It seemed to me that the person who completed this ritual of baptism might be given a bodily experience of the story of all humanity, and one that had the capacity to correct our misperceptions about God and increase our trust.

One more thing crossed my mind when I reflected on this ritual of baptism. In the stories of Jesus' followers, I noticed baptism was presented

29. E.g., Acts 2:37–41; 8:12–13, 36–38; 9:18–19: 10:47–48; 16:15; 18:8; 19:5.
30. Matt 3:13–17; Mark 1:9–11; Luke 3:21–22; John 1:29–34.
31. John 4:1–2.

as a voluntary response to an invitation, accepted and surrendered to—with consent. I was reminded then of the story of Jesus in the garden of Gethsemane, where he seemed aware that his body was about to slip under the water's surface where he would be unable to breathe. In that story, Jesus prayed to be spared this trial, but ultimately expressed his consent to it. And it seemed to me then that the practice of consent was perhaps an essential component of the ritual.[32] It may be understood as a practice of saying "yes" to the Spirit moving us in a direction that did not originate with us. It may also be a practice of saying "yes" to being lifted and carried where we need to go, which we seem unable to do for ourselves. And finally, I thought it might be understood as a practice of trust—in God, and in others. Through the process of reminder and repetition, then, when we participate in, perform, and witness baptism, this fundamental story of trust and trustworthiness was perhaps being reinforced in the circuits of our brain in a manner that was neurobiologically helpful to us.

Eucharist

Jesus' followers are said to have also practiced a ritual of reenacting Jesus' Last Supper.[33] I looked through the stories of Jesus to remind myself of the narrative of this final meal he had shared with his friends on the night before he died.[34]

> While they were eating, Jesus took a loaf of bread,
> and after blessing it he broke it, gave it to the disciples, and said,
> "Take, eat; this is my body."
> Then he took a cup, and after giving thanks he gave it to them, saying,
> "Drink from it, all of you;
> for this is my blood of the covenant,
> which is poured out for many
> for the forgiveness of sins."[35]

I wondered then about the ritual of participating in this reenactment called by many names, the Lord's Supper, Holy Communion, or the Eucharist,[36]

32. We might find a similar giving of consent in the story of Paul's conversion in Acts 22:6–21.

33. 1 Cor 11:23–26.

34. Matt 26:26–29; Mark 14:22–25; Luke 22:14–22.

35. Luke 22:19–20.

36. The word *eucharistia* (giving thanks) is translated elsewhere in Scripture as

and the potential impact it may have on those who practiced it. I thought here too that the ritual involving food, drink, the body, the blood, and for-giveness of sins might also be understood as a tiny story of everything. I thought when Jesus broke the bread, this might represent the fragility of the human brain and body. And by giving it to his friends, he was com-municating his consent to having his body be broken—scapegoated—as a way of releasing them from the trap in which they were caught in. By giving the cup to his friends, it appeared to me that Jesus was communicating his consent to having his skin pierced and his blood spilled, which, according to the story, would occur a few hours later. And when the moment came that night and Jesus was arrested, something else stood out to me.

When those who were around [Jesus] saw what was coming, they asked,
"Lord, should we strike with the sword?"
Then one of them struck the slave of the high priest
and cut off his right ear.
But Jesus said, "No more of this!"
And he touched his ear and healed him.[37]

In this account of Jesus' arrest, I noticed that his friends were prepared to become his Rescuers. In fact, we read that one of them inflicted violence as a form of punishment against those who came to arrest him. In this scene, it occurred to me the trap of punishment was already in motion. Even as some of his followers asked Jesus' permission to strike out violently, one of them did not wait for instruction. He lashed out with his sword and cut off the enemy's ear—an act of punishment almost certain to inflict stress to the point of a threat-reaction.

If Jesus' friends at this point, having known Jesus for three years and observed him never to be violent toward another human being, were still misperceiving God to be punishing, I thought Jesus' response here served as a powerful correction of misperception. First we read that Jesus corrected his friends, stopping them from any further punishment. Next we read that Jesus reached out and touched his enemy, and *healed* him, restoring him to wellness and trust.

I reflected on that for some while.

What must that moment have been like? It appeared to me that in heal-ing his enemy, Jesus was bodily telling the story of forgiveness; it seemed to

"thanksgiving," as in, "Yes, everything is for your sake, so that grace, as it extends to more and more people, may increase thanksgiving, to the glory of God" (2 Cor 4:15).

37. Luke 22:49–51.

be a fractal story within the larger story, containing every bit of the pattern inside of it. I wondered then if it might be possible that every time Jesus' friends reenacted that last supper, and remembered him saying, "This is my blood, poured out for the forgiveness of sins," if they might be reminded too of this moment of tender forgiveness—the healing of his enemy—the moment where Jesus came near, and decreased stress, and increased safety. I wondered if they would be moved by this remembrance to have any lingering misperceptions about God as punishing corrected once more.

That is to say, over time, when Jesus' friends, through stress and daily life, may have slipped back into disconnection and mistrust of God, I wondered if the ritual of the Eucharist might have served as an opportunity for reconnection. Gustavo Gutiérrez once put it this way: "'To make a remembrance' of Christ is more than the performance of an act of worship . . . it is to accept the meaning of a life that was given over to death—at the hands of the powerful of this world—for love of others."[38] And for us too, I wondered if each time we participate in, perform, or witness the reenactment of the Last Supper, if this fundamental story of trust may perhaps be reinforced in the circuits of our brain in a manner helpful to us.

Sanctuary

From there, I traced the unfolding story of Jesus' followers over the centuries as they continued gathering regularly and maintaining a rhythm of common practices. As history tells it, they persisted in sharing meals, retelling the stories of Jesus, reflecting on the Scriptures, and practicing rituals such as baptism and the reenactment of Jesus' Last Supper. They spent time in contemplative prayer and they wrote songs expressing the joy, creativity, kindness, relationality, and life that they had discovered, facilitated by trust. And when I reflected on this new type of community—the body of Christ through the ages—two things stood out to me about it.

First, it occurred to me that when the body of Christ was practicing trust and forgiveness as Jesus had seemed intent on them doing, this type of community served as a great *equalizer*. Which is to say, those who had committed crimes or who were at risk of being scapegoated could find *sanctuary* within the community of people known as the body of Christ, and the grounds which that body considered to be sacred.[39] By turning to the body of Christ, criminals could be spared punishment in the form of torture—loss of life or limb—and Scapegoats could find protection from

38. Gutiérrez, *Theology of Liberation*, 150.
39. For reflection, Behrman, *Law and Asylum*, 6–30.

the mob. This fundamental and embodied practice of forgiveness accessible in the body of Christ played a significant role in community life throughout Europe for over a millennia.

Reading about the practice of offering sanctuary—protection and forgiveness—appeared to me to be a great equalizer by virtue of the fact that it undid the two deceptions upon which the trap of punishment functions: the first being the lie about the "badness" of the Scapegoat and the second being the misperception that punishment is helpful or necessary. When a person requested sanctuary in the body of Christ, the community organized to both protect and restore that person. Some stories I encountered described the buildings that the body of Christ deemed sacred to have doors with large knockers where a person seeking sanctuary could knock and be ushered inside, and given a special robe to signify the person's status as an asylum seeker.

Sometimes watchers would be stationed around the building to both protect the asylum-seeker and prevent them from leaving until a safe solution could be negotiated. The various methods of restoration that I read about included instructions to the asylum seeker to perform spiritual practices such as prayer and fasting, amends to victims—often monetary—and sometimes the asylum-seeker fleeing the region and starting life afresh.[40] That last method reminded me of God's approach with Cain after he had murdered his brother.[41]

By the sixteenth century, I read that the practice of sanctuary appeared less common, having been replaced even among members of the body of Christ with the notion that punishment of the criminal was necessary.[42] This led me to a second thought, which was that the body of Christ is also human and subject to the neurobiological processes of growth and development, which include progression and regression.[43] And that sparked in me a curiosity. If for the past five hundred years or so, the body of Christ had been experimenting with the reverse of the practice of sanctuary—choosing punishment over forgiveness—what might a reconnection with this practice in the twenty-first century look like?

I did not know, but the question brought to mind the work of Gary Slutkin, an epidemiologist who for two decades has studied violence and how it moves through a community in a pattern similar to a contagious

---

40. McSheffrey, "Sanctuary Seekers in England, 1380–1557."
41. Gen 4:15–16.
42. Shoemaker, "Sanctuary for Crime," 15–26.
43. For reflection, Bowen, "On Emotional Process in Society," 211–17.

virus.[44] Slutkin has experimented with the use of "violence interrupters" to restore trust in neighborhoods following a shooting or homicide; his research has found that this intervention serves as a form of "antibiotic," decreasing stress, increasing safety, preventing gun violence, and in some places reducing retributive homicides and other crimes by up to seventy percent.[45]

What might it look like for the body of Christ in the coming decades to practice trust and forgiveness in such a way that the nervous system of entire communities might be regulated, stress decreased, and safety increased? I was not sure. But when I thought about that, it occurred to me that Jesus' friends in those early years had a bodily encounter with Jesus that had corrected their misperceptions about God and restored their trust. From there, they had awoken to find themselves on the inside of a communication that did not originate with them. And as they practiced listening, and living that communication, the neural anatomy in their brain appeared to change. Their trust increased, and when they were broken, forgiveness poured out. And I wondered if, in that story of the body of Christ, we might find the image of God reflected and able to be perceived.

Here is a summary of this seventh chapter:

The Story of the Body of Christ

As we gathered together
to pray and reflect on the Scriptures,
we were practicing being the body of Christ.

We observed baptism and the Eucharist
and were reminded
of what the Christ story reveals
about God's trustworthiness.

We practiced the holy rhythms of
connection, disconnection, and reconnection
and we grew in trust.

And we became a sanctuary
where punishment was transformed
into forgiveness and restoration.

44. E.g., Ransford et al., "Positive Effects."
45. Whitehill et al., "Interrupting Violence," 84–95.

A Prayer to God Who Is Trustworthy

Oh God of ancient laughter and light,
let the shadows learn my name.

They will call me "one who shines"
for I trust in You, and You are reflected in me,

and no shadow exists
which can eclipse You forever.

In the name of God,
the light of Christ,
and the laughter of the Holy Spirit,
Amen

A Blessing for One Who Is Trusting

May you know the One
who goes behind us,
and gathers our fallen leaves,
grinding them into tea
to nourish our soul.

May you be intimate with the One
who walks beside us,
gathering our discarded scraps
for soup
to feed our roots.

May you be comforted by the One
who watches over you,
spreading green branches above your head,
saying "Look up! Give no thought to the ground;
it's always been there, catching everything."

May you marvel at the earthy stuff
from which you are made:
part silver, part soil,
and trust that nothing in your plot will be wasted;
the Composter is thorough and the tea so sweet.

In the name of God who is trustworthy,
Christ who walks with us,
and the Spirit who renews all things,
Amen

Postscript
The Shape of the Story

I CONTEMPLATED ENDING WITH eschatology, which takes up concerns about our future. Many colleagues were gracious to spend time in conversation with me about their thoughts on eschatological questions, and I practiced listening slowly to the text of Revelation and other Scriptures that scholars consider to hold eschatological themes. But until I have something clear to add from a neurobiological perspective that might amplify something helpful on the subject, I would rather continue listening for now. In chapter 5, we took up questions about life after death, and the resurrection of the body, and those were matters related to the future about which I ventured some thoughts. But questions related to Jesus' second coming, prophecy, and the end of the world, while important, are matters about which I want to continue listening and perhaps living a bit longer before endeavoring to speak. Many thoughtful scholars have engaged eschatology,[1] and I will continue learning from them for the time being.

So instead, I thought it might be more helpful for our purposes to conclude this theological reflection—which thus far has considered creation, humanity, sin, Christ, salvation, the Spirit, and the body of Christ—by inviting us now to become curious where in the Christ story we might find ourselves today. When I began writing this manuscript, I anticipated we would be facing some unprecedented global challenges in coming years; however, in the time it has taken to write this, even more crises have surfaced than I could have predicted. How might the Christ story continue to nourish us as we practice listening to it and consenting to be shaped by it in the years to come, while we face the pressing challenges in today's modern world?

---

1. Alison, *Raising Abel*, 117–97; Daniels, *Resisting Empire*, 23–32; Fiorenza, *Revelation*, 39–116; Jennings, *Liturgy and Theology*, 111–29.

It has been said that a coherent story is one with a beginning, middle, and end,[2] and the significance of earlier events is often illuminated by what occurs after it. When I reflected on the question of where we might be today in the unfolding Christ story, I thought it might be helpful to draw some possible diagrams for the narrative structure of the story we have been listening to. Narrative structures allow us to plot the key elements on a diagram, and many possible narrative structures exist.[3] Here is an example of one of the first diagrams I drew when reflecting on the Christ story:

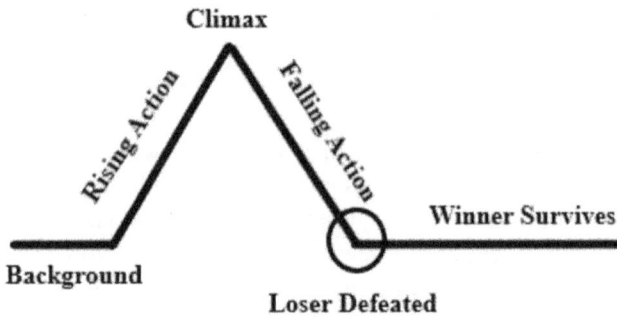

"Fight to the Death" Plot Diagram

This is an example of a narrative structure popular in ancient Greek literature,[4] and we might recognize it from many superhero stories of today.[5] This story typically begins with some elements of background that set the stage. Next there's a period of rising action where we are introduced to protagonists and villains. Tension then builds to a climactic peak, often an epic battle. Then there's a period of falling action while the heroes and villains fight; finally, someone wins. We might call this a "Fight to the Death" or "Winner Takes All" story, and we may find many examples of this narrative in Western media.

So I wondered then if and how the Christ story might map onto this narrative structure. Here is what came of my first attempt:

2. Aristotle, *Poet.* 7.25, 26.
3. For reflection, Freytag, *Technique of the Drama*, 114–40.
4. E.g., Homer, *Iliad*, 1–22.
5. Forbes, "Battling the Dark Side," 351–62.

Background:

We once lived in paradise.

Rising Action:

Satan deceived us into sinning; God gave us laws to save us.

Climax:

Christ came and . . .

At this point I reached a dead end. I could not see a way to fit Christ's peaceful, nonviolent, forgiving response to his enemies into this narrative of a great battle with heroes and villains fighting to the death until someone wins. There may be a way to do it, but the way did not present itself to me. It occurred to me, however, that by inserting the notion that God is punishing into this story, we might succeed in getting it to fit a "Fight to the Death" narrative structure. So I tried a few more versions, and here is one example of what came from my attempt:

Background:

We once lived in paradise.

Rising Action:

We sinned; God punished us with death.

Climax:

Christ came and took God's punishment in our place.

Falling Action:

Christians and "sinners" now fight for control over the world.

Someone Wins:

Christ will emerge as the "winner;" God will punish "sinners."

You might map these points and characters differently; I think there are various ways to do it. And I noticed that, by inserting the element of God as a punisher, there did seem to be way to make this story fit with a "Fight to the Death" narrative structure, so that the falling action unfolds as a great battle. It seemed to me, however, that a key element of story was missing: the non-punishing, forgiving response we encounter in Jesus, and the notion that Jesus is God. But in reflecting on this narrative structure a bit longer, it occurred to me that this "Fight to the Death" story is one for which our lower subcortical threat networks are primed. This plot structure gives the illusion of a clear distinction between heroes and villains, and suggests that villains can be punished or fought into "right thinking" and "right behavior" (or eliminated).

The problem I saw here, from a neurobiological perspective, was that this plot structure flattens the three-dimensional processes occurring in the human brain. That is to say, this plot diagram seems more fitting for two-dimensional characters like those in comic books (though even then, the line between hero and villain often becomes blurred). The "Fight to the Death" narrative structure is one that may better fit humanity as we wish we were—two-dimensional Victims or Persecutors or Rescuers, only—rather than us as we actually are: three-dimensional characters swapping roles around the Triangle of Punishment, at the mercy of our nervous systems.

Even still, I thought this "Fight to the Death" narrative structure might appeal to the lower circuitry of our brain that exists to help us to avoid overthinking things. Our lower networks are there to help us navigate the occasional actual threat. The problem with engaging a "Fight to the Death" story as if it were the foundational reality of our existence, however, is that it will likely keep our lower networks perpetually on high alert. In that case, we could expect our stress to hover in the "too high" range, without us being able to name precisely what is keeping it there. Under these neurobiological conditions, our day-to-day resources may indeed be taxed and our ability to access our upper circuitry reduced. It occurred to me then that we may find life, relationality, kindness, creativity, and access to joy diminished by our attempts to live this story.

From there, I began to wonder if there might be another possible structure that could even better fit the narrative of the Christ story, without flattening any of the characters or inserting elements that did not seem to fit the revelation, through Christ, that God is not punishing.

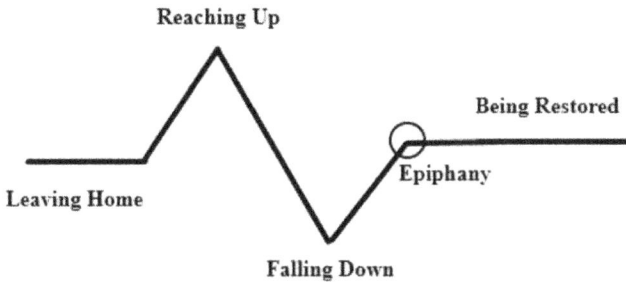

"Epiphany" Plot Diagram

When I considered other possible narrative structures that might fit the shape of the overarching Christ story, from Genesis through the Greek epistles, and incidentally many stories and parables of Jesus as well, here is the diagram I came up with.[6] A distinctive feature of this narrative structure appeared to me to be an emphasis on three movements: reaching up, falling down, and then being restored after an "epiphany"—a sudden appearance, by God or spark of insight that expands one's perspective.

This narrative structure typically begins with the protagonist leaving home or being lured away by curiosity. Next the protagonist reaches up toward a lofty goal, sometimes as a result of being tricked or deceived. The protagonist loses their footing, falls, and is in danger of jeopardizing everything. This part of the story may be dramatic or comical and is usually humbling for the protagonist. Then the protagonist has an epiphany—an "ah ha!" moment—when some element of truth is revealed, wisdom imparted, or help finally received. The story concludes with a restoration, reconciliation, or a "welcome home" event; I came to think of this as the "Epiphany" narrative structure.

I wondered then what it might sound like if we attempted to map the Christ story along this narrative structure. Here is one example I came up with:

6. E.g., Cain (Gen 4:8–16); Moses (Exod 2:11–24); Miriam (Num 12:10–15); Job (42:10); Jonah (4:6), David (2 Sam 11–12); Elijah (1 Kgs 19:4–5); the parables of Jesus such as the prodigal son (Luke 15); the woman saved from a stoning (John 8:7–11); the woman who anointed Jesus' feet (Luke 7:36–50); the restoration of Peter (Matt 18:21); and the transformation of Saul into Paul (Acts 9:1–20); there may be some common elements between the "Epiphany" plot diagram and "Voyage and Return" stories; Booker, *Seven Basic Plots*, 87–106; I also saw common elements between the "Epiphany" plot diagram and the phases of attachment: symbiosis, differentiation, and *rapprochement*; Mahler et al., *Psychological Birth of the Human Infant*, 39–121.

Background:

We trusted God and all our needs were met.

Reaching Up:

Satan deceived us; we misperceived our needs.

Falling Down:

Our trust was broken and we misperceived God as a punisher and a threat.

Epiphany:

Jesus died a forgiving death and revealed God to be non-punishing.

Being Restored:

The Spirit is restoring our trust, and helping us come to perceive our needs more accurately.

I noticed in this narrative structure that quite a bit of the story appeared to be behind us; but I also thought it was possible that the process of being restored could conceivably extend long into our future. I wondered if we could perhaps be living through the part of the story now where the Spirit is in the process of restoring our trust. And if so, I was curious how we might practice saying "yes" to that process. I wondered what practices might help us heal, grow, and mature spiritually and neurobiologically, so that we might come to perceive reality more as Jesus did and respond with a similar trust. I took out a page and wrote down a few questions that now, as a result of this listening process, had begun to crystallize:

How might we support one another's contemplative practices so the Spirit may help us regulate our stress?

How might we gather to pray, reflect on the Scripture, and observe baptism and the Eucharist so we may be helped to remember the Christ story which restores our trust?

How might we practice connection, disconnection, and reconnection in our relationships, so we may grow in trust and trustworthiness?

How might we create among us sanctuaries where punishment is transformed into forgiveness and restoration?

After reflecting on these questions, I wondered then if others were perhaps arriving at similar ones and would be interested in discerning potential steps forward and practices that might support the life, relationality, kindness, creativity, and access to joy rendered possible by trust. I wondered too about individual and societal practices that might help us become more trustworthy for one another. When I thought of this, I felt a renewed desire to say "yes" to being helped by the Spirit to learn whatever we need to learn, in order to restore trust between us and the planet, and to discern creative solutions to the global problems facing us now and in the future. And I hoped that, as our trust was restored, perhaps we might find the image of God reflected increasingly more clearly in us as human beings, individually and collectively.

May it be so, in Christ.

Bibliography

Alexander of Alexandria. "Letter to Alexander of Thessalonica." In *The Trinitarian Controversy*, translated by William G. Rusch, 27–36. Philadelphia: Fortress, 1980.

Alison, James. *The Joy of Being Wrong: Original Sin through Easter Eyes*. New York: Crossroad, 1998.

———. *Raising Abel: The Recovery of the Eschatological Imagination*. New York: Crossroad, 1996.

———. "Worship in a Violent World." *Studia Liturgica* 34 (2004) 133–46. doi:10.1177/003932070403400201.

Amanpreet, Kaur, et al. "A Systemic Review of Meditation and Psychophysiology." *Indian Journal of Public Health Research & Development* 9 (2018) 212–219.

Anderson, Bernhard W., et al. *Understanding the Old Testament*. 5th ed. Upper Saddle River: Pearson Prentice Hall, 2007.

Aquinas, Thomas. *On Evil*. Translated by Richard Regan. Oxford: Oxford University Press, 2003.

———. *Summa Theologica*. Translated by Fathers of the English Dominican Province. 1948. Reprint, Notre Dame: Christian Classics, 1981.

Aristotle. *Poetics*. Translated by Anthony Kenney. Oxford: Oxford University Press, 2013.

———. *Rhetoric*. Translated by W. Rhys Roberts. Fairhope: Mockingbird Classics, 2015.

Athanasius of Alexandria. "Letter to the Bishops of Egypt and Libya." In *Historical Tracts of St. Athanasius*, translated by Members of the English Church, 125–53. Oxford: John Henry Parker, 1843.

———. *On the Incarnation*. Translated by John Behr. Yonkers: St. Vladimir's Seminary Press, 2011.

Augustine of Hippo. *City of God*. Translated by Marcus Dods. Edinburgh: T. & T. Clark, 1871.

———. *The Confessions*. Translated by Henry Chadwick. Oxford: Oxford University Press, 1991.

———. *On Genesis: A Refutation of the Manichees*. Translated by Edmund Hill. Edited by John E. Rotelle. New York: New City, 2002.

Avi-Yonah, M. "The Development of the Roman Road System in Palestine." *Israel Exploration Journal* 1 (1950) 54–60.

Badenoch, Bonnie. *The Heart of Trauma: Healing the Embodied Brain in the Context of Relationship*. New York: Norton, 2018.

————. "Safety Is the Treatment." In *Clinical Applications of the Polyvagal Theory*, edited by Stephen Porges and Deb Dana, 73–88. New York: Norton, 2018.

Bader-Saye, Scott. *Following Jesus in a Culture of Fear*. Grand Rapids: Brazos, 2007.

Baker, Anthony D. *Diagonal Advance: Perfection in Christian Theology*. London: SCM, 2011.

Baldwin, Jennifer. *Trauma-Sensitive Theology*. Eugene, OR: Cascade, 2018.

Bangasser, Debra A., and Tracey J. Shors. "Critical Brain Circuits at the Intersection between Stress and Learning." *Neuroscience and Biobehavioral Reviews* 34 (2010) 1223–33.

Banks, Amy. *Wired to Connect: The Surprising Link between Brain Science and Strong, Healthy Relationships*. New York: Tarcher Perigee, 2016.

Banks, Amy, and Leigh Ann Hirschman. *Four Ways to Click: Rewire Your Brain for Stronger, More Rewarding Relationships*. New York: Penguin, 2015.

Barth, Karl. *Church Dogmatics*. Louisville: Westminster John Knox, 1961.

Bartlett, Anthony. *Theology Beyond Metaphysics: Transformative Semiotics of René Girard*. Eugene: Cascade, 2020.

Beckes, Lane, and James A. Coan. "Social Baseline Theory: The Role of Social Proximity in Emotion and Economy of Action." *Social and Personality Psychology Compass* 5 (2011) 976–88.

Behrman, Simon. *Law and Asylum: Space, Subject, Resistance*. New York: Routledge, 2018.

Bergoeing, Jean Pierre. "Sodom and Gomorrah and Plates Tectonic." *Mercator* 17 (2018) 1–8.

Block, Daniel. *The Book of Ezekiel, Chapters 1–24*. Grand Rapids: Eerdmans, 1997.

Bolte Taylor, Jill. *My Stroke of Insight: A Brain Scientist's Personal Journey*. New York: Viking, 2006.

Booker, Christopher. *Seven Basic Story Plots: Why We Tell Stories*. New York: Continuum, 2004.

Borucke, Michael, et al. "Accounting for Demand and Supply of the Biosphere's Regenerative Capacity." *Ecological Indicators* 24 (2013) 518–33.

Bowen, Murray. "On Emotional Process in Society." In *Bowen: Theory and Practice*, edited by Ruth Riley Sager, 211–17. Washington, DC: Georgetown Family Center, 1979.

Cannon, Katie Geneva. "The Wounds of Jesus: Justification of Goodness in the Face of Manifold Evil." In *A Troubling in My Soul: Womanist Perspectives on Evil and Suffering*, edited by Emilie M. Townes, 219–31. Maryknoll: Orbis, 1993.

Cardoso, Christopher, et al. "Stress-Induced Negative Mood Moderates the Relation between Oxytocin Administration and Trust: Evidence for the Tend-and-Befriend Response to Stress?" *Psychoneuroendocrinology* 38 (2013) 2800–2804.

Cartwright, Martin, et al. "Stress and Dietary Practices in Adolescents." *Health Psychology* 22 (2003) 362–69.

Clough, David L. *On Animals, II: Theological Ethics*. New York: T. & T. Clark, 2019.

Clowry, Gavin, et al. "Renewed Focus on the Developing Human Neocortex." *Journal of Anatomy* 217 (2010) 276–88.

Cone, James H. *God of the Oppressed*. Maryknoll: Orbis, 2012.

Cooper, David L. *The World's Greatest Library Graphically Illustrated*. Los Angeles: Biblical Research Society, 1942. https://www.biblicalresearch.info/The_World's_Greatest_Library.pdf.

Cruwys, Tegan, et al. "When Trust Goes Wrong: A Social Identity Model of Risk Taking." *Journal of Personality and Social Psychology* (2020) 1–27. http://dx.doi. org/10.1037/pspi0000243.

Damerow, Peter. "Sumerian Beer: The Origins of Brewing Technology in Ancient Mesopotamia." *Cuneiform Digital Library Journal* 2 (2012) 1–20.

Daniels, Wess C. *Resisting Empire: The Book of Revelation*. Newberg: Barklay, 2019.

Darvill, Timothy, and Geoffrey Wainwright. "Stonehenge Excavations 2008." *The Antiquaries Journal* 89 (2009) 1–19. https://doi.org/10.1017/S000358150900002X.

Doll, Anselm., et al. "Mindful Attention to Breath Regulates Emotions via Increased Amygdala–Prefrontal Cortex Connectivity." *NeuroImage* 134 (2018) 305–13.

DuBois Gilliard, Dominique. *Rethinking Incarceration: Advocating for Justice that Restores*. Downer's Grove: InterVarsity, 2018.

Ecker, Bruce, et al. *Unlocking the Emotional Brain: Eliminating Symptoms at their Roots Using Memory Reconsolidation*. New York: Routledge, 2012.

Edwards, Jonathan. "Sinners in the Hands of an Angry God. A Sermon Preached at Enfield, July 8th, 1741. Edited by Reiner Smolinski. *Electronic Texts in American Studies* 54 (1741) 1–31. https://digitalcommons.unl.edu/etas/54.

Eisenberger, Naomi I., and Matthew D. Lieberman. "Why Rejection Hurts: A Common Neural Alarm System for Physical and Social Pain." *Trends in Cognitive Sciences* 8 (2004) 294–300.

Eisenberger, Naomi I., et al. "Does Rejection Hurt? An fMRI Study of Social Exclusion." *Science* 302 (2003) 290–92.

Feldman Barrett, Lisa. *How Emotions Are Made: The Secret Life of the Brain*. New York: Houghton Mifflin Harcourt, 2017.

Feltman, Charles. *The Thin Book of Trust: An Essential Primer for Building Trust at Work*. Bend, OR: Thin Books, 2009.

Ferguson, R. Brian. "Violence and War in Prehistory." In *Troubled Times: Violence and Warfare in the Past*, edited by Debra L. Martin and David W. Frayer, 321–355. New York: Routledge, 1997.

Figueiredo, Miguel F. P. "The Effect of Punishment on Recidivism and Social Cost." *Arizona State Law Journal* 47 (2015) 1017–97.

Fiorenza, Elisabeth Schüssler. *Revelation: Vision of a Just World*. Minneapolis: Fortress, 1991.

Flood, Derek. *Healing the Gospel: A Radical Vision for Grace, Justice, and the Cross*. Eugene: Cascade, 2012.

Foo, Stephanie. "Rosie's Paradox." *This American Life* (podcast), May 19, 2017. https:// www.thisamericanlife.org/617/fermis-paradox/act-three-5.

Forbes, Bruce David. "Battling the Dark Side: Star Wars and Popular Understandings of Evil." *Word and World* 19 (1999) 351–62.

Fosha, Diana. "Emotion, True Self, True Other, Core State." *Psychoanalytic Review* 92 (2004) 513–51.

Freytag, Gustav. *Technique of the Drama: An Exposition of Dramatic Composition and Art*. Translation by Elias J. MacEwan. Chicago: Scott, Foresman, 1900.

Garrett, Greg. *Stories from the Edge: A Theology of Grief*. Louisville: Westminster John Knox, 2008.

Gilligan, Carol. *In a Different Voice: Psychological Theory and Women's Development*. Boston: Harvard University Press, 1982.

Girard, René. *The Scapegoat*. Translated by Yvonne Freccero. Baltimore: Johns Hopkins University Press, 1986.

———. *Violence and the Sacred*. Translated by Patrick Gregory. Baltimore: Johns Hopkins University Press, 1972.

Goodman, Martin. *Rome and Jerusalem: The Clash of Ancient Civilizations*. New York: Vintage, 2008.

Greenstein, Edward L. *Job: A New Translation*. New Haven: Yale University Press, 2019.

Gregory of Nazianzus. *On God and Christ: The Five Theological Orations*. Translated by Frederick Williams and Lionel Wickham. Crestwood: St. Vladimir's Seminary Press, 2002.

Grypeou, Emmanuel, and Helen Spurling. "Abraham's Angels: Jewish and Christian Exegesis of Genesis 18–19." In *The Exegetical Encounter between Jews and Christians in Late Antiquity*, edited by Emmanouela Grypeou and Helen Spurling, 181–203. Lieden: Brill, 2009.

Guillaumont, Antoine. "Esquisse d'une Phénoménologie du Monachisme." *Numen* 25 (1978) 40–51.

Gutiérrez, Gustavo. *A Theology of Liberation: History, Politics, and Salvation*. Maryknoll: Orbis, 1988.

Haidt, Jonathan. *The Righteous Mind: Why Good People are Divided by Politics and Religion*. New York: Random House, 2012.

Harvard Medical School. "Survey Finds U.S. Has High Rate Of Mental Illness, Low Rate Of Treatment Compared To Other Countries." *Science Daily*, May 7, 2003. www.sciencedaily.com/releases/2003/05/030507080958.htm.

Henderson, Julian. *Ancient Glass: An Interdisciplinary Exploration*. Cambridge: Cambridge University Press, 2013.

Henry, Donald O., et al. "Blame It on the Goats? Desertification in the Near East during the Holocene." *Holocene* 27 (2017) 625–37.

Hillar, Marian. *From Logos to Trinity: The Evolution of Religious Beliefs from Pythagoras to Tertullian*. Cambridge: Cambridge University Press, 2012.

Hitchner, Bruce R. "Roads, Integration, Connectivity, and Economic Performance in the Roman Empire." In *Highways, Byways & Road Systems in the Pre-Modern World*, edited by Susan E. Alcock et al., 222–34. West Sussex: Wiley Blackwell, 2012.

Hoffman, Alexandra A. "Mass Incarceration's Second Generation." *Race and Social Justice Law Review* 7 (2017) 247–74.

Hölzel, Britta K., et al. "Mindfulness Practice Leads to Increases in Regional Brain Gray Matter Density." *Psychiatry Research: Neuroimaging* 191 (2011) 36–43.

Homer. *The Illiad*. Translated by Rodney Merrill. Ann Arbor: University of Michigan, 2010.

Hooker, Richard. *Of the Laws of Ecclesiastical Polity*. Edited by Arthur Stephen McGrade. Cambridge: Cambridge University Press, 1989.

Hume, David. *Dialogues Concerning Natural Religion*. Edited by Dorothy Coleman. Cambridge: Cambridge University Press, 2007.

Iacoboni, Marco. *Mirroring People: The Science of Empathy and How We Connect with People*. New York: Picador, 2008.

Ignatius of Loyola. *The Spiritual Exercises of St. Ignatius*. Translated by Louis J. Puhl. New York: Vintage, 2000.

Immordino-Yang, Mary Helen, and Antonio Damasio, "We Feel, Therefore We Learn: The Relevance of Affective and Social Neuroscience to Education." *Mind, Brain, and Education* 1 (2007) 3–10.

Irenaeus of Lyons. *Against Heresies*. Translated by Alexander Roberts and William Hautenville Rambaut. 1885. Reprint. South Bend, IN: Ex Fontibus, 2020.

Jebb, Andrew T., et al. "Happiness, Income Satiation and Turning Points around the World." *Nature Human Behavior* 2 (2018) 33–38. https://www.nature.com/articles/s41562-017-0277-0.

Jennings, Nathan G. *Liturgy and Theology: Economy and Reality*. Eugene: Cascade, 2017.

Jennings, Wesley G., et al. "A Longitudinal Assessment of the Victim-Offender Overlap." *Journal of Interpersonal Violence* 25 (2010) 2147–74.

Jennings, Willie James. *Acts*. Louisville: Westminster John Knox, 2017.

Jensen, Mark P., et al. "Brain Oscillations, Hypnosis, and Hypnotizability." *The American Journal of Clinical Hypnosis* 57 (2015) 230–53.

Jordan, Judith. "Recent Developments in Relational-Cultural Therapy." In *The Power of Connection*, edited by Judith Jordan, 1–4. New York: Routledge, 2010.

———. "A Relational-Cultural Model: Healing through Mutual Empathy." In *Bulletin of the Menninger Clinic* 65 (2000) 92–103.

Josephus, Flavius. *The Antiquities of the Jews*. Translated by William Whiston. https://www.gutenberg.org/files/2848/2848-h/2848-h.htm#link142HCH0015.

Kant, Immanuel. *Lectures on Ethics*. Translated by Louis Infield. Indianapolis: Hackett, 1980.

Karpman, Stephen B. "Fairy Tales and Script Drama Analysis." *Transactional Analysis Bulletin* 7 (1968) 39–43.

Keller, Helen. *The Story of My Life and Selected Letters*. New York: Quarto, 2016.

Keller, Timothy. *Walking with God through Pain and Suffering*. New York: Dutton, 2013.

Kemp, Elyria, et al. "The Calm before the Storm: Examining Emotion Regulation Consumption in the Face of an Impending Disaster." *Psychology and Marketing* 31 (2013) 933–45.

Kirk-Duggan, Cheryl. "African-American Spirituals: Confronting and Exorcising Evil through Song." In *A Troubling in My Soul: Womanist Perspectives on Evil and Suffering*, edited by Emilie M. Townes, 150–71. Maryknoll: Orbis, 1993.

Kohler, Timothy A., et al. "Greater Post-Neolithic Wealth Disparities in Eurasia than in North America and Mesoamerica." *Nature* 551 (2017) 619–22.

Kohls Niko, et al. "The Relationship between Spiritual Experiences, Transpersonal Trust, Social Support, and Sense of Coherence and Mental Distress—A Comparison of Spiritually Practising and Non-Practising Samples." *Mental Health, Religion and Culture* 12 (2009) 1–23.

Kuhn, Peter J., et al. "The Own and Social Effects of an Unexpected Income Shock: Evidence from the Dutch Postcode Lottery." *UC Santa Barbara Departmental Working Papers* (2008) 1–56. https://escholarship.org/uc/item/07k895v4.

LaCugna, Catherine Mowry. *God for Us: The Trinity and Christian Life*. New York: HarperCollins, 1991.

Lashier, Jackson Jay. *Irenaeus on the Trinity*. Leiden: Brill, 2014.

Lazarus, R S. "From Psychological Stress to the Emotions: A History of Changing Outlooks." *Annual Review of Psychology* 44 (1993) 1–21.

Lereya, Suzet Tanya, et al. "Bully/Victims: A Longitudinal, Population-Based Cohort Study of their Mental Health." *European Child and Adolescent Psychiatry* 24 (2015) 1461–71.

Lewis, C. S. *The Great Divorce*. New York: Collier, 1984.

———. *The Problem of Pain*. New York: HarperCollins, 1996.

Lieberman, Matthew D., and Naomi I. Eisenberger. "Pains and Pleasures of Social Life." *Science* 323 (2009) 890–91.

Loader, William. "Homosexuality and the Bible." In *Two Views on Homosexuality, The Bible, and the Church*, edited by Preston Sprinkle et al., 17–68. Grand Rapids: Zondervan, 2016.

Luke, Chad, et al. "Addiction, Stress, and Relational Disorder: A Neuro-Informed Approach to Intervention." *Journal of Mental Health* Counseling 40 (2018) 172–86. https://doi.org/10.17744/mehc.40.2.06.

MacArthur, John. *Alone with God*. Ontario: Cook, 2011.

MacLean, Paul D. *The Triune Brain in Evolution: Role in Paleocerebral Functions*. New York: Plenum Press, 1989.

Maeda, Osamu, et al. "Narrowing the Harvest: Increasing Sickle Investment and the Rise of Domesticated Cereal Agriculture in the Fertile Crescent." *Quaternary Science Reviews* 145 (2016) 226–37.

Mahler, Margaret, et al. *The Psychological Birth of the Human Infant: Symbiosis and Individuation*. New York: Basic, 2000.

Mankarious, Amanda, et al. "The Pro-Social Neurohormone Oxytocin Reverses the Actions of the Stress Hormone Cortisol in Human Ovarian Carcinoma Cells in Vitro." *International Journal of Oncology* 48 (2016) 1805–14.

Martyr, Justin. *Dialogue with Trypho*. Translated by Henry Brown. Cambridge, Deightons, 1846. https://play.google.com/books/reader?id=YCRLAQAAMAAJ&hl=en&pg=GBS.PP1.

Maximus the Confessor. "Opuscule 7." In *Maximus the Confessor*, edited by Andrew Louth. New York: Routledge, 1996.

McFague, Sally. *The Body of God: An Ecological Theology*. Minneapolis: Augsberg Fortress, 1993.

McGilchrist, Iain. *The Master and His Emissary: The Divided Brain and the Making of the Western World*. New Haven: Yale University Press, 2009.

McSheffrey, Shannon. "Sanctuary Seekers in England, 1380–1557 (Ordered by Surname)." https://shannonmcsheffrey.files.wordpress.com/2018/10/mcsheffrey-sanctuary-seekers-name-order.pdf.

Miller, Jean Baker. "What Do We Mean by Relationships?" *Work in Progress*, No. 70. Wellesley: Stone Center Working Paper Series (1986) 1–13.

Milsum, John H. "A Model of the Eustress System for Health/Illness." *Behavioral Science* 30 (1985) 179–86.

Ming, Fang, and Zhaoyu Liao. "The Influence of Adlai Silk on the Cultural Value of Xinjiang." *Advances in Economics, Business and Management Research* 29 (2017) 934–40.

Moltman, Jürgen. *God in Creation: A New Theology of Creation and the Spirit of God*. Minneapolis: Fortress, 1993.

Mulch, Matthew. "Crime and Punishment in Private Prisons." *National Lawyers Guild Review* 66 (2009) 70–94.

Mureriwa, Joachim Fana Lance. "Common Factors in Psychotherapy: The Autonomic Nervous System Final Common Pathway." *Current Advances in Neurology and Neurological Disorders* 1 (2017) 1–12.

National Scientific Council on the Developing Child. "Excessive Stress Disrupts the Architecture of the Developing Brain: Working Paper 3." https://developingchild.harvard.edu/wp-content/uploads/2005/05/Stress_Disrupts_Architecture_Developing_Brain-1.pdf.

Newton, Ruth P. *The Attachment Connection: Parenting a Secure and Confident Child Using the Science of Attachment Theory.* Oakland: New Harbinger, 2008.

Nishida, Masaki, et al. "REM Sleep, Prefrontal Theta, and the Consolidation of Human Emotional Memory." *Cerebral Cortex* 19 (2009) 1158–66.

Nissenbaum. Aerie. "Utilization of Dead Sea Asphalt throughout History." *Reviews in Chemical Engineering* 9 (1993) 365–83.

Norman, Greg, et al. "Social Neuroscience: The Social Brain, Oxytocin, and Health." *Social Neuroscience* 7 (2012) 18–29.

Onaka, Tatsushi, et al. "Roles of Oxytocin Neurones in the Control of Stress, Energy Metabolism, and Social Behavior." *Journal of Neuroendocrinology* 24 (2012) 587–98.

Onaka, Tatsushi, and Yuki Takayanagi. "Roles of Oxytocin in the Control of Stress and Food Intake." *Journal of Neuroendocrinology* 29 (2019) 1–20.

Oord, Thomas Jay. "An Open Theology Doctrine of Creation and Solution to the Problem of Evil." In *Creation Made Free: Open Theology Engaging Science*, edited by Thomas Jay Oord, 28–52. Eugene, OR: Pickwick, 2009.

Oughourlian, Jean-Michel. *The Genesis of Desire.* Translated by Eugene Webb. East Lansing: Michigan University Press, 2010.

———. *The Mimetic Brain.* Translated by Trevor Cribben Merrill. East Lansing, MI: Michigan University Press, 2016.

Our World in Data. "Share of Population with Mental Health and Substance Abuse Disorders, 2017." https://ourworldindata.org/grapher/share-with-mental-and-substance-disorders.

Packer, J. I. *Rediscovering Holiness.* Grand Rapids: Baker, 2009.

Palmer, Parker. *On the Brink of Everything: Grace, Gravity, and Getting Old.* Oakland: Berrett-Koehler, 2018.

Pargament, Kenneth I., et al. "The Brief RCOPE: Current Psychometric Status of a Short Measure of Religious Coping." *Religions* 2 (2011) 51–76.

Park, W. A. "A Brief History of Asphalt." *American Asphalt Journal* (1901) 14–17.

Parpola, Asko. "Study of the Indus Script." *Transactions of the International Conference of Eastern Studies* 50 (2005) 28–66.

Philo of Alexandria. *On the Creation of the Cosmos According to Moses.* Translated by David T. Runia. Leiden: Brill, 2001.

Piff, Paul K., et al. "Awe, the Small Self, and Prosocial Behavior." *Journal of Personality and Social Psychology* 108 (2015) 883–99.

Pinker, Steven. *The Better Angels of our Nature.* New York: Penguin, 2011.

Piper, John. *Desiring God: Meditations of a Christian Hedonist.* Colorado Springs: Multnomah, 2011.

Porges, Stephen. "Polyvagal Theory: A Primer." In *Clinical Applications of the Polyvagal Theory*, edited by Stephen Porges and Deb Dana, 50–69. New York: Norton, 2018.

Possehl, Gregory L. *The Indus Civilization: A Contemporary Perspective*. Lanham: AltaMira, 2002.

Puwar, Nirmal. *Space Invaders: Race, Gender, and Bodies out of Place*. Oxford: Berg, 2004.

Ramachandran, Vilayanur Subramanian. *The Tell-Tale Brain: A Neuroscientist's Quest for What Makes Us Human*. New York: Norton, 2011.

Ransford, Charles, et al. "The Positive Effects of the Cure Violence Model for Families and Children." https://1vp6u534z5kr2qmrow11t7ub-wpengine.netdna-ssl.com/wp-content/uploads/2019/04/BVL_Report_final.pdf.

Rhor, Richard. *Things Hidden: Scripture as Spirituality*. Cincinnati: St. Anthony Messenger, 2016.

Ricoeur, Paul. "'The Image of God' and the Epic of Man." *Cross Currents* 11 (1961) 37–50.

———. *The Symbolism of Evil*. Translated by Emerson Buchanan. Boston: Beacon, 1967.

Riedl, René, and Andrija Javor. "The Biology of Trust: Integrating Evidence from Genetics, Endocrinology, and Functional Brain Imaging." *Journal of Neuroscience, Psychology, and Economics* 5 (2012) 63–91.

Rizzolatti, Giacomo, and Corrado Sinigaglia. *Les Neurones Miroirs*. Translated by Marilène Raiola. Paris: Odile Jacob, 2008.

Robb, Christina. *This Changes Everything: The Relational Revolution in Psychology*. New York: Picador, 2006.

Russo, Michael, and Gregory Heide. "Shell Rings of the Southeast US." *Antiquity* 75 (2001) 491–92.

Sacks, Vanessa, and David Murphy. "The Prevalence of Adverse Childhood Experiences, Nationally, by State, and by Race/Ethnicity." *Child Trends Research Brief* (2018) 1–20. https://www.researchgate.net/publication/330397979_The_prevalence_of_adverse_childhood_experiences_nationally_by_state_and_by_raceethnicity.

Sanders, E. B. "Jesus and the Sinners." *Journal for the Study of the New Testament* 6 (1983) 5–36.

Sandi, Carment, and József Haller. "Stress and the Social Brain: Behavioural Effects and Neurobiological Mechanisms." *Nature Reviews Neuroscience* 16 (2015) 290–304.

Sapolsky, Robert M. *Behave: The Biology of Humans at Our Best and Worst*. New York: Penguin, 2017.

Schore, Allan. *Affect Regulation and the Repair of the Self*. New York: Norton, 2003.

Schneiderman, Neil, et al. "Stress and Health: Psychological, Behavioral, and Biological Determinants." *Annual Review of Clinical Psychology* 1 (2005) 607–28.

Schwartz, Richard C., and Martha Sweezy. *Internal Family Systems Therapy*. New York: Guilford, 2020.

Selye, Hans. *Stress without Distress*. Philadelphia: Lippencott, 1974.

Shapiro, Francine. *Getting Past Your Past: Take Control of Your Life with Self-Help Techniques from EMDR*. New York: Rodale, 2012.

Shoemaker, Karl. "Sanctuary for Crime in the Early Common Law." In *Sanctuary Practices in International Perspectives: Migration, Citizenship and Social Movements*, edited by Lippert, Randy. K. and Sean. Rehaag, 15–26. London, Routledge, 2013.

Shuster, Marguerite. "Preaching the Trinity." In *The Trinity: An Interdisciplinary Symposium on the Trinity*, edited by Stephen T. Davis, et al., 357–81. Oxford: Oxford University Press, 1999.

Siegel, Daniel. *The Developing Mind: How Relationships and the Brain Interact to Shape Who We Are*. New York: Guilford, 2012.

Siegel, Daniel, and Tina Payne Bryson. *The Whole-Brain Child: 12 Revolutionary Strategies to Nurture Your Child's Developing Mind*. New York: Bantam, 2012.

Siever, Larry J. "Neurobiology of Aggression and Violence." *The American Journal of Psychiatry* 165 (2008) 429–42.

Sneath, Julie Z., et al. "Coping with a Natural Disaster: Losses, Emotions, and Impulsive and Compulsive Buying." *Marketing Letters* 20 (2009) 45–60.

Solis, R. S., et al. "Dating Caral, A Preceramic Site in the Super Valley on the Central Coast of Peru." *Science* 292 (2001) 723–26.

Sproul, R. C. *Essential Truths of the Christian Faith*. Carol Stream: Tyndale House, 1992.

Straus, Murray A. "Prevalence, Societal Causes, and Trends in Corporal Punishment." *Law and Contemporary Problems* 73 (2010) 1–30.

Sun, Yan, et al. "Reports of Empirical Studies Brain Network Analysis of Cognitive Reappraisal and Expressive Inhibition Strategies: Evidence from EEG and ERP." *Acta Psychologica Sinica* 52 (2020) 12–25.

Tanner, Kathryn. *Jesus, Humanity, and the Trinity: A Brief Systematic Theology*. Minneapolis: Fortress, 2001.

Taylor, Shelley. E., "Biobehavioral Responses to Stress in Females: Tend-and-Befriend, Not Fight-or-Flight." *Psychological Review* 107 (2000) 411–29.

Teresa of Avila. "The Book of Her Life." In *Collected Works*, translated by Kieran Kavanaugh and Otilio Rodriguez, 54–354. Washington, DC: Institute of Carmelite Studies, 1987.

Tertullian. *Apology for the Christians*. Translated by T. Herbert Bindley. Strand: Parker, 1890. https://play.google.com/books/reader?id=C57DRKAPzLoC&hl=en&pg=G BS.PP1.

Theophilus of Antioch. *To Autolycus*. Translated by Marcus Dods. 1885. Reprint. Veritatis Splendor, 2012.

Thompson, Curt. *Anatomy of the Soul*. Carol Stream: Tyndale, 2010.

Tickle, Phyllis, and Jon M. Sweeney. *The Age of the Spirit: How the Ghost of an Ancient Controversy Is Shaping the Church*. Grand Rapids: Baker, 2014.

Tippett, Krista. *Becoming Wise: An Inquiry into the Mystery and Art of Living*. New York: Penguin, 2016.

———. "The Drugs Inside Your Head." *On Being* (podcast), Sept 19, 2019. https://onbeing.org/programs/erik-vance-the-drugs-inside-your-head/.

———. "Shaping Grief with Language." *On Being* (podcast), May 30, 2019. https://onbeing.org/programs/gregory-orr-shaping-grief-with-language/.

Tung, Monica L., et al. "Observation of Limb Movements Reduces Phantom Limb Pain in Bilateral Amputees." *Annals of Clinical and Translational Neurology* 1 (2014) 633–38.

United Nations. "Fast Facts: The State of the World's Land and Water Resources." http://www.fao.org/fileadmin/user_upload/newsroom/docs/en-solaw-facts_1.pdf.

———. "World Population Prospects 2019." https://population.un.org/wpp/Download/Probabilistic/Population/.

van der Kolk, Bessel. *The Body Keeps the Score: Brain, Mind, and Body in the Healing of Trauma*. New York: Viking, 2014.

Volf, Miroslav. *After Our Likeness: The Church as the Image of the Trinity*. Grand Rapids: Eerdmans, 1998.

Warneken, Felix, et al. "Young Children Share the Spoils after Collaboration." *Psychological Science* 22 (2011) 267–73.

Watson, John B., and Rosalie A. Watson. *Psychological Care of Infant and Child*. London: Allen & Unwin, 1928.

Whitehill, Jennifer M., et al. "Interrupting Violence: How the CeaseFire Program Prevents Imminent Gun Violence through Conflict Mediation." *Journal of Urban Health: Bulletin of the New York Academy of Medicine* 91 (2014) 84–95. doi:10.1007/s11524-013-9796-9.

Williams, David, and Pamela Braboy Jackson. "Social Sources of Racial Disparities in Health Policies." *Health Affairs* 24 (2005) 325–34. https://www.healthaffairs.org/doi/pdf/10.1377/hlthaff.24.2.325.

Williams, Monnica T., et al. "Assessing Racial Trauma within a DSM-5 Framework: The UConn Racial/Ethnic Stress & Trauma Survey." *Practice Innovations* 3 (2018) 242–60. https://doi.org/10.1037/pri0000076.supp.

Williams, Rowan. *Tokens of Trust: An Introduction to Christian Belief*. Louisville: Westminster John Knox, 2007.

———. *The Truce of God*. London: Fount, 2005.

World Health Organization. "Cross-National Comparisons of the Prevalences and Correlates of Mental Disorders." *Bulletin of the World Health Organization* 78 (2000) 413–26.

———. "World Health Statistics Overview, 2019." https://apps.who.int/iris/bitstream/handle/10665/311696/WHO-DAD-2019.1-eng.pdf?ua=1.

Yanagisawa, Kuniaki, et al. "Does Higher General Trust Serve as a Psychosocial Buffer against Social Pain? An NIRS Study of Social Exclusion." *Social Neuroscience* 6 (2011) 190–97.

Zak, Paul J., et al. "The Neurobiology of Trust." *Annals of the New York Academy of Sciences* 1032 (2004) 224–27.

Zizioulas, John D. *Being as Communion: Studies in Personhood and the Church*. New York: St. Vladimir's Seminary Press, 1985.

———. *The One and the Many: Studies on God, Man, the Church, and the World Today*. Edited by Gregory Edwards Alhambra: Sebastian, 2010.

Index

Abel, 58–60, 68
  See also violence
Abraham, 13, 61–66, 82–85, 169
  See also Scriptures
abuse. *See* violence
accountability, 31
  See also body of Christ; relational-
    ity; sanctuary
Adam. *See* original couple
agony, 11, 19, 26–29, 63, 109–14
  See also hell; nervous system; stress;
    torment
agriculture. *See* climate crisis
Alison, James, 13, 69, 117
anger, 59, 83, 107
  See also justice; nonviolence
animals. *See* climate crisis
aphiemi, 92
'arbeh, 55
Aristotle, 12
atonement. *See* scapegoat mechanism

baptism. *See* ritual
behavior change. *See* learning
belief. *See* trust
Bible. *See* Scriptures
blood of Christ. *See* crucifixion
body of Christ, 153–55, 160–62, 165
  See also relationality; ritual;
    sanctuary
brain
  development of, 50, 52, 110,
    130–31, 150, 152, 161
  hemispheres, 125–31

imaging, 5, 7, 79, 141
  impairment of, 126
  lower networks, 19–20, 27–33, 37,
    40–41, 48–55, 59, 83, 88–90, 96,
    126–33, 168
  mapping of, 5–10
  neural networks, 6–7, 10, 114, 118
  neurotransmitters, 5, 29–30, 32,
    56–58, 91–92, 96, 116, 152
  upper networks, 19–21, 26–41,
    48–61, 66, 83–84. 88, 90–92, 96,
    104–5, 108, 116–17, 126–40,
    149, 156–57, 168
  waves, 15, 79, 130, 138, 141
  See also fMRI technology; mirror
    systems; neuroscience
breath, 11–15, 20, 29, 34, 113, 133–35,
  157–58
  as prayer, 137–38
  synchronizing of, 79
  See also life; nervous system; Spirit

Cain, 58–64, 66, 68, 161
  See also forgiveness
centering prayer. *See* prayer
chatta'ah, 61
childbirth, 28, 55–56
  See also nervous system; pain; trust
children, 36, 49–52, 60, 81, 118,
  127–30, 149–51
Christ. *See* Jesus
Christology, 74, 77–97
  See also crucifixion; forgiveness;
    incarnation

choice, 19–20, 30, 50, 61, 88, 109, 130
    See also learning; nervous system;
        stress
church. See body of Christ
Clement of Alexandria, 114
climate crisis
    agriculture, 61
    animals, 35, 39, 61, 63
    food, 34–41, 56–57, 61–62, 80–81,
        110, 113, 151, 154, 159
    plants, 35, 38, 57, 63
    population, 36
    vegetarianism, 35, 38
    See also overconsumption
cloning of God
    avoidance of, 17
    correspondence with image, 17–20,
        134
    See also creation; God; stress; time
commandments. See law
community. See relationality
compassion, 8–9, 19, 27–28, 30, 92,
        105–6, 128, 131–32
confession. See forgiveness
conflict, 40, 66, 81, 152, 155
    See also relationality; rivalry; stress;
        trust
connection. See Relational Cultural
    Theory
consent, 136–42, 158–59
    saying "yes," 136, 138–39, 141–42,
        158, 170
    See also prayer; ritual; spiritual
        practice
contemplation. See prayer
correspondence. See likeness
Cosmology, 1, 3–21
    See also creation; God
covenant. See Israel
creation, 11–21, 35, 85, 139
    as self portrait of God, 16–17
    created existence, 11–12, 16, 21,
        155
    See also creativity; humanity
creativity
    as a reflection of God, 21, 27, 57,
        70, 91, 96, 111, 160

neuroscience of, 19, 28, 33, 37, 39,
        41, 51–52, 92, 106–7, 116, 135,
        139
    See also God
criminal justice system, 50–51, 94,
        160–61
    See also learning; punishment;
        sanctuary
cross. See crucifixion
crucifixion, 108, 114, 116, 153
    "let it be me," 96, 111, 118
    See also enemy; forgiveness; incar-
        nation; scapegoat mechanism;
        violence
cruelty, 19, 26–27, 63, 109–10, 114
    See also sin
culture, 80, 125, 150

David, king, 83, 85, 113, 169
    See also Scriptures
death. See crucifixion
debt. See sin
deescalation, 55, 57, 59, 89,
desire, 78, 80–82, 86, 113, 132
    See also Girardian theory; mimesis
        rivalry
destructiveness, 10, 15, 19, 26, 85,
        109–10, 114
    See also sin
devil. See serpent
dikaiosyne, 63
discernment. See listening
disciples, 158
    See also body of Christ; friendship;
        relationality; ritual; witness
disconnection. See Relational Cultural
    Theory
disease, 66, 94, 113
distress, 9–10, 27, 29, 83, 84, 106–7,
        126, 130–31, 138, 153
    See also eustress; stress; trust
diversity, 150, 155
    See also relationality

'ebrah, 83
Ecclesiology, 145, 147–62
    See also body of Christ; relational-
        ity; ritual; sanctuary

Egypt, 64, 68, 138
ehyey, 12
Elijah, 169
  See also Scriptures
Elohim, 12
EMDR therapy, 130
emotion, 5–8, 10, 28, 34, 51–52, 69,
  78, 104, 110, 126–27, 130, 132,
  134, 151
  See also anger; brain; fear; shame
empathy, 19, 51, 79, 131
  See also brain; neural networks
enemy, 111, 113, 118, 159–60
  See also forgiveness; rivalry; scapegoat mechanism
epiphany. *See* plot diagram
equity. *See* justice
Eschatology, 165
Esther, 83
  See also Scriptures
eternal life, 109–10, 118
  See also heaven
  hell
Eucharist. *See* ritual
eucharistia, 158
eustress, 27
  See also "just right conditions;"
  nervous system
  stress, trust
evangelism. *See* witness
Eve. *See* original couple
evil
  definition of, 62–63
  knowledge of, 37–40, 57, 89
  See also sin; stress; violence
evil one. *See* serpent
existence. *See* Cosmology
exodus, 53, 64, 67–68
  See also Scriptures
"eye for an eye," 86, 92, 140, 156
  See also punishment
  violence

faith, 11, 91–92, 94, 113–14, 116–17
  See also trust
faithfulness, 83, 92
fall. *See* garden of Eden

false alarm, 33, 54, 57, 69–70, 84, 88,
  104, 108, 110
  See also nervous system; perception; stress
falsehood. *See* lie
fasting. *See* prayer
fear, 35–36, 41, 113
  See also brain; stress; trust
Fertile Crescent, 60–61, 85
fight-or-flight, 130, 151
  See also nervous system; threat
  reaction
fight to the death. *See* plot diagram
fMRI technology, 5–7, 141, 152
forgiveness
  definition of, 91–92, 111, 117, 135,
  140
  of God, 91–93, 95–97, 108, 111–12,
  114, 118, 135, 140, 142, 154,
  158–60
  neuroscience of, 91–92
  toward others, 66, 106, 136, 141,
  155–56, 160–62
  See also peace; salvation;
  transformation
free will. *See* humanity
friendship, 48, 153–54, 158–60, 162
  See also body of Christ
  relationality

garden of Eden, 34–41, 54, 84, 89,
  107–8, 111, 157
  See also evil; lie; original couple;
  serpent
garden of Gethsemane, 140–41, 158
  See also Jesus; prayer
gardening, 56–57
Gilligan, Carol, 150
  See also Relational Cultural Theory
Gilligan, James, 51
  See also criminal justice system
Girardian theory, 86–89
  See also mimesis; rivalry; scape-
  goat mechanism; Theological
  Anthropology
God
  coming near, 54, 57, 89, 114–15
  Creator, 11, 14, 17, 133

God *(continued)*
  image of, 11–14, 17–18, 20, 133,
    162
  non-punishment of, 85, 97, 107,
    138, 168, 170
  perception of, 60, 67, 83–85, 88,
    114, 117, 135
  reflection of, 17–21, 37, 41, 66, 70,
    89, 91, 96, 104, 109, 115–17, 142
  See also forgiveness; Jesus; Spirit
good news. *See* salvation
gospel. *See* salvation
grace, 116, 159
  See also forgiveness; integration;
    Spirit
Greek literature. *See* plot diagram
Gregory of Nazianzus, 11, 12, 14, 114
  See also three-in-one
growth, 10–11, 27, 50, 105, 108, 114,
    118, 130, 141, 161
  -fostering relationships, 149–52,
    155
  See also healing; learning;
    relationality
Gutiérrez, Gustavo, 160

ha-satan, 140
hamartiai, 63, 140
Hamartiology, 45, 47–71
  See also evil
  sin
healing
  forgiveness and, 94, 110, 117,
    159–60
  neuroscience of, 78, 80, 104–7, 114,
    117–18, 126–27, 130–31
  spirituality and, 131–32, 137, 141
  See also integration; learning; spiri-
    tual practices
  story
heaven, 13, 15, 110–14, 118, 139
  See also perception; salvation; trust
hell, 109–10, 114, 116
  See also perception; stress; torment
Herman, Judith Lewis, 150
  See also Relational Cultural Theory
Holy Communion. *See* ritual
Holy Spirit. *See* Spirit

hope. *See* trust
humanity, 34, 41, 84, 89, 117, 125, 157
  See also Theological Anthropology

"I Am," 13
Iacoboni, Marco, 78, 80
  See also mirror systems
incarnation, 13, 90, 93, 107, 114, 138,
    168
  See also Christ; God; Jesus
Indus Valley Civilization, 85
integration, 124–33
  crossing the midline, 127, 129–30
  right-left, 125, 127, 132–33
  spiritual practices for, 133–42
  top-bottom, 126–27, 129
  See also brain; consent; "just right"
    conditions; learning; Spirit
intimacy, 38, 108, 111, 150
  See also relationality
Isaiah, 83
  See also Scriptures
isolation, 26–27, 63, 109–10, 114,
    151–52
  See also sin
  torment
Israel, 68, 85–86
  See also Scriptures

Jesus, 12–14, 16, 55, 63, 89, 96–97,
    107, 109, 115–16
  as scapegoat, 82, 93–95, 108, 113
  birth, 84–85, 90
  brain of, 91, 110–11
  forgiveness of, 91–92, 95, 107,
    111–14, 117–18
  nonviolent teaching, 90–91, 93, 96,
    111, 113–14, 154, 156, 159, 167
  See also crucifixion; nonviolence;
    salvation; scapegoat mechanism;
    three-in-one
Job, 11, 83, 140, 161
  See also Scriptures
John the Baptist, 84
  See also Scriptures
Jonah, 169
  See also Scriptures
Jordan, Judith, 150

Joshua, 83
See also Scriptures
joy, 11, 19, 21, 27, 33, 36–37, 39, 41,
57, 66, 91, 92, 96, 107, 108, 111,
115, 116, 126–27, 135, 139, 160,
168
See also God
Judaism. See Scriptures
judgement, 31, 64–65, 90
See also heaven; hell; forgiveness
"just right" conditions, 85, 115
for learning, 10–11, 48–50, 55, 57,
60, 89, 96, 131, 133, 138, 149
stress and, 10–11, 18–20, 21, 27–28,
52, 80, 115, 117
See also nervous system; stress;
trust
justice, 90–93
See also criminal justice system;
learning; punishment
justification. See forgiveness

Karpman, Stephen, 69
Keller, Helen, 15
kindness, 11, 18, 19, 21, 27, 28, 33, 36,
37, 39, 41, 57, 66, 91, 92, 96, 107,
108, 115–16, 135, 139, 160, 168
See also God
kingdom of God. See body of Christ
Kohlberg, Lawrence, 150

Last Supper. See ritual
law, 63, 64, 66–67, 70, 86, 88, 91–92,
153, 167
See also Moses; scapegoat
mechanism
learning, 7, 10, 20, 27, 39, 55, 60, 66,
69, 80, 89, 117, 149, 155
forgiveness and, 92, 96
impact of punishment on, 49–52,
56, 70, 93
neuroscience of, 8, 48–49, 50, 53,
57, 70, 96, 108, 116, 129–32, 138,
141
See also brain; stress; trust
lie
original couple and, 40–51, 55, 57,
71, 84, 89, 108, 157, 167

scapegoat mechanism and, 88, 90,
92, 95, 108, 116, 161
See also perception; stress; trust
life, 11, 16, 18, 19, 21, 27, 33, 36, 37,
39, 41, 57, 66, 67, 85, 91, 92, 96,
107, 108, 111, 115, 116, 126–27,
135, 139, 160, 161, 168
breath of, 14, 34
See also God; resurrection
likeness, 14, 18
See also God
linkages. See learning
listening, 13, 52, 150, 162
See also prayer; relationality; spiritual practices
liturgy. See ritual
logos, 12–15, 90
See also God; Jesus; three-in-one
Lord's Supper. See ritual
love. See God

mᵉrachefet, 133
Martyr, Justin, 13
Mary, mother of Jesus, 136–37
Matthew, the apostle, 82, 140
McGilchrist, Iain, 125
See also brain; integration
meditation. See prayer
memory, 5, 7, 9–10, 31, 52, 53, 104–6,
126, 130–32, 138
See also brain; healing; story
mercy, 82, 91–92, 113, 138
messiah. See Jesus
Miller, Jean Baker, 150–51
See also Relational Cultural Theory
mimesis, 78, 80–81
See also mirror systems
mindfulness. See prayer
Miriam, 169
See also Scriptures
mirror systems, 78–82, 86
See also desire; nervous system;
relationality
misperception. See perception
"missing the target," 63
See also sin
mistrust. See trust

Moses, 13, 64–68, 82–83, 85
    See also Scriptures
murder. *See* violence

narrative. *See* story
nervous system, 35, 37, 69, 81, 88, 90,
    110, 117, 155
    hijack of, 19, 29, 39, 54–55, 60, 89,
        106, 108–9, 114, 130, 168
    regulation of, 26, 35, 91–92, 130–
        31, 135, 138–40, 156–57, 162
    See also brain; learning; trust
neural networks. *See* brain
neuroscience, 11, 20, 34, 35, 49,
    51–53, 69, 82, 92, 106, 126, 130,
    132–33, 152–53
    See also fMRI technology
neurotransmitters. *See* brain
nonviolence, 90, 111, 114, 156, 167
    See also forgiveness; God;
        incarnation
nothingness, 12

obedience. *See* learning
offspring, 55
opheilemata, 140
original couple, 34, 39–40, 54–55, 64,
    66, 85, 108, 157
    See also perception; serpent; sin;
        stress; trust
original sin. *See* garden of Eden
overconsumption, 53, 89, 139, 54
    See also scarcity; stress; trust

pain. *See* stress
paqad, 63
Paul, the apostle, 13, 39, 55, 84, 158
payment for sin. *See* scapegoat
    mechanism
peace, 55, 66, 70, 82, 86–88, 167
    neuroscience of, 8, 126
    See also nervous system; relational-
        ity; trust
peirasmon, 140
penal substitution. *See* scapegoat
    mechanism

perception, 7, 27, 36–37, 41, 55, 58,
    80–81, 87, 94, 96, 108, 110, 138,
    141, 161
    correction of, 60, 70, 84, 89, 95–96,
        107, 115, 117, 135–36, 155, 159,
        162, 157, 159
    impact of stress on, 27, 40, 79, 134,
        160–61, of God, 60, 67, 83–85,
        88, 93, 95, 114, 160
    relationship to trust, 31–33, 39,
        155, 162
    See also brain; incarnation;
        salvation
perfection, 17, 19, 28, 110, 155
persecutor, 69–70, 87–97, 116
    See also scapegoat mechanism
Peter, the apostle, 169
pistis, 116
plot diagram, 166–70
Pneumatology, 122, 130–42
    See also Spirit
prayer, 83, 93, 131–32, 137–41, 156,
    158, 160–62
    See also breath; healing; integration;
        learning; Spirit
predicted outcome, 62
prescribed outcome, 62
propitiation. *See* scapegoat
    mechanism
punishment
    definition of, 51–52
    impact on learning, 49–53, 55–57,
        69–70, 93, 96
    in scripture, 59–60, 63–64, 66,
        83–84, 91
    triangle of, 67–71, 86–97
    See also nervous system; stress;
        violence

ra, 61
racism, 36, 38
    See also evil; sin; trauma
radah, 35
reality. *See* perception
reconnection. *See* Relational Cultural
    Theory
recursivity, 7, 27–28, 30
redemption. *See* salvation

reflection. *See* likeness
regulation. *See* nervous system
Relational Cultural Theory, 149–52
  See also relationality
relationality, 5, 8, 11, 14, 18, 19,
  26–29, 33, 35–37, 91–92, 115,
  126–27, 135, 149–52, 155, 160,
  168
  See also God; learning; trust
religion. *See* body of Christ
REM sleep, 130
  See also brain
repentance. *See* learning
rescuer, 69–70, 86, 88, 93–97, 116,
  159, 168
  See also scapegoat mechanism
resilience, 105, 155
  See also healing; learning;
  transformation
restoration. *See* trust
resurrection, 109–10, 114, 118, 153,
  157
  See also eternal life; heaven; hell
revelation, 93, 95–97, 107, 111–12,
  116–18, 162, 168
  See also God; Jesus; incarnation;
  perception; Spirit; story
ritual, 156–62
  baptism, 157–58
  Eucharist, 158–60
  See also learning; prayer; spiritual
  practices
rivalry, 69, 81–82, 86–87, 89, 111, 155
  See also mimesis; scarcity; scapegoat mechanism
ruach, 11
Rome, 85

sacrifice, 82, 86–88, 95–96, 113
  See also crucifixion; punishment
safety. *See* "just right" conditions
salvation, 41, 63, 107–10, 114,
  116–19, 135–36, 167
  See also incarnation; nonviolence;
  sin; trust
sanctuary, 160–62
  See also forgiveness; learning; trust
Satan. *See* serpent

scapegoat mechanism, 82, 86–90,
  93–97, 108–9, 111, 116, 159–61
  See also sacrifice; punishment;
  violence
scarcity, 37, 80–81, 139
  See also climate crisis; stress
Scriptures, 35, 38, 58, 63–64, 82–85,
  109–10, 140, 158, 160, 162
  Hebrew, 12–13, 62–63, 83, 85
self awareness, 7–10, 19, 28, 50–52,
  105–6
serpent, 39–40, 54–55, 60, 89, 107,
  157
  See also evil; lie; perception; sin
service. *See* relationality
sexuality, knowing, 38
shame, 35–36, 41, 89, 131–32
  See also brain; stress; trust
share-and-care, 151
sickness. *See* disease
Siegel, Dan, 125–26
sin, 59, 62–64, 69, 71, 81–84, 90–92,
  94, 107, 113, 135, 138, 140, 154,
  156, 158–60
  See also brain; forgiveness; perception; stress; trust
Slutkin, Gary, 161–62
social pain, 152
  See also relationality; stress; trust
Sodom, 62–64
  See also Abraham; forgiveness;
  Scriptures
sola confidere, 116
sola fide, 116
sola gratia, 116
Solomon, 83
  See also Scriptures
Soteriology, 100, 105–19
  See also crucifixion; forgiveness;
  God; Jesus; incarnation; perception; salvation; Spirit; trust
sozo, 117
Spirit, 11–14, 16, 153, 156
  as movement, 133–34
  like ocean current, 137, 141
  receiving of, 135–37
  saying "yes" to, 141–42, 158
  See also consent; spiritual practices;
  three-in-one

spiritual practice, 131, 141, 161
    See also breath; learning; prayer
Stephen the martyr, 156
story, 7, 19, 26, 87–88, 125, 129
    as revelation, 17, 20–21, 84–85, 90,
        94, 96–97, 114–19, 134, 157–60,
        162
    healing through, 104–7, 125,
        135–38
    See also plot diagram; time;
        transformation
stress, 7, 10, 17, 26, 39, 40–41, 48,
        57–58, 63, 67, 104–5, 138, 152,
        155
    collective, 37, 39, 53, 66, 83, 86, 89,
        117, 135
    continuum of, 10–11, 18–21,
        27–28, 31, 115, 117, 131, 149
    learning and, 49–53
    perception and, 53–54, 80–82, 84,
        139
    punishment and, 51–52, 60, 69, 93,
        135, 159
    regulation of, 29–31, 34, 42, 51, 55,
        59, 61, 66, 85, 89, 92, 107–10,
        113–14, 116, 118, 133–34,
        141–42, 151, 154, 156, 160, 162
    relationship to pain, 51, 55–56, 83,
        91, 116, 131–32, 152
    safety and, 48–49, 51, 65, 68,
        70–71, 96, 106, 111
    tolerance of, 20, 26–27, 59, 157
    See also nervous system; trust
stroke. *See* brain
substitutionary death. *See* scapegoat
    mechanism
suffering. *See* stress

Tanner, Kathryn, 18, 114
temptation, 20, 140
    See also serpent
tend-and-befriend, 151
Teresa of Avila, 137
Theological Anthropology, 24, 26–71
    See also sin; stress; trust
Thompson, Curt, 117
threat reaction. See *nervous system*
three-in-one, 13–16, 18–19, 21, 133

    See also image of God; relationality
time, 12, 13, 15, 109, 117–18, 125–26,
        130, 132, 134–35
    necessity for, 16
    relationship to stress, 17, 21
    See also creation; story; stress
torment, 19, 84, 106, 109–10, 114
    See also nervous system; sin; stress;
        trust
transformation, 8, 50, 105, 114, 132,
        141
    See also brain; healing; learning
trauma, 38, 105
    See also healing; nervous system;
        racism; stress; transformation
trials, 140–41, 158
    See also garden of Gethsemane
triangle of punishment. *See*
    punishment
trinity. *See* three-in-one; trust
    crisis of, 29, 39, 42, 57–58, 63, 84, 89,
        108, 110, 114, 131, 157
    neuroscience of, 29–30, 34–36, 92,
        96, 116–17, 127, 133, 152
    relationship to belief, 84, 113, 117,
        153
    relationship to faith, 91–92, 94,
        113–14, 116–17
    relationship to learning, 48–49, 60,
        140–42
    relationship to perception, 27,
        31–37, 40–41, 50, 59, 91, 136,
        162
    relationship to salvation, 110, 114,
        116–19, 135–36
    relationship to stress, 31, 51, 61, 81,
        83, 86, 109, 111, 113, 131, 139,
        151, 154, 156
    restoration of, 54–56, 58, 60, 62, 64,
        66, 68–71, 85, 90, 107, 150, 159
    See also brain; perception; nonvio-
        lence; transformation
trustworthiness, qualities of, 30, 65,
        97, 115, 116, 155
    See also trust
truth, 108
    See also revelation

van der Kolk, Bessel, 5, 26
victim, 69–71, 86–91, 93–96, 107–8,
    116, 156, 161, 168
    See also scapegoat mechanism
victimization, 70, 87, 96, 107–8, 156,
violence, 35, 36, 39, 50, 51, 61, 62, 70,
    87–88, 159, 161–62
    See also stress

wages of sin. *See* scapegoat
    mechanism
will, 139
    See also consent; listening; prayer
window of tolerance. *See* tolerance

witness, 156, 158, 160
    See also body of Christ; ritual; story
worship. *See* ritual
woundedness. *See* stress
wrath, 83–84
    See also hell; perception; punish-
    ment; stress; trust

yada, 38

zest, 151
    See also Relational Cultural Theory
zoom, in or out, 125, 127
    See also brain; perception

www.ingramcontent.com/pod-product-compliance
Lightning Source LLC
Chambersburg PA
CBHW030305100426
42812CB00002B/573